"I THINK I KNOW WHO I AM"

– the anatomy of a family –

by
Anthony Russell

RB
Rossendale Books

Published by Lulu Enterprises Inc.
3101 Hillsborough Street
Suite 210
Raleigh, NC 27607-5436
United States of America

Published in paperback 2016
Category: Family History
Copyright Anthony Russell © 2016
ISBN : 978-1-326-89270-8

All rights reserved, Copyright under Berne Copyright Convention and Pan American Convention. No part of this book may be reproduced, stored in a retrieval system, or transmitted in any form or by any means, electronic, mechanical, photocopying, recording or otherwise, without prior permission of the author. The author's moral rights have been asserted.

CONTENTS

Introduction 7

A Note on Sources and Materials 15

Some History Headlines 33

Part I – Tracing the Tuttles 36

   Chapter 1: The Origins of the Tuttle Family of Norfolk 36

   Chapter 2: Known Tuttle Ancestors 48

   Chapter 3: Henry Tuttle 55

   Chapter 4: Ebenezer Tuttle 65

   Chapter 5: A History of Tuttles 75

   Chapter 6: Air Marshal Sir Geoffrey Tuttle KBE CB DFC 80

   Chapter 7: The Berretts of Orford 89

   Chapter 8: The Duckers of Great Yarmouth 95

   Chapter 9: The Langmaids of Polperro 97

Part II – Tracing the Eyres 104

   Chapter 10: Beginnings 104

   Chapter 11: Further Discoveries from
the Census Returns 114

   Chapter 12: Thomas Eyre and his family 118

   Chapter 13: Earlier Eyre ancestors – cordwainers, peruke
makers and clergy 131

   Chapter 14: Wing Commander Anthony Eyre DFC 142

Chapter 15: Leslie Appleton OBE 152

Chapter 16: The Stephens Family.. 155

Chapter 17: Angela Mortimer.. 164

Part III – Tracing the Russells 169

Chapter 18: The Starting Point.. 169

Chapter 19: The Russells of Somerset and Hampshire 175

Chapter 20: The Hibberds of Hampshire and Dorset
and related families... 184

Chapter 21: The Right Hon. Sir Patrick Russell 203

Part IV – Tracing the Potters.. 211

Chapter 22: A Paucity of Information.. 211

Chapter 23: The Potters of Lancashire – inspecting nuisances. 217

Chapter 24: Discovering the Byrom Family 229

Chapter 25: Some Interesting Links... 251

Chapter 26: A Connection to the Plantagenet Kings............... 264

Part V – Some Thoughts And Conclusions 282

Chapter 27. Kings and Princes, Saints and Sinners - some
further Royal Connections 282

Chapter 28. Other less glamourous ancestors........................... 289

Chapter 29. Some Themes which have emerged 293

Introduction

This book is the product of two periods of ill-health which kept me away from work and confined to the house for lengthy periods. On the first occasion I was urged to take up a project and I decided, having spent some time sorting out old family photographs and papers, that I should make some notes for the benefit of younger family members so that information about family relatives would not be lost. As this progressed I realised that the results could be put into a short book and under the title "Passing through this world but once" I privately published a volume for distribution to members of the family and close friends which was well-received. Some of this book is replicated in the current work in the biographical chapters which, where appropriate, have been updated.

All of the material for that book came from family papers and information within my knowledge augmented by some information available in various publications and the Internet. However my researches using the Internet made me appreciate that the likelihood was that there was much more to be discovered about ancestors of whom I knew nothing. Further the interest in discovering more about one's past has become widespread as the popularity of television programmes such as "Who do you think you are?" indicates.

I realised that to embark on such an investigation was not something that I could do whilst working in the demanding office of a senior circuit judge and apart from the occasional foray into my past by making the odd search on a genealogical website I did little about it for a couple of years. However a further period of illness which kept me off work for four months gave me the opportunity to take this project further and once I began to find out what was available I made systematic and thorough investigations which have led to the results set out in this book. Having taken early retirement I was able to devote more time to the project and compile comprehensive notes, from which I have distilled the details which seemed to me to be of interest not only to the family but the general reader, because I found the social history which has emerged to be as interesting as the simple identification of my ancestors.

The structure of this book is based upon the way in which I conducted my researches. I decided that what I wished to find out was who my ancestors were rather than to make contact with current members of the family, although I have made contact with some long lost cousins as a consequence of my investigations. I had the experience about 15 years ago of discovering a first cousin of my mother's and arranging an introduction between them – they had last seen each other 70 years previously when they had been bridesmaids at the wedding of the parents of Angela Mortimer about whom more will be read later in this book. However discovering distant relatives currently living was not my main purpose and so, knowing the names of each of my four grandparents I used them as my starting point and worked backwards.

My father was Michael Hibberd Russell, 1921-1987, and my mother was Pamela Eyre, 1920-2011.

I knew only one of my grandparents, my maternal grandmother Dorothy May Eyre, a daughter of Ebenezer Tuttle, my great grandfather. Her husband, George William Booth Eyre, died in

1935 when my mother was 15. A few years after his death my grandmother returned to live in Lowestoft from where her family, the Tuttle family, came. The Tuttles were a well-known local family whose business was a high class department store. My grandmother was the company secretary and one of the directors of the business. As a child family holidays were often spent with her and her family in Lowestoft. Consequently I knew more about my mother's family than my father's although this knowledge was heavily skewed in favour of the Tuttles, because, following the early death of her father and the intervention of the Second World War when my mother's home was destroyed in a bombing raid, almost all of my mother's contact with the Eyres was lost. My mother's brother, Anthony Eyre, was a Battle of Britain fighter pilot who was shot down later in the War, survived as a prisoner of war, but he was killed in an air crash in 1946.

My paternal grandfather, Sidney Arthur Russell, died in 1953 when I was aged two, so I have no recollection of him. His wife, Elsie, had died in 1948, shortly after the marriage of my parents. Her maiden name was Potter, and although I knew my father's aunt, Marion Potter, and my father's two brothers, Peter Byrom Russell and Thomas Patrick Russell, little was ever spoken about their families. In particular neither my father, whose second name was Hibberd, nor my uncle Peter, whose second name was Byrom, knew the precise origins of their unusual names, although it was always said (correctly as it turns out) that there was a connection to the Byrom family of Manchester.

Born in 1951, I was named Anthony Patrick after my maternal uncle and my father's younger brother, both of whom were men of distinction. Anthony Eyre rose to the rank of Wing Commander in the RAF and would probably have risen further but for his untimely death. Sir Patrick Russell concluded an outstanding career in the law as a judge of the Court of Appeal. More about their lives will be found later in this book.

So, knowing more about them than the other families making up my ancestry, I started my researches with the Tuttles, about whom there was more material available than for any of the others, then the Eyres, then the Russells and finally the Potters about whom I knew next to nothing.

Thus the book consists of four principal parts:

Part I - Tracing the Tuttles;

Part II - Tracing the Eyres;

Part III - Tracing the Russells;

Part IV - Tracing the Potters.

The final part (Part V) contains some conclusions & observations.

One of my purposes in publishing this book is to show what can be discovered and how one can go about making the discoveries and I have set out how I made progress in relation to each family in the relevant part. I have also set out at the beginning of each section some information about the family name and some general family history known to relate to that name which may or may not amount to information about direct ancestors.

As the project progressed and more information came to light I compiled detailed notes in four parts based on each of these families and their ancestors and this book is set out in the same way to reveal the structure of each of these families which make up my own ancestry. In the process I discovered a number of interesting characters, some of whom are given little biographies in the text. I have also included more detail about some of the family members who have made a worthwhile contribution and acquired some distinction – these were the subjects of my earlier book so those who have that volume will find some duplication, although my researches have resulted in some updating of the particulars.

The result is to reveal the anatomy of a family which contains some characters who have distinguished themselves in various ways, but others who have led ordinary but worthwhile lives. It is a family to which I am proud to belong, and the preparation of this book has given me much pleasure. My intention is that it will be of interest not only to my relatives but to others - and it shows what it is possible to discover about one's ancestors with the assistance of the material which is so readily available now because of the Internet, but above all it enables me to say with confidence that I think I know who I am!

My researches resulted in many unexpected results as will be seen, discovering many ancestors including some from the very distant past, but in addition to identifying these people I also found out much more than I thought was possible about the lives they led and thus my knowledge and appreciation of social history expanded significantly out of my findings.

In speaking to others I have found that distant relationships are frequently misunderstood. For example what is the relationship to oneself of a second cousin once removed? In an effort to help understand this I set out the following explanation. First cousins are the children of two siblings – first cousins share a pair of grandparents. Second cousins are the children of two first cousins and they share a pair of great grandparents. Third cousins are the children of two second cousins and the grandchildren of two first cousins who share a pair of great great grandparents and so on. The use of the term "removed" indicates the fact that the cousins are in different generations – so, for example the child of one's first cousin is a first cousin once removed, or in reverse the first cousin of a parent is one's first cousin once removed. Similarly the child of one's second cousin or the second cousin of a parent is a second cousin once removed, to answer the question posed at the beginning of this paragraph. If a cousin is twice removed then the cousin relationship is two generations apart, so the grandchild of one's first cousin or the first cousin of one's grandparent is a first cousin twice removed.

The table set out below may help to understand this point more clearly. All those whose names appear in bold type are direct descendants of Henry and Mary. Henry and Mary's children are Thomas and Jane, Arthur and Elizabeth are their grandchildren, David and Alice their great grandchildren and Charles and Kate their great great grandchildren. Thomas and Jane are brother and sister. Arthur and Elizabeth are first cousins, David and Alice are second cousins and Charles and Kate are third cousins. Arthur and Alice are first cousins once removed, as are David and Elizabeth. Charles and Alice are second cousins once removed as are David and Kate. Charles and Elizabeth are first cousins twice removed as are Arthur and Kate.

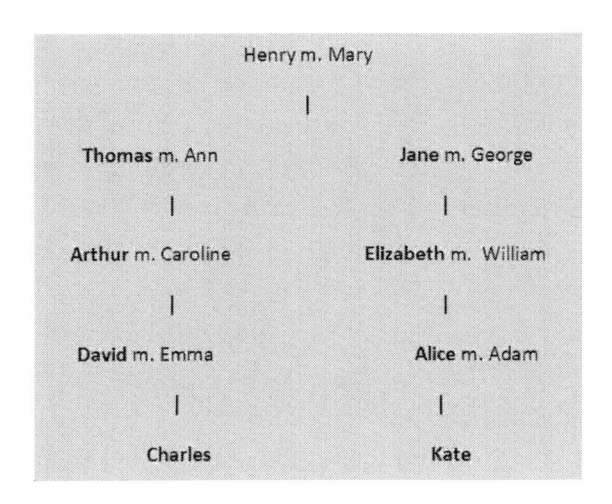

```
                    Henry m. Mary
                         |
      Thomas m. Ann              Jane m. George
           |                           |
    Arthur m. Caroline        Elizabeth m. William
           |                           |
      David m. Emma              Alice m. Adam
           |                           |
         Charles                      Kate
```

I wish to acknowledge the considerable assistance I have gained from subscribing to Ancestry.co.uk without which gaining access to much of the material upon which I have relied would not have been possible except by travelling to various record offices around the country, a time-consuming exercise which would not have proved as productive. I also wish to acknowledge the support and encouragement I have received from my family and friends who have urged me to put the results of my researches into an accessible form more widely available than to just themselves. Because of the nature of the material available it is likely that some errors in interpretation will have been made. As my researches progressed I have corrected those mistakes which have come to light, particularly as more records have become publicly available, but the responsibility for any errors which remain is mine alone.

As will be seen, from time to time I have departed from the main theme and recounted or commented on some of the events of the time or aspects of the life of a named person, or have inserted short biographies. There is a distinguished precedent for such an approach in the work of the 12th century monk, William of Malmesbury, whose work "The Deeds of the English Kings" in the magnificent Folio Society edition I have recently had the pleasure of reading as translated by R.A.B. Mynors. William himself refers to his digressions justifying them as being interesting and entertaining for his readers, and with due humility I venture the same excuse. To quote William, translated by Mynors "…let me for such long digressions…bespeak the reader's pardon."

The majority of the illustrations in this book comprise old family photographs in my possession or photographs I have taken myself. A few illustrations have been copied from sites on the Internet where no copyright has been claimed.

As I was completing my work on this book I learnt that one of my history teachers at the King's School, Chester, Keith Lysons, had died at the age of 95. He was an inspirational teacher who encouraged his pupils to "think outside the box". The older I have become the more I have appreciated the good fortune of having been taught by him and some of his colleagues and with gratitude I dedicate this volume to him and the several others, including my late father and mother, who have encouraged my lifelong interest in history.

A Note on Sources and Materials

When embarking on a project of this kind it is important to set some parameters and a starting point. I know who my close living relatives are and although it would be interesting to extend my knowledge to third and fourth cousins etc. of the current generation, the chances of thus gaining new relatives with whom I might form a close personal relationship seemed remote. So I took a decision to work backwards from my parents to trace direct ancestors, although occasionally I found some interesting relatives who were not direct ancestors, but closely related to them such as siblings or cousins, and where such interesting characters were discovered I extended the boundaries of my researches. I have been fortunate in that my ancestry, so far discovered, is almost exclusively English as far back as the Norman Conquest which has meant that I have been able to confine my researches into English records. I comment on some of these records below, in the hope that those making similar researches may be assisted, but because my experiences are limited to searching English records this section should by no means be regarded as a comprehensive guide as to how to proceed.

I was also fortunate in having some family information to get me started which was a considerable help. From family records and talking to some of my relatives from preceding generations I knew the full names of each of my grandparents, and in some cases great grandparents, where they lived and their occupations. On my mother's side there was further detail which was of itself very useful. But what was most useful about this knowledge was that it enabled me to gain accurate access to and to use information contained within the 1911 United Kingdom census, the details of which are readily available on line. This in turn enabled me to trace back through the 19th century to the 1841 census which is the earliest published UK national census. I will say some more about the material contained within the census records later.

Genealogy Websites

An easy way to gain access to these records is to subscribe to one of the genealogy sites available over the Internet. This is a wonderful resource now available through recent advances in information technology, and an essential tool for any serious research. There are several of these sites and it would be wrong for me to recommend a particular one because each has its advantages, and it may be sensible as findings are revealed to use more than one. There are some sites which are free, but those with large amounts of data available charge a subscription, although some will grant free access for a trial period. Testing them to find which suits you best from the point of using the site and which contains the best range of source materials for your researches is a sensible idea. For example, if it seems likely that your ancestry is contained within the United Kingdom, as mine is, the choice of a site with the most UK records is sensible. If, however, you are descended from an early settler family in North America or Australia, then another site which specialises in the records of those continents would be better. If you have potential lines of descent from European roots or the various colonies of Europe or other countries careful analysis of the records available on the site needs to be undertaken and it may be necessary to subscribe to multiple sites, particularly if your ancestry appears to result from a variety of different places in the world.

In addition to census records these sites enable searches of birth, marriage and death records, parish records, military records, migration records, trade directories, and many other sources including the researches of other enthusiasts. Some of the results will enable the record itself to be viewed, others will consist of a transcription of the record or simply an index note. Some of the records may be incomplete for a variety of reasons, for example if a parish church was burnt down or a record office damaged by flood the records will probably have become lost, so there are inevitable gaps and a dead end may be reached. It is also important to remember that any collection of records is dependent upon the accuracy of the information placed within it, so there is always a possibility of error. Reliance upon the researches of other enthusiasts can be dangerous because the person compiling a family tree of his or her ancestors may have misinterpreted information, plugged a gap by guesswork, or recorded what was hoped would be the outcome from inadequate material, perhaps motivated by a desire to establish distinguished ancestry.

A subscription to one or more of the available websites is strongly recommended. It is usually possible to keep your own family tree on the site, which will mean that your own records are constantly cross referenced against other records available to the site and any potential links will be indicated by way of alerts which can be followed up. As the site accesses more records this process continues and you will sometimes be rewarded by a new discovery about an ancestor [See Chapter 27 for an example of this]. Some of the websites offer to analyse your DNA which may also be of interest.

I also strongly recommend keeping comprehensive notes of any findings. Whilst the tree itself and some information can be kept on the website, together with links to the documents discovered, keeping one's own notes is essential for ease of reference. I did this on my computer with separate sections for each family and numbered entries for each generation, building up as much biographical detail as possible for each person. The use of numbering made it easy to add new generations as they were discovered and update the notes in a logical manner. I was also able to add photographs or scanned copies of documents in the relevant place. Such an approach has enabled me to copy sections for distribution to any interested family member. Other methods of keeping such information include the use of spread sheets, card indexes or simply a notebook whichever is most convenient – as with all note-keeping it is best to use a system that you are comfortable with and we all have our own preferences.

It is important to use as many sources as possible to confirm a line of ancestry and to seek corroboration of each piece of material and evidence discovered. In a Chapter 26 I set out how I was misled as to a line of ancestry because of the existence of two people born at the same time, with the same name, but who were unrelated (except possibly very distantly), and how tracing each back by completely different routes led back to the early Plantagenet Kings of England, one of which was the correct route for my own ancestry, the other being completely wrong for me, although an accurate line of descent.

Extending enquiries beyond the mere discovery of the identity of ancestors by searching for information about the district where they lived or, for example, the church where they were baptised, married or buried, can put flesh on the bones uncovered and is very worthwhile. The distant Jane Austen connection referred to in Chapter 19 is an example in point. The Internet enables such enquiries to be carried out with ease.

The Census Records

When beginning my enquiries I found the United Kingdom Census records to be the most helpful source to trace back my ancestors through the nineteenth century. The census was taken every ten years, as is still so, and the earliest one for which records have been kept and are available is the census of 1841 and currently the last to be published is the census of 1911. The reason why no further census records are publicly available is that there is a one hundred year embargo on publication of the details to protect the privacy of the individuals named.

The census records the people resident in a household on a particular date. As with all other records this depends upon the diligence and accuracy of the person completing the return. The details in the 1841 census are quite sparse. The records are for each parish within a city, borough or county, and noted by place of abode. Listed should be every person who resided at each address the preceding night. The age and sex of each person is recorded, however the age of adults given in the 1841 census can be misleading because all that was required was to place an adult's age within a five year range, so for example a person aged 43 would be within the range 40 to 45, which would be recorded as 40. The ages of children up to the age of 15 should have been correctly recorded. Whether a person had a profession, trade, employment or was of independent means should be stated, and, finally, whether the person was born in the same county or abroad should be noted.

More details are recorded in the census records for the following decades. Those for 1851 to 1901 are in almost identical format and record the address, the name and surname of each person who was residing in the house on the night of the census, the relationship of that person to the head of the family (which might indicate, for example, that a person was a servant or lodger if not a relative), the "condition" of the person (which refers to whether married or single), the age and sex of each person, the age being the exact age, the "rank, profession or occupation" of the person and where the person was born (usually the county and parish or town).

The most detailed records are contained within the 1911 census. In addition to full names, relationship to head of the family, age and sex, more details of the marriage are recorded, more details of employment, more precise details as to birthplace, details of nationality and whether any person was suffering from an infirmity, such as being deaf, blind or "an imbecile". Further there is a separate sheet for each household, signed by the head of the household certifying that the information is correct. The 1911 census is an excellent starting point for research because it is the most recent and most comprehensive census currently available.

Starting with the information gleaned from the 1911 census it is usually possible to trace the family back through previous census records to 1841 which will provide information for 3 generations or so. Using the search facilities available on the on-line websites makes this a relatively easy task although if the name you are sourcing is a common one it is important to beware against errors arising because of duplication of names – the fact that all the members of a household are listed with ages in these records means that it is usually possible to cross-reference the details and build up an accurate history.

However the census records reveal more than simply the details of the family members living in a household. Even a family of quite modest means may have a domestic servant, sometimes surprisingly young, living in the home. People with small businesses sometimes had an assistant or assistants living with their family. Lodgers were often taken in to provide some additional income. Thus a picture of the circumstances in which a family lived can emerge. It is usually possible by means of a search engine to discover whether the address still exists and if so by use of mapping facilities now available on line to see exactly where the house was and often find an aerial picture of it. Putting an address into a search engine may reveal all manner of interesting information; for example some of my ancestors lived in central Southampton in streets where members of the crew lost in the sinking of the Titanic were recorded as having their homes. It is well worth reading the entries for other families living in the vicinity which give further clues about the social history but may also reveal other relatives living nearby, because people tended not to move very far away.

Civil Registration

From 1st July 1837 all births marriages and deaths in England and Wales were recorded. Other dates apply for Scotland and Ireland. The English and Welsh details are available from the General Register Office and copies of certificates will be provided for a fee. There is a website [www.gro.gov.uk] which enables this service to be used. However most of the genealogy websites can supply the bare essentials of this information from indexes on their sites which may give sufficient detail, particularly if what is sought is corroboration of other evidence. For Scotland and Ireland the respective General Register Offices should be approached, but for most purposes the information available on genealogy websites will suffice. Obtaining birth, marriage and death certificates for all one's ancestors is expensive, but the certificates can provide valuable information which may not otherwise be readily available, such as occupations, and careful analysis of a certificate may solve problems of identification which arise from time to time.

Parish Records of baptisms, marriages and burials

Although Parish Records have been required to be kept from Tudor times, not all have survived, and of course some may not have been kept very diligently. Before the Dissolution of the Monasteries in 1535, the monks were the principal register-keepers. In 1538, Thomas Cromwell, then Vicar-General, issued a mandate requiring each parish to keep registers of baptisms, marriages and burials. Subsequent orders and legislation confirmed this obligation and it was a requirement that copies should be made and kept centrally by each diocese. However this was not always done and many records have been lost or destroyed by accident and in some cases by design.

Until these became more widely available on the Internet it was necessary for the researcher to make a physical search of the records, some of which were held in county record offices, others still being in the possession of the incumbent of the parish. Enquiries could be made of the relevant office or the parish priest who were usually very helpful, but fees were charged, so the exercise could become quite expensive and time-consuming. Now many of these records are held on genealogy websites and other sites and they are indexed, so searching them is relatively easy. There are a large number of sites, some of which are limited to particular localities, others have a wider coverage. Some sites have links to the records themselves, which can be examined, others consist of a simple database prepared from the records. Finding appropriate sites is not always straightforward, but for example if you have ancestors in a particular county entering "X-shire parish records" in a search engine should produce some results. For a number of counties there may be an on-line parish clerks website which can be very useful. In Chapter 18 I set out how by using such a site I was able to trace several generations of my Russell ancestors. This experience is an indication of how important it is to check as many sources as possible before coming to a conclusion. Simply because one line of enquiry appears to be exhausted one should not give up because other researches may achieve the desired result.

Examining these records is one of the most interesting aspects of research but it can also be exasperating. It is important to appreciate that the records may be incomplete, so a dead end can be reached. Some parish priests kept more detailed records than others, so there may be information of occupation, address, cause of death, age at death and parentage of the parties to a marriage. However sometimes the details are very brief – no more than the record of the baptism of "William son of William Smith" is not very informative. Spellings can be very varied. In the case of the Byrom family with which I am connected, the name is variously spelt, Byrom, Byram, Byrome, Biram, Buyroum and Burom. One of my ancestors bore the unusual forename "Melior"; in the short parish marriage record her name is spelt two ways "Mellyear" and "Milyear". In searching the parish records, as in other aspects of research, sometimes a degree of lateral thinking is required.

These records are in handwriting, which can be difficult to decipher. However in many cases the writing is very beautiful. One early 18th century parson in the parish of Gillingham in Dorset which I was researching wrote all his records in Latin, so my rusty "O Level" Latin was brought into play. If researches take you into Quaker Records these documents can give a fascinating insight into how, for example, a Quaker marriage was conducted. [See Part III, Chapter 20, for more about this]

Until 1752 church and legal records used a dating method by which the year started on 25th March, which might lead to confusion. So, for example, a legal document dated 3rd February 1740 would by modern dating methods be dated 3rd February 1741. Some records refer to the regnal year of the monarch, which in this example would be the 14th year of the reign of King George II. An illustration of how this dating system operated can be seen from the extract from a parish record copied below. Under the present system all the entries would be recorded as being in 1716. The reference to "Georgii secundo" is not to King George II but to the second year of the reign of King George I, who would at that time have been known as King George, there having been no other Kings of England named George at that date.

Extract from a parish record recording burials from January to May 1716 using the old dating system

Until 1754 boys could marry at the age of 14 and girls at 12, so what might appear to be an unlikely marriage of an ancestor because the age of one or both parties seems too young may well be correct. There are many pitfalls for the unwary!

Although parish records are still kept and can be readily searched, they are most useful for the period before general registration, and can provide valuable evidence of ancestry from the mid-sixteenth to the early nineteenth century. As with all such evidence using the information in conjunction with that obtained from other sources is desirable, and I have found that these records have been particularly helpful in confirming or refuting the ancestry recorded by others in their family trees.

Military Records, Trade Directories etc.

Having discovered the identity of ancestors it is sometimes possible to discover more information about them than appears in the parish or census records. A number of military and naval records are available on line, many of them linked to genealogy websites. The award of campaign medals is usually well-recorded. If an ancestor was engaged in business, a trade or profession then this is likely to be recorded in the comprehensive trade directories which have been published in the 18th, 19th and 20th centuries. Again many of these can be accessed on line, and because they have been digitised entering an ancestor's name in the search facility will frequently provide interesting details so that a picture of the ancestor's life will emerge and a greater understanding of social history is the result.

There are many such avenues of research, and to detail them all would take too much time and space, but for example lists of clergy, members of universities and other educational establishments, criminal records and migration records can all reveal interesting results.

Probate Records

For a person who died in England and Wales after 1858 it is possible by referring to a Government website (probatesearch.service.gov.uk) to see the short probate record of their estate and if desired, for a fee, obtain a copy of the will. This has the potential to reveal other aspects of the ancestor's history, and by use of a calculator, again readily available on line, assess the wealth of the ancestor in terms of current values. Other records are sometimes available on the genealogy websites.

Family Knowledge

A very valuable source of information can be family knowledge. This may come from documents retained, family bibles, and photographs etc. Photographs can be particularly interesting because they may record important events and show how people dressed, but frequently you have no idea who the subjects are or what events are recorded. So to assist yourself, and provide help to future generations, noting up as many family pictures as possible is essential, and if there is an elderly relative who has the information obtain it from them before it is too late. I was able to persuade my elderly mother to record the identity of the subjects on the reverse of many old family photographs which enabled me to identify pictures of some of my great great grandparents' generation.

It is also very important to discuss family history with one's relatives. It has been a source of considerable regret to me that I did not do this as much as I should have done. I never got the opportunity to discuss with my uncle his career as a Battle of Britain pilot and his incarceration in Stalag Luft III because he died shortly after the end of the Second World War, but what a tale he could have told[1]. I have found that members of the generation which survived that experience are often reluctant to speak about it, but it is important that their knowledge and experiences and those of more recent generations are preserved.

From time to time on television programmes such as "Flog it" one sees someone bringing in an unwanted family heirloom, which always makes me sad. However the sale of old family photographs, documents or medals is more than sad – it is consigning family history to the dustbin, and while the individual seller may have no interest in his or her past disposing of such material deprives other members of the family of information about their roots. Even if they are kept in a box in the attic, for future members of the family these items may have much more real value than the few pounds for which they are sold to contribute towards a holiday, car repairs, a meal or a garden makeover. Hang on to such objects – they are part of history and an invaluable aid to researching ancestry.

The Researches of Others and Family Trees

Many of the various genealogy and ancestry websites encourage their subscribers to build up their own family trees on the database. This is an immensely helpful aid to research, because the recording of a name on such a site will result in cross-referencing with other data on the site and suggested lines of enquiry are thrown up. So, for example, if you enter the name of

---

[1] See Chapter 14

a relative several generations back, say a 3rd great grandparent who lived from 1800 to 1862 using family knowledge, the website may be able to refer you to parish records of baptism and marriage, a death record from the General Register Office, the Probate records, census records and perhaps trade directories.

In addition there will be cross-referencing of the person against the family trees which other enthusiasts have recorded. Again this can reveal much information and is an invaluable tool which can often corroborate your own researches and provide new leads to follow up. These family trees may contain links to source material such as parish records which you have not been able to discover.

However, some of this information may not be well-researched and I have sometimes found serious anomalies which can be apparent on the face of the family tree itself – it is not very usual for a child to be born to parents aged in their nineties, or for someone to marry a spouse who died 10 years earlier! I have even come across an example, repeated without question in other family trees, of a couple who achieved the remarkable feat of having a child 600 years after they had died! It is vital, before relying on such sources, to seek for corroboration such as a parish record. These trees can be very helpful and guide you in new directions, but it is wise to be wary of them, particularly if they stand alone, because as with all such information the end result is only as good as the material entered into the equation.

Sometimes other subscribers to the site will make contact with you to request or exchange information, or you may choose to make an enquiry of one of them. This can be very helpful and interesting. I have enjoyed exchanging notes with another person named Russell, who so far as we were able to ascertain is no relation, but in his investigation of his ancestry he had been misled into believing that an ancestor of mine was an ancestor of his. Discovering his mistake and coming across my own family tree he very kindly provided me with the results of his researches into my family which filled some gaps in my own results. What would once have been called a pen-pal friendship has developed by email (e-pal?) which has been most entertaining.

General On-Line Searches

Sometimes a simple entry of a name, and perhaps dates or a place associated with the person, into a general search engine can reveal interesting results. This is especially so if the person researched is distinguished or famous and it is certainly worth trying with any name. In Part II I have included some information about the Revd. John Eyre which came to light as a result of such an enquiry [Chapter 13]. Similarly when researching John Byrom [Part IV, Chapter 24], although I knew something of him and I had a volume of his poems the Internet search revealed much more of interest. The Byrom ancestry revealed distant links to many important figures in the Middle Ages about whom I was able to learn much from the Internet and from various histories and biographies.

Professional Help

Finally, if all else fails or you do not have the time or inclination to do your own research, which even with the Internet is time-consuming, although most interesting and enjoyable, it is always possible to instruct a professional genealogist. Without a doubt the highest quality service for England and Wales will be obtained from the College of Arms, sometimes referred to as the College of Heralds. The heralds are highly skilled professionals who will undertake genealogical research for a fee. The College of Arms holds numerous pedigrees and other original records, and has a huge library at its premises in Queen Victoria Street, London.

The College of Arms is also the official repository for all armorial records and handles all grants of arms. If researches lead to the discovery of a coat of arms which may belong to your family then it is to the College of Arms that enquiry should be made to ascertain the true position. In Scotland the Lord Lyon King of Arms and the Scottish heralds perform a similar function.

A Final Word on Sources and Material

While some of the information discovered can be regarded as absolutely conclusive, some of it may be erroneous for a variety of reasons, one of which is that the researcher has, in good faith and based on a proper interpretation of the material available, come to an incorrect conclusion which subsequent researches challenge. This can apply to one's own researches, so all such research should be regarded as an on-going project, and checks should be made from time to time to ensure that conclusions are based upon the best evidence available. As more material becomes available on the Internet this is an important and interesting aspect of the amateur's genealogical researches.

The results of my researches are set out in this book. I am satisfied that the details back to the early 19th century are accurate. The existence of the census records from 1841 and compulsory registration of births marriages and deaths from 1837 provide reliable source material which is sometimes supported by other material such as parish records, military records, trade directories, passenger lists etc.

The further back one goes beyond the early 19th century, unless you are very fortunate, the less material is available and the accuracy of some of the records may be suspect, particularly if all that is available is a family tree prepared by someone else without identifying the sources of the information. In these cases, of course, the researcher may have had some source material, such as private papers which have not been disclosed. We all have ancestors, so for example we each have over 60,000 fourteenth great grandparents to be traced, in my case living in the 15th century. They all actually existed – the difficulty is discovering their identities. So far I have been able to name fourteen of this number, so there is a long way to go!

Before claiming an ancestor I have applied the test used in the English courts to decide a civil case, by assessing the evidence and asking myself whether on the balance of probability the relationship is proved – in other words is it more likely than not that the person is an ancestor? So, if there is more than one piece of evidence, and if satisfied as to reliability, the balance shifts firmly in favour of ancestry, but even if there is only one source, if everything fits, such as dates all corresponding and making sense, in the absence of any contrary evidence then the balance of probability test would be satisfied. This is a good test which has withstood the test of time in the English civil courts, but it does require an exercise of judgement, and as with all such exercises mistakes can occur, but I believe the conclusions I have drawn are correct. As I was completing this book further material became available on line in relation to parish records for Somerset and Norfolk where some of my ancestors had lived. Aware that new records could shift the balance of probability in a different direction I checked these carefully and was glad to find my findings confirmed and thus strengthened, but it could have been otherwise, which emphasises the fact that genealogical research is ongoing and that all possible sources should be checked in the search for corroboration and confirmation of one's interpretation and conclusions.

Some History Headlines

While many readers will have a good knowledge of British and European history, others may not, and the table below is designed to assist with some important dates and events in chronological order which may enable some of the events referred to in this book to be put into their historical context. It is highly selective and chosen with reference to some of the information discovered in my researches rather than an attempt to set out all events of importance.

Date	Event
814	Death of Charlemagne
839	Death of Egbert, King of Wessex
899	Death of Alfred the Great
1016	Death of Ethelred the Unready
1066	The Norman Conquest and commencement of rule of William the Conqueror and the House of Normandy
1135	King Stephen assumes the throne, disputed by the Empress Matilda until 1153 when Stephen acknowledged her son Henry as his successor
1154	Henry II crowned, the first Plantagenet King (House of Anjou)
1215	Magna Carta
1265	Henry III grants the Lancaster Estate to his younger son Edmund Crouchback
1327	Edward II deposed
1337	The Hundred Years' War commences
1346	The Battle of Crecy

1381	The Peasants' Revolt
1399	Richard II deposed Henry Bolinbroke (Henry IV) usurps the throne becoming the first King of the House of Lancaster
1415	The Battle of Agincourt
1453	The Fall of Constantinople
1455-1487	The Wars of the Roses
1461	Edward IV crowned as the first King of the House of York
1485	Henry VII (House of Tudor) crowned following his defeat of Richard III at the Battle of Bosworth.
1492	Christopher Columbus discovers America
1533	The Break with Rome
1535	Dissolution of the Monasteries
1538	Parishes required to keep registers of baptisms, marriages and burials
1588	The Defeat of the Spanish Armada
1603	Queen Elizabeth I dies and is succeeded by King James VI of Scotland, the first Stuart King of England as James I
1620	The first Pilgrim Fathers sail to America in the Mayflower
1649	The Execution of King Charles I following the English Civil War
1660	The Restoration of the Monarchy and coronation of King Charles II
1688	The Glorious Revolution as a result of which William of Orange and Mary II succeeded James II
1712	Thomas Newcomen invents the steam engine – the Industrial Revolution is generally recognised as having developed following this and other such advances during the 18th century
1714	King George I invited to become King of England as the first King of the House of

	Hanover
1745	The last Jacobite rising in which Prince Charles Edward Stuart (Bonnie Prince Charlie) marched with his troops as far south as Derby
1775-1783	The American War of Independence
1789	The French Revolution commences
1805	The Battle of Trafalgar
1815	The Battle of Waterloo
1832	The Great Reform Act
1837	Civil Registration of births marriages and deaths in England and Wales
1851	The Australian Gold Rush commences
1857	The Indian Mutiny
1870-1871	Franco-Prussian War
1901	Death of Queen Victoria
1914-1918	The First World War
1939-1945	The Second World War
1952	Accession of Queen Elizabeth II

Part I – Tracing the Tuttles

Chapter 1: The Origins of the Tuttle Family of Norfolk

The name Tuttle is believed to derive from natural or artificial mounds called tot-hills (hill of god, the reference is said to refer to Tot or Thot, an Egyptian deity - an alternative suggestion is that there is an association with the Norse god Thor). One such mound, called tut-hill is near Thetford, Norfolk, one of several tumuli raised by the Danes to cover their dead, slain in a battle with King Edmund in A.D. 871. Such hills were often used as lookout posts. The name Toteles, which may derive from the same source, appears in the roll of Battle Abbey (1066) identifying some of those who took part in the Battle of Hastings. There are suggestions of ancient descent in Ireland dating back to the sept or tribe of O'Toole (sometimes written "O'Tothill") in the pre-Christian era. The name is most likely to have been used to refer to someone who was a dweller by a hill used as a lookout. The name Tuttle can also be spelt

Tuthill, Totyl, Totehill, Toothill, Towtill, or Tuttell and other variants.

The earliest Tuttle of whom I was aware from family sources was my 3rd great grandfather William Tuthill. In an article for the series "Worthies of Lowestoft" compiled by the Lowestoft Historical Society about his son, Henry, who founded the family business in Lowestoft, Henry Tuttle was referred to as the son of William and Mary Tuthill of Norwich, who are also named in the family Bible. It was not difficult to trace William Tuthill who was born in 1792 in Wymondham, Norfolk and who died in 1842, the year after the first recorded census, in which he appears, living in Norwich, about which more later.

This evidence confirmed information from a family tree on line compiled by a distant relative that the Tuttle family from which I am descended came from the area to the south and west of Norwich, in particular the villages of Barford, Hockham, Tharston and Saxlingham Nethergate and the small town of Wymondham, all within a few miles of each other.

There is some very interesting Tuttle history to be found in a privately published pamphlet entitled "The Tuthill Family of Tharston, Norfolk County, England and Southold, Suffolk County, New York" by Lucy Dubois Akerly, New York 1898. The information is derived from the papers of Judge W. H. Tuthill and other sources. The name Tuttle is quite common in the United States because the early settlers included some of the name Tuttle or its alternatives, particularly a number of members of a family called Tuttle in Northamptonshire and a number of members of the Tuthill family from Norfolk.

There is an important family of Tuthills from the area south and west of Norwich. Given that mobility of families was unusual before the 19th century and that Tuttle is an uncommon surname in England it seems highly probable that our Tuttles are descended from this family. Henry Tuttle (1816-1897), my great great grandfather, who founded the family business in Lowestoft, was born in Barford, a small village about five miles south west of Norwich. Tuthill or Tutthill seems to have been the favoured early spelling of the Norfolk family. Barford is one of several small villages to the south and west of Norwich from where all the people mentioned in the American pamphlet and living in England were baptised or lived and died. These villages are all within a radius of no more than five miles. The coincidence of two unconnected families with the same relatively uncommon surname in such a small area seems highly unlikely. The College of Heralds Visitation of Essex of 1634, one of several such visitations throughout the country to establish the pedigree of local families, is an authoritative document with reference to the Tuthills of Norfolk. Although there is no certainty, the evidence is compelling that the Tuttle family to which we belong has its origins in the family of John Tuthill of Saxlingham who is stated to be the founder of the family in the College of Heralds' Visitation.

In the parish church at Saxlingham Nethergate dedicated to St. Mary the Virgin are a number of Tuttle references. The Rector of the Church from 1512-1530 was William Totehill (Totehill being a recognised early spelling of the name Tuttle). There is a tomb in the floor of the chancel, a simple slab unfortunately now covered by carpet, bearing the names "John Tuthill, gent. died October 1684" and "Elizabeth Mingay, wife of John Mingay, daughter of John Tuthill, died May 1716".

The Church of St Mary the Virgin, Saxlingham Nethergate

Saxlingham is about four miles from Wymondham where William Tuthill, my 3rd great grandfather was born and a similar distance from Barford where Henry Tuttle, my great great grandfather, was born. Close by is the village of Tharston where some of the Tuthills mentioned below lived. In the parish church at Tharston (St. Mary's), which is in an isolated spot with few surrounding houses, are listed recent baptisms (dating back to about 1940) including a Michael Tuttle.

The Tuthills of Norfolk have an armorial achievement, more usually referred to as a coat of arms, as I shall do in this book – "Or, on a chevron azure, three crescents argent. Crest, a leopard passant, sable, crowned or, on a mound vert". The "mound vert" or green mound is probably an allusion to the tot-hill from which the name is derived. These arms are found in the church of Trowse-with-Newton, Norfolk, now part of South Norwich, not far from Barford, on the tomb of Elizabeth, wife of Sir Roger Dalyson, daughter of William Tuthill of Newton and granddaughter of John Tuthill of Saxlingham. She died on 27th September 1585 in her nineteenth year. John Tuthill of Saxlingham is recorded as the founder of the family in "The Pedigree of Tuthill of Norfolk Co., Eng" in the College of Heralds, London. William Tuthill of Newton died in 1591. Trowse and Newton are about four miles north of Saxlingham.

The Coat of Arms of the Tuthills of Norfolk

There were direct descendants of the Tuthills of Saxlingham using the family coat of arms as late as the beginning of the 19th century. In the Norwich church of St. George Colegate (known as St. George over the water) is a memorial to John Tuthill, Merchant, who died in 1801 in his 65th year, and his wife Rachael, died 1818 aged 74, and their daughter Lucy, the wife of Edward Daniell, who died in 1820, aged 43. The memorial displays the Tuttle crest and shield illustrated above.

Putting all the evidence together it appears highly probable that my Tuttle ancestors are part of this family of Tuthills based in the villages to the south and west of Norwich.

William Tuthill of Newton, Elizabeth's father, had a brother, John Tuthill of Saxlingham, who had three sons, William, John and Henry Tuthill. William's third son Henry Tuthill was born in 1580 and lived in Tharston, Norfolk. Henry Tuttle married Alice Gooch (b. 1584). Alice Gooch was the daughter of John Gooch (b. 1558) and Margaret Rau (b 1562). Henry Tuthill's will, dated 20th March 1618, mentions John Gooch, father (in-law), Margaret Rau, mother-in-law, Ann Woodyard, kinswoman, John Tuthill, brother, wife Alice, and five children. Henry Tuthill was buried on 26th March 1618 at St. Mary's, Tharston. It seems probable that Henry's brothers, William and John, also remained in Norfolk as did their families and that it is their descendants from whom the later Norfolk Tuttles are descended.

St. Mary's Church, Tharston

However unfortunately the trail goes cold when one tries to trace William and John Tuthill, the two brothers of Henry Tuthill (1580-1618) whose three sons, also called John, William and Henry all emigrated to America – see below. The American descendants are all well recorded in many American family trees as early settlers. In effect, if the Norfolk Tuttles are descended from one or other of the other two (William or John), there is a gap of approximately a century before the three William Tuthills of the 18th century mentioned below, who do come from the same part of Norfolk. Such parish records as exist on line do not help, although more may come to light, and despite having conducted an extensive search I have so far been unable to make the link, although I consider it likely that my theory as to the ancestry from the early Tuthills from the Saxlingham area is correct.

A possible line is as follows:

i. John Tuttell (1485-1543) born in Saxlingham
ii. John Tuthill (1510-1579) born in Saxlingham, married to Elizabeth Hodgkin
iii. John Tuthill (1550-1618) born in Saxlingham, married to Elizabeth Woolmer (born 1545). [He was the brother of William Tuthill of Newton, who died in 1591, referred to above, whose daughter's tomb (Elizabeth, Lady Dalyson) is in the Church of Trowse-with-Newton, bearing the Tuthill arms.]
iv. Brothers William Tuthill (probably born in 1576 but other dates and descendants unknown), John Tuthill (probably born in 1578 but other dates and descendants unknown – however he was alive in 1618 because he is mentioned in his brother, Henry's, will dated 1618) and Henry Tuthill (1580-1618) – see below for a note on Henry Tuthill under "The American Connection".

There are a large number of American family trees on line which mention either William or John Tuthill of this last generation as ancestors. However in my view these must be taken with a large pinch of salt because there are many obvious errors, and no supporting records to corroborate the assertions. For example according to some of the trees William Tuthill managed to be baptised in Yorkshire three years before his birth in Norfolk and achieved the remarkable feat of fathering a daughter seven years after his death. However his birth in 1576 to John Tuthill of Saxlingham and Elizabeth Woolmer seems likely to be correct. Apart from the posthumous daughter born seven years after his death no descendants are identified, but it is asserted he married Susan Osborne.

John Tuthill is confused in some of the family trees with his cousin Henry Tuthill of Newton because he is said to have married Alice Gooch. Again no records have been identified to corroborate any of the assertions. However the evidence does point to there having been at least three brothers in this generation of the Saxlingham Tuthills, and the likely birth dates are William (b. 1576), John (b. 1578) and Henry (b. 1580). In addition there may have been another brother, Thomas (1586-1648) and three sisters, Jane (b. 1583), Elizabeth (b. 1584) and Judith (b. 1589). There is evidence of the existence of these further possible siblings, but the connection between them and their potential brothers is not established and they may be descendants of a relative from an earlier generation of Tuthills. The probability is that the later Tuttles or Tuthills who lived in the Saxlingham area of Norfolk were descended from one of the Tuthills mentioned above.

The American Connection

Most of this information comes from the American pamphlet, "The Tuthill Family of Tharston, Norfolk County, England and Southold, Suffolk County, New York" by Lucy Dubois Akerly, New York 1898.

Henry Tuthill (1580-1618), the third son of John Tuthill and Elizabeth Woolmer, had a number of children, three sons and two daughters. Each of the three sons, John, baptised 25th October 1607, William, baptised 29th October 1609 and Henry junior, baptised 28th June 1612, were early settlers in North America. The daughters were Alice (b. 1614) and Elizabeth (b. 1616).

The three sons, John, William and Henry, all emigrated to New England, possibly on board the "Planter" in 1635, but some of the documentation refers to Henry Tuthill having sailed on board the "Mary Anne" of Yarmouth in 1637. There were numerous ships taking settlers to the American Colonies at this time and the records are inevitably somewhat confusing and vary in detail. John Tuthill (b.1607), known as Pilgrim John, settled in New Haven (Connecticut, where the University of Yale was founded) – he was one of the earliest settlers of Southold and its first civil magistrate, being appointed Constable for Yennicok or Southold in 1642. He subsequently returned to Ireland, settling in Galway along with a number of disheartened settlers from the American colonies and is said to have died in Carrickfergus.

William Tuthill (b.1609) seems to have definitely sailed to America aboard the ship "Planter" in 1635 and settled in New Haven. Henry Tuthill (b.1612), who appears more likely to have sailed on the "Mary Anne", settled in New Hingham in 1637 where he was Constable in 1640. He moved to Southold in 1644 and died before 1650. His wife Bridget survived him and remarried William Wells. The descendants of these two families remained in North America.

There is some fascinating information about the American Tuthills. They bred prolifically and appear to have been very devout Protestants. There are some wonderful names recorded including Deliverance, Freegift, Noah, Azariah, Lazarus, Mehitable, Bethia, Zipporah, Desiah, Parnel, Jared, Elisha, Gamaliel, Lucretia, Selah, Eliphaz and Micah.

Some members of the family lived at Salem at the time of the Salem witch trials. Some of them became Army and Navy Officers in the American war of Independence and subsequently. Anna Tuthill Symmes, who was a descendant of Henry Tuthill (b 1580) via Henry Tuthill (b. 1612), mentioned above, married Brigadier General William Henry Harrison (1773-1841), who became the ninth President of the United States of America in 1841, the last Whig President, who was the first to die in office, of pneumonia, after only three months as President. He had the nickname "Old Tippecanoe" as a result of leading the Army in a major battle at the Tippecanoe River in Indiana of which he was the Governor, defeating an Indian uprising in 1811. He also led the American forces in the short war against the British in 1812. Their grandson, Benjamin Harrison (1833-1901) was elected President of the United States in 1888, defeating the incumbent, Grover Cleveland. Known as "Little Ben" because of his diminutive stature he was defeated by Grover Cleveland in the 1892 presidential election. He was a Republican. Presidents William Henry Harrison and Benjamin Harrison share a common ancestor, Captain Thomas J. Taylor, (4th great grandfather of William Henry Harrison) with the actress Elizabeth Taylor who is Captain Taylor's 7th great granddaughter.

The ship "Planter" sailed to the American Colonies in 1635 and the "Mary Anne" in 1637. The first Pilgrim Fathers sailed on the "Mayflower" in 1620 and in the twenty years which followed many ships containing disaffected Protestants set sail from Britain to the British colonies in North America. This was a time of religious unrest in England when the King (Charles I) and the Archbishop of Canterbury (Archbishop Laud) were imposing anti-Puritan and less Protestant practices in the Church of England. As a consequence many devout Protestants left the country for New England where Protestant Churches were established. Whole congregations left for the American colonies to practice their religion away from the control of the King and Archbishop. The early settlers became known as the Pilgrim Fathers. The emigration became so considerable that consideration was given by the King to banning it. The religious differences between the King and Parliament were one of the factors which led to the English Civil War in the 1640s. Norfolk was a major stronghold of Protestantism.

The "Planter" appears to have been full of Tuttles. There was a Richard Tuttle, his wife Ann, his mother Isobel and 3 children, Ann, Anna and John. There was another William Tuttle, his wife Elizabeth and 3 children, John, Ann and Thomas. These two families had their origins in Northamptonshire. There were also other passengers named Tuttle (or the name's various alternative spellings) on board including those mentioned above.

Some of the descendants of the Northamptonshire Tuttles were the subject of serious criminal charges. Mercy Tuttle (b. 1650) a daughter of the William Tuttle who emigrated from Northampton on the "Planter", was convicted of murdering her son, Samuel, by chopping him to death with an axe as he lay in bed. She pleaded insanity but was convicted of murder and sentenced to death. However the public outcry led to her escaping execution. Mercy's brother, Benjamin Tuttle, was also convicted of murder, the victim being his sister Sarah, who he killed "for losing her virginity", and he was executed.

The American descendants of the Norfolk Tuttles and others descended from the Northamptonshire Tuttles became prominent citizens of the New England colonies and subsequently the United States, and the name is quite common amongst old-established American families.

There are no records to prove any connection between the Norfolk Tuttles and the Northamptonshire Tuttles although such records as may exist in Tudor times and earlier are inevitably very sparse, so a connection must be a possibility.

Chapter 2: Known Tuttle Ancestors

My grandmother was born Dorothy (Dolly) May Tuttle in 1889, one of ten children, five boys (two of whom died in infancy) and five girls, born to Ebenezer Tuttle[2] and his wife Mary Jane. Dolly Tuttle married George William Booth Eyre in 1917 at Lowestoft. Until her marriage she lived with her parents at the family homes in Lowestoft, firstly 4, Commercial Road, over one of the shop premises comprising the family business, and latterly at Cliff House, a grand house on the cliff at the south of the resort with commanding views of the coast. As will emerge she suffered a number of serious blows during her life, becoming widowed at the age of 46 and losing her son in an air accident shortly after the Second World War during which he had been held a prisoner of war for over three years.

My grandmother's surviving siblings were: Arthur Ebenezer Tuttle (1878-1937), Ernest William Tuttle (1879-1955), Herbert Stanley Tuttle (1880-1937), Ethel Jennie Tuttle (1882-1942), Violet Emma Tuttle (1888-1966) who married Arthur Reynolds, Olive Mary Tuttle (1891-1960) and Kathleen Hope Tuttle (1894-1974). Her brothers all married, as did her sister Violet. My grandmother died in 1970 aged 81. My grandmother and her four sisters were known as Ellie, Vi, Dolly, Olly and Kacky!

Ebenezer Tuttle died in 1921 and his widow, Mary, remained living at Cliff House until her death in 1930, when the house was sold – a fisheries research establishment now stands on the site.

---

[2] See Chapter 4 for a short biography of Ebenezer Tuttle

The three unmarried daughters, Ethel, Olive and Kathleen, had a house built nearby at Oulton Broad, where following Ethel's death and the bombing of her home in Surrey my grandmother moved.

It was at summer holidays at this house, "Old Meadows", that I came to know my Tuttle relatives. In addition to my grandmother, there were her sisters Olive and Kathleen, and later for the last few years of her life, Violet, living at "Old Meadows". Ernest's son, John Tuttle, who was the managing director of the family business, his wife, Marjorie, and their two sons, my second cousins Christopher and Stephen were frequent visitors. John's brother, Air Marshal Sir Geoffrey Tuttle[3], visited from time to time - he was very close to my mother so we also saw him elsewhere. John Tuttle was regarded as the head of the family and he was the chairman and managing director of the family business, Tuttles, a department store in the centre of Lowestoft which operated until 1960 when it was sold to Debenhams[4]. Uncle John as we knew him had a withered arm as a result of polio. My grandmother was the company secretary. It was from these relatives that I learnt about my family origins and the particular influence of Ebenezer Tuttle whose portrait in the robes of Mayor of Lowestoft dominated the sitting room at "Old Meadows" where any members of the family visiting Lowestoft would call to pay their respects to my grandmother and her sisters.

---

[3] See Chapter 6 for a short biography of Sir Geoffrey Tuttle
[4] See Chapter 5 for a short history of Tuttles

A photograph taken at the wedding of my great uncle Ernest Tuttle, the second son of Ebenezer Tuttle, to Florence May Whittaker, in 1904

We saw very little of Arthur Tuttle's family who had all left the area. Two of his sons, Tom and Donald, lived in South Africa. His other son, Richard (Dick), lived in Kent and his daughters were married and lived elsewhere. The three sons were educated at Gresham's School in Holt, North Norfolk. Ernest Tuttle had another son in addition to John and Geoffrey, Henry, known as Bunny. He and his family would visit from time to time and I also met him when visiting his brother, Geoffrey, in the London area. Ernest's three sons had been educated at St. Paul's School, London. Ernest's daughter, Pauline, was married to a bank manager, Tom Fairbairn, and the family lived in Scotland, but they sometimes visited their Lowestoft relatives. Stanley Tuttle had two daughters who both lived in Suffolk and they were occasional visitors. Violet Reynolds and her husband Arthur had twin sons, Paul and John. Paul Reynolds and his family regularly took holidays in Sheringham in Norfolk, so they were frequent visitors, particularly when Violet was living at "Old Meadows", and Paul became very close to my mother. My second cousin Christopher Reynolds, Paul's son, and his wife Mary now live in

Norwich a few hundred yards from where our mutual 3rd great grandparents William and Mary Tuthill resided.

Ebenezer Tuttle, my great grandfather, was born in 1851, the second son of Henry Tuttle (1817-1897)[5]. He married Mary Jane Berrett from Orford in 1878. Ebenezer was a distinguished citizen of Lowestoft whose life is set out in Chapter 4. Something of a mystery surrounds his elder brother Henry William Tuttle (b. 1850), who appears to have set himself up as a grocer and draper in Pakefield at the south of the town of Lowestoft, but of whom nothing is known after 1888. The 1881 census shows him living at 12, Dagmar House, Pakefield, with his wife Minnie who was born in the West Indies. Also living in the house was a servant and Henry William is described as a grocer and draper employing three assistants. A trade directory refers to him trading in 1888, but neither Henry William nor Minnie appear in any subsequent census returns, nor is there a record of their deaths in any British records. There was occasional talk of a member of the family who emigrated to the Americas, which may be him, but I have been unable to trace any record of this, so his fate remains unknown.

The life of Henry Tuttle is set out in detail in Chapter 3. He moved from Norwich to Lowestoft in the 1840s and founded the family business. He was born in Barford a small village just outside Norwich, but by the time of the 1841 census he was living with his parents in the centre of Norwich. His parents were William and Mary Tuttle, sometimes recorded as Tuthill. In 1845 he married Mary Ann Ducker whose Ducker family had lived in Great Yarmouth for generations.

---

[5] See Chapter 3 for a short biography of Henry Tuttle

Henry's father, William Tuthill (1792-1842), married Mary Smith in 1815. He was born in Wymondham and baptised in the magnificent abbey church. It is clear from records of the births of the family's various children that the family moved from place to place within the Norwich area, including the villages of Hockham and Barford. This may fit with William Tuthill's occupation as stated in the 1841 census of "hawker", a sort of door to door salesman, although in a record of the baptism of a son, James, in 1829, he is stated to be a labourer. Clearly at this time the family was of relatively humble means and it would appear that Henry bettered himself when he took up the grocery trade. It is interesting to note that while Henry was already a grocer at the time of the 1841 census, his sisters Mary (aged 19) and Ann (aged 15) and brother Robert (aged 16) were working as silk or cotton weavers. Mary subsequently married Henry Betts who was a grocer and draper in Norwich. So grocery and drapery were clearly the sorts of business that this family worked in and were connected with. There are a number of graves at Barford in the name of Betts. Following the death of William Tuthill in 1842 his widow, Mary, went to live with her daughter Mary and son-in-law, Henry Betts, in the Lakenham area of Norwich – in the census returns for 1851 and 1861 she is described as an "annuitant" which presumably means she was receiving an income from an annuity. There is a record of the burial of Maria Tuttle in the parish of Lakenham in 1869 which seems more likely to refer to her than the death of a Mary Tuttle in Yarmouth in 1878, particularly as there is no appropriate record of her living with the Betts family in the 1871 census.

It has been possible to trace back at least three, and possibly five further generations. William Tuthill's father was also called William, my 4th great grandfather (1766-c.1815), as were his father and grandfather before him. Little is known about them except what can be gleaned from the parish records which reveal them all living in the village of Hockham, one of the small villages between Norwich and Wymondham, where it appears that the family ended up at the end of the 18th century. It is clear that there have been Tuttles living in the vicinity of Wymondham for many generations and there is a road called Tuttles Lane on the outskirts of the town. The parish records for Hockham reveal the marriage of William Tuttle (so spelt) and Mary Balls in 1736, my 6th great grandparents, the birth of their son, William, in 1738 and his marriage to Elizabeth Chapman in April 1765, my 5th great grandparents, and the birth of their son William, my 4th great grandfather in September 1766. In all the Hockham parish records up to the middle of the 18th century the surname is spelt Tuttle, as it is today, but later records give the spelling Tuthill until the early 19th century. Unfortunately none of the parish records give any clue as to the occupation of any of these Tuttles, but they do indicate that each of the parties to the respective marriages came from Hockham.

A large number of the parish records for Norfolk have been made available on line by the Norfolk County Record Office. I was able to find the records relating to all my Tuttle ancestors back to William Tuttle, my 6th great grandfather, who was born in 1709. His baptismal record at Ketteringham, one of the villages to the south and west of Norwich from where the family clearly comes, names his parents as Benjamin and Joanna Tuttell, and the only Benjamin Tuttell in the records was baptised in the same parish in 1685, the son of another Benjamin Tuttell and his wife Mathy. If these are correctly identified as ancestors they will be my 7th and 8th great grandparents respectively. Unfortunately the records do not reveal earlier ancestors so it is still not possible to identify a definite link to the Tuthills of Newton and Saxlingham referred to in the last chapter, but since these people all lived in the same small district the possibility becomes ever more probable and further records may come to light to confirm this.

Chapter 3: Henry Tuttle

The Tuttle family to which my close relatives belonged was always associated with Lowestoft where the family business was located. From my grandmother and her sisters I gained much knowledge about their father, Ebenezer Tuttle [see Chapter 4], but there was little known about earlier generations. However many years ago I came across an article published by the Lowestoft Historical Society in a series entitled "Worthies of Lowestoft" about Ebenezer Tuttle's father, Henry, from which much of the information in this chapter and Chapter 5 has been drawn.

Henry Tuttle (1817-1897) was my great great grandfather. He was born on 12th December 1817 at Barford, a small village seven miles west of Norwich. He was the son of William and Mary Tuthill and was baptised at Barford on 15th February 1818. The surname is spelt Tuthill in the record and William Tuthill's occupation is given as "labourer". By the time of the 1841 census the name was usually spelt "Tuttle".

St. Botolph's Church Barford

In 1833, aged 18, he became employed by Bennet and Bream of 12, Upper Market, Norwich, wholesale and retail grocers and later joined Messrs. Copeman and Son, 12, Gentlemen's Walk, Norwich, also wholesale and retail grocers.

In 1843 Henry Tuttle moved to Lowestoft and established himself as a grocer and provision merchant at 66, High Street. On 2nd June 1845 he married Mary Ann Ducker, who was born on 7th October 1818 at Great Yarmouth. The marriage took place at Mundesley in Norfolk.

Henry and Mary Ann Tuttle had 6 children, Rebecca (born 30th August 1846), twins Mary Ann and Louisa Ann the second of whom died within days of her birth (born 27th March 1848), Henry William (born 31st January 1850) Ebenezer (born 13th September 1851) [See Chapter 4] and Emma (born 5th March 1855, died 23rd March 1920, the day before my mother was born).

The business flourished and in 1850 Henry Tuttle purchased land and erected another shop at 58, High Street, Lowestoft. These premises were known as Victoria House and were operated by the Tuttle family until 1920 when the shop was closed down. However shortly after this the premises were operated as "The International Tea Company Stores" and continued in business until 15th February 1941 when the building suffered a direct hit in a bombing raid.

Henry Tuttle opened further premises in 1854 at the junction of Raglan Street and Barn Street, in 1856 at 4, Denmark Road and in 1866 at 4, Commercial Road, which also marked the expansion of the business into drapery and millinery.

Henry Tuttle served as a Town Constable for Lowestoft (in those days an elected office) in 1846 and 1849. In the Handbook for Lowestoft of 1871 there is an entry which reads: "The Post Office in the New Town is near the harbour and is in the care of Mr. Henry Tuttle". The development of Lowestoft in the latter part of the nineteenth century as a holiday resort and the building of the new town to the design of Sir Moreton Peto is itself a most interesting history and no doubt this expansion assisted the development of the Tuttles business which can be followed in Chapter 4 about Ebenezer Tuttle, Henry's son, and Chapter 5 about the history of Tuttles.

From the census returns it is possible to discover quite a lot of information about the circumstances of how the family lived. In 1851 the family which comprised Henry, his wife Mary, and their children, Rebecca (1846-1888), Mary Ann (1848-1899) and Henry William (b. 1850) were living at Dukes Head Street in Lowestoft. Henry Tuttle's occupation was grocer, and also living in the household were a male grocer's assistant and two female servants. Ebenezer Tuttle was born later in 1851 after the date of the census.

By 1861 the family had moved to 58, High Street, Lowestoft. Henry is described as a grocer and merchant employing six men. Henry William Tuttle, who would have been 11 years old, is not listed as one of the children at this address, but this may mean no more than that he was staying away on the day of the census. Also residing in the household were a grocer's assistant called Edwin Wise and a servant called Caroline Stubbs.

Henry's wife, Mary Ann, died in 1870. In 1871 his daughter, also named Mary Ann, son Henry William and daughter Emma were living with him at 58, High Street. Henry is now described as a grocer merchant employing nine people. Also living in the household were Henry Welch and James A Butler, described as assistants, and Eliza Folkard, general servant. Ebenezer Tuttle was living in Peterborough at the date of the census, working as a draper's assistant, probably to gain experience of the business in other premises.

In the 1881 census Henry Tuttle's daughter Emma, described as housekeeper, was living with him as was his ten year old granddaughter, Constance Creak, born Great Yarmouth and daughter of Rebecca Creak (Henry's eldest daughter – see below). There was a boarder, called E W Webber and a general servant, Honor Hardy, in the household. Henry is described as a family grocer and wine and spirit merchant.

By 1891 Henry Tuttle, still at 58, High Street, is described as a grocer and draper. Of his children only Emma is living with him, described as housekeeper. A domestic servant called Emma Tuthill is listed as a member of the household, as are William Webb and James Brown, grocer's assistants

Henry Tuttle died on 24th May 1897. He left effects valued at nearly £11,000, a huge sum which using the assessment of the economic power of that value of wealth today would equate to approximately £10 million.

Henry Tuttle's shop premises and home at 58 High Street Lowestoft

It has been possible to trace Henry's children. Ebenezer's story was well known to me and is set out in Chapter 4. As I have stated earlier there is a mystery surrounding the elder son, Henry William. Two of Henry's daughters married and had children.

Rebecca Tuttle (1846-1888) married William Philip Creak (1844-1911). The Creaks had six children: Edith May (b. 1869); Constance Ethel (b.1871) who became a music teacher; Lillian (b. 1872); Herbert William (1875-1947); Evan Victor (1880-1966); and Gladys Christine (b.1887). William Creak was born in King's Lynn. His occupation was stated as grocer in the 1881 census and thereafter he was a commercial traveller.

Evan Victor Creak, the younger son, married Marie Grace von Goldstein (1884-1924) in Shimla, Bengal, India in 1906. Marie Grace von Goldstein was born in Shimla of German origins. Her father, Felix Carl von Goldstein (1834-1892), came from Leipzig and her mother, Adolphina Caroline Sophia Kirsten (1842-1910), was born in Wiesbaden (see below). Evan and Marie Creak were close to Ebenezer and Mary Tuttle and stayed with them when they visited England from India and they are mentioned several times in Mary Tuttle's journal. Evan Creak served as an officer in the Indian Army and the family resided in Delhi. He died in a motor accident in Hastings in 1966, aged 86. Gladys Creak, his sister, makes an interesting appearance in the 1911 census return as one of the staff of Marshall and Snelgrove Ltd, the well-known Oxford Street Store, one hundred of whom were residing in a hostel for the store's staff at 16, Marylebone Lane. All the named staff were single, many described as a draper's assistant as was Gladys Creak, and some of the others were described as shopwalkers.

Evan Creak, Ebenezer Tuttle's nephew and my first cousin twice removed, pictured at Cliff House in 1921

A Creak family picnic on New Year's Eve 1922 at Delhi

Felix Carl von Goldstein (1834-1892)

Although not an ancestor of mine, Evan Creak's father-in-law, Felix Carl von Goldstein, is an interesting character worthy of note. He was a German Baron who came from an aristocratic catholic family in Leipzig but he was disinherited by his family when he became a protestant. He went to England where as a professional musician he gained the appointment as bandmaster of one of the native regiments in India. He arrived in India shortly before the outbreak of the Indian Mutiny of 1857. He took up a post as Regimental Bandmaster of the 10th Native Infantry (a civilian post) and was stationed at Fatehgarh. He was one of the few civilians to be awarded the Indian Mutiny Medal for his courageous service in escorting the wives of English officers from Fatehgarh to Calcutta ensuring their safety. Fatehgarh was a military station on the banks of the Ganges and was the site of one of the first rebellions of the Indian Mutiny. From there the mutiny spread rapidly to Cawnpore, an important garrison town for the East India Company. Some of the most brutal murders of the Indian Mutiny took place in this area, then known as Bengal. Following the recapture of Fatehgarh, as the British forces advanced upon Cawnpore approximately 200 British women and children from Fatehgarh and Cawnpore, who had not been able to escape and who were held captive by the rebels, were massacred and their bodies were thrown into a well.

Felix and Adolphina von Goldstein c. 1870

Felix von Goldstein married Adolphina Kirsten, also of German stock, in 1858 at Fort William in Calcutta – Fort William was the headquarters of the East India Company. They had no fewer than 17 children, one of whom, Marie, married Evan Creak (Ebenezer Tuttle's nephew, and my first cousin twice removed). Felix von Goldstein's musical career led to his being appointed Director of Music to the Viceroys of India, directing the various bands and orchestras which were maintained by the Government. He served 4 Viceroys, namely Lord Lytton, The Marquess of Ripon, Earl Dufferin and the Marquess of Lansdowne, between 1876 and 1892, the year of his death. The von Goldstein family lived in

Simla which was the summer capital of the Government when Calcutta was vacated because of the oppressive heat. Felix von Goldstein appears to have become quite wealthy acquiring two old Simla properties, first Benmore and then Wildflower Hall, Natasu. Benmore became the public assembly rooms of Simla. Wildflower Hall was let to the Government and was the official residence of Lord Kitchener when he was Commander in Chief from 1902 to 1909. Wildflower Hall is now a luxury hotel, reputed to be one of the best in India.

Rudyard Kipling spent some of his early life living in Simla, and as a journalist in the late 1880s wrote many articles and reports commenting on life in the summer capital. Some of these included references to musical events including some at Benmore in which Felix von Goldstein will have been involved. His book "Plain Tales from the Hills" is a collection of stories based on his experiences at Simla. In his poem "The Plea of the Simla Dancers", published in 1886, Kipling bemoans the fact that Benmore had been taken over for Government Offices.

Mary Ann Tuttle (1848-1899) married Edward Lang (1849-1925). They had 2 children: Daisy (b.1883) and Constance Mary (1884-1961). Following his wife's death in 1899 Edward Lang married a second time in 1900 to Annie Betts. Edward Lang was born in Heavitree, Exeter, and he became a Methodist Minister, serving in Middlesbrough, Huddersfield, Grimsby and Louth, where he died in 1925.

Constance Mary Lang (1884-1961) became a lecturer at The Diocesan Training College at Ripon (Church of England), and is listed amongst the ten lecturers in the 1911 census. This was a teacher training college for ladies with at that time 105 students.

It and its associated college for men, St. John's College, are the two institutions which were the constituent colleges for what is now York St. John's University. Another lecturer at the college was Mary Eleanor Whitaker, whose brother The Revd Charles Frederic Mann Whitaker married Constance Lang – they had three children, Edward, Christine and John.

Emma Tuttle (1855-1920) was the youngest of Henry Tuttle's children. She never married and until her father's death in 1897 she lived with him. Thereafter she lived in the household of her brother, Ebenezer.

Chapter 4: Ebenezer Tuttle

Ebenezer Tuttle (1851-1921), the second son of Henry Tuttle [See Chapter 3], was my great grandfather. He was born at Lowestoft on 13th September 1851. Educated at Lowestoft College, and following a period working in Peterborough as a draper's assistant (revealed in the 1871 census) he joined his father in the family business which by now was flourishing having branched out from grocery to drapery, millinery and furnishing. It was Ebenezer Tuttle who was responsible for the major development of the business into a leading department store of the highest quality at the Bon Marche premises, but retaining the two grocery outlets at 4, Commercial Road and 58, High Street, all in Lowestoft. The growth and expansion of the family business coincided with the development of Lowestoft from a small fishing village into a major holiday resort, fishing port and commercial and naval port, its location at the most easterly point in the country rendering it well placed to meet the threats posed by the rise of Germany as a naval power at the end of the nineteenth century. Lowestoft was the victim at least one major Zeppelin raid and a naval bombardment in World War I and bombing in World War II as a result of its naval importance. It is clear that both Henry and Ebenezer Tuttle showed considerable business acumen in adapting their business to the growing needs of the town.

In 1877 Ebenezer married Mary Jane Berrett of Orford and they had ten children, two of whom (Edwin Garfield and Percy) died in infancy. The three sons, Arthur, Ernest (father of John and Geoffrey [see Chapter 6] and others) and Stanley, all went into the family business. There were five daughters, three of whom (Ethel, Olive and Kathleen) remained unmarried. Violet married Arthur Reynolds and had twin sons, Paul and John. Dorothy (Dolly) married George Eyre and had a son, Anthony [see Chapter 14] and a daughter, Pamela, my mother.

Ebenezer and Mary Tuttle

After living for several years at 4, Commercial Road, over one of his shop premises, Ebenezer Tuttle acquired a magnificent home, Cliff House, at the edge of the cliffs at the south of the town where it merged with the village of Pakefield. This lovely house and garden were the family's residence for about 30 years until the death of Ebenezer's widow in 1930 after which it was sold and the unmarried daughters moved to a newly built home at nearby Oulton Broad – Old Meadows. Cliff House stood immediately above the spot on the beach where the family retained a beach hut (Number 2) until the early 1970s. The site of Cliff House is now occupied by a fisheries research establishment. Living with the family there until her death was Mary Jane's mother, Celia Jane Berrett (1826-1915), and there was a live-in housekeeper, Edith Simmonds.

A gathering at Cliff House – possibly for a family wedding – current members of the family now refer to this as the staff photograph!

There was however considerably more to Ebenezer Tuttle than being a very successful businessman. He played an important role in the civic life of Lowestoft, so much so that when he died in 1921 the Lowestoft Journal referred to his death as "Lowestoft's Great Loss" in its headline and devoted almost a whole page (of closely typed broadsheet) of its edition of Christmas Eve 1921 to a "Special Memoir".

Ebenezer Tuttle served as a town councillor and for some time alderman from 1890 until his death. He was a staunch Liberal and Treasurer of the Lowestoft Liberal Club. He served for two terms as Mayor of Lowestoft from 1904 to 1906. When his first term of office came to an end which would usually be relinquished to another, the council unanimously elected him to a second term. He was the Chairman of the Sea Defence Committee in Lowestoft, under which auspices the sea wall and promenade were built.

Ebenezer Tuttle when Mayor of Lowestoft

He also served as a member for Lowestoft on Suffolk County Council for several years, chairing the committee which administered St. Audry's Hospital, formerly known as Molton Asylum. This was just one of his many social and charitable interests. He was Chairman of the local YMCA, Honorary Secretary of the Sailor's and Fishermen's Bethel and Sailors' Home, and a devout and loyal member of the Lowestoft United Methodist Church.

Ebenezer Tuttle was a Justice of the Peace, serving as a member of the Lowestoft Magistrates' Bench and the Suffolk County Bench for many years. He was a highly respected magistrate who took a special interest in juvenile offenders (it is perhaps worth noting that it was only in 1909 that the Juvenile Court – then referred to as the Children's Court - was established and before then little special account was taken of the youth of offenders). The obituary in the Lowestoft Journal is worth quoting verbatim, for his judicial approach could be a model to be followed by all who occupy judicial office whether high or lowly:

"As a magistrate he was fair and impartial. Although he held strong views on certain matters he never allowed prejudice to blind him. He was painstaking to a degree, and would never be satisfied until everything brought in evidence was sifted to the full. Sometimes he was considered too particular, but he had a high sense of duty, and nothing ever deterred him from exercising it. He was a regular attendant at the Children's Court, and when juvenile offenders were brought before him he tempered sternness with kindness. He recognised that the fault was not so much that of the youngsters as of their parents, and to the latter he gave reasoned and pointed advice, which it is known was very affective. The youthful delinquents he urged with all earnestness to be better boys and girls, and as often with tears in their eyes they were leaving the Court he admonished them with: 'Now go and be good and don't come here again.' Afterwards he would

visit their homes and in this way he was able to make for domestic betterment."

Having been in poor health for some time, on Saturday 17th December 1921, as was his usual practice, Ebenezer Tuttle went to the Free Methodist Church to ensure that all was ready for the Sunday service and to place flowers on the rostrum. When he did not return home to Cliff House for lunch there was some concern and his two sons Arthur and Ernest went to the church where they found their father in his pew, in a leaning attitude. Having completed his duties, for everything was in its rightful place, in the church which meant so much to him, Ebenezer Tuttle died peacefully, aged 70. As the Lowestoft Journal stated: "May it be said, with due reverence, the painless death of a righteous man in the House of God."

So respected was he that the streets of Lowestoft were lined with mourners as the horse-drawn funeral cortege passed by and the curtains of many windows were drawn closed as a mark of respect on the route of the funeral procession. Ebenezer's estate was valued at £24,217 12s. 6d. which equates to approximately £8 million using the assessment of the economic power of that value of wealth today.

Ebenezer Tuttle's influence as the head of the family should not be underestimated. The character of some of his descendants is apparent from this volume. Several of us knew some of his children well and can recall them wondering "what Daddy would have done" when faced with difficult decisions or circumstances many years after his death. He was clearly a very loving father and his children and their descendants have done him proud. In my brother's and my possession are some of the journals he wrote about holidays he took at home and abroad with a selection of his daughters. From these a very warm character emerges and having read them I feel I know the man. The most interesting is an account of a cruise along the Norwegian coast in the summer of 1914 a few weeks before the outbreak of the Great War. By all accounts the party, which comprised Ebenezer and his three elder daughters, Ethel, Violet and Dorothy, was fortunate not to be shipwrecked. There is a description of a terrible storm as the small vessel crossed the North Sea from Newcastle which was so severe that some of the railings were wrenched off the ship. On board were some survivors of the "Empress of Ireland" disaster who said that the experience was more frightening than the sinking they had experienced. (On 28th May 1914 the Canadian Pacific liner "Empress of Ireland" was in collision with another ship in the St. Lawrence River with a huge loss of 1,012 lives, the third greatest civilian maritime loss of life of the decade after the sinkings of the "Titanic" and "Lusitania").

At the time of the 1911 census only two of Ebenezer and Mary Tuttle's children were living with their parents at Cliff House - Dorothy (my grandmother) and Olive. Arthur and Ernest were married and living in their own homes in Lowestoft. Stanley, Ethel and Violet were living at 4, Commercial Road, over one of the shops, where Stanley was the grocery manager. At some stage Olive moved to 4, Commercial Road, possibly when Stanley married in 1913 and moved to his own home. Ethel and Olive remained living at 4, Commercial Road until the building was sold in 1920, when they returned to Cliff House to live with their mother and father. Kathleen Hope Tuttle was at boarding school in Llandudno at the time of the 1911 census. She worked in a munitions factory during the Great War and remained unmarried, living with her parents until her mother died in 1930.

Ebenezer and Mary Tuttle and their children (from L to R) Ethel, Arthur, Olive, Violet, Ernest, Kathleen, Stanley & Dorothy (Dolly) - photograph c.1897, possibly to mark the Diamond Jubilee of HM Queen Victoria

Following the death of Ebenezer his widow, Mary Jane Tuttle (1852-1930), lived at Cliff House until her death. Her unmarried daughters, Ethel, Olive and Kathleen, lived with her. She kept a book of days in which she recorded significant events. The First World War from her perspective is documented in this journal. These include a description of several air raids including a major Zeppelin raid on Lowestoft in 1916, and a sea battle in the North Sea which she observed from her house. The entry for 25th April 1916 reads: "Naval engagement by German warships etc off Lowestoft. Terrible time – saw it from Cliff House. Fled to the cellar".

This refers to a battle fought between the British and German navies. A German battle cruiser squadron accompanied by cruisers and destroyers bombarded Lowestoft and Great Yarmouth, in order to entice the Royal Navy ships to sea to be picked off by the battle cruiser squadron or by the full German High Seas Fleet which was stationed at sea ready to intervene. The result was inconclusive. Each navy lost a submarine, two British light cruisers were damaged, a German cruiser was damaged and a German submarine was captured. 200 houses in Lowestoft were damaged by shellfire and four people were killed and nineteen were wounded in the attack. Lowestoft was an important base for mine-laying and sweeping and Great Yarmouth was a submarine base. The engagement is sometimes referred to as "The Lowestoft Raid". The Battle of Jutland took place at the end of May 1916.

Afternoon tea in the garden of Cliff House in 1920 – overlooking Lowestoft Beach

Mary Jane Tuttle also noted the receipt of letters from her three sons, Arthur, Ernest and Stanley, and later her son-in-law, my grandfather George Eyre, from the conflict arenas where they were stationed in the First World War including Gallipoli, Egypt, Palestine and France. From these it is possible to follow their military careers. Remarkably all of them survived, but alas the letters are lost. Her notes of the 1920s are an interesting account of an upper middle class existence at the time and contain very personal accounts of her grief following the death of her husband to whom she was clearly devoted.

Ebenezer Tuttle's youngest daughter, Kathleen, died in 1974 aged 79, and was laid to rest in the family tomb alongside her beloved father and other family members in Lowestoft Cemetery.

Chapter 5: A History of Tuttles

There are still people who live in or have connections with Lowestoft who remember "Tuttles" the department store situated in the centre of the town close to the railway station. The business was operated by my family for 117 years.

Henry Tuttle, having worked in grocers businesses in Norwich, arrived in Lowestoft and set himself up in business as a grocer and provision merchant at 66, High Street in 1843. In 1850 he opened a further shop at 58, High Street, known as Victoria House [see illustration in Chapter 3]. The business continued to expand and in 1854 a branch was opened at the junction of Raglan Street and Barn Street. A further branch was opened in 1856 at 2, Virant Place, Denmark Road, later known as No, 4 Denmark Road.

Tuttles' Department Store, London Road, Lowestoft, late 19th or early 20th century

In the 1850s Henry Tuttle issued the "Tuttle Token". Such tokens were issued by businesses, redeemable by customers making purchases, the early equivalent of the vouchers often distributed today. The design was as follows:

"Obverse – Victoria. Queen of Great Britain. Head of Queen Victoria to the left.

Reverse – H. Tuttle. Lowestoft. Grocer and tea dealer. High Street"

1866 saw a significant expansion of the business which had hitherto been predominantly a grocery operation with the opening of premises at 4, Commercial Road with drapery and millinery departments.

In 1876 Ebenezer Tuttle, Henry's son, became a partner in the business which became known as H. Tuttle and Son, later Tuttle and Son. In 1886, by which time Ebenezer Tuttle was running the business, the firm purchased a large plot of land on London Road and the premises known as "The Bon Marche" were established bringing into being the largest shop in Lowestoft, later proudly boasting that it was the most easterly department store in Great Britain. The business continued to operate from these very fine premises until 1960 and the building still stands - parts of it are now rather shabby, but a smart public house and restaurant has been established at the end of the building furthest from the harbour.

In 1902 two of Ebenezer's sons Arthur and Ernest Tuttle joined the firm and a limited company was formed – Tuttle and Sons Limited. The third son, Stanley, also joined the firm a few years later. Various members of the family were directors during the 20th century.

When Ebenezer Tuttle died in 1921 his eldest son Arthur Tuttle became Chairman. Arthur died in 1937 and Ernest Tuttle succeeded his brother, remaining Chairman until his death in 1955. His eldest son John Tuttle succeeded as Chairman, having been a director since 1936. John Tuttle had been sent to work at Selfridges in London in the mid-1920s to gain business experience after being educated at St Paul's School, London.

It is worth noting that three generations of Tuttles (Ebenezer, Ernest and John) served as Justices of the Peace for Lowestoft. Known as caring employers the business even had its own football team, Tuttles United Football Club, which played in a local league.

The Tuttles United Football Club Team, 1908-9
Ebenezer Tuttle is seated on the right of the picture, wearing a bowler hat, Arthur Tuttle to the left seated with a riding crop, Ernest Tuttle standing behind him and Stanley Tuttle standing behind his father.

By the end of the 1950s there was no member of the family of the next generation in a position to carry on the business and in the modern age a single high quality department store had probably had its day, so it was decided to sell up to Debenhams Ltd who took over the company on 8th December 1960. The whole of the issued capital in the company was acquired by Debenhams in consideration of the issue of 45,900 10 shilling ordinary shares in Debenhams Ltd which were distributed amongst the family according to their respective shareholdings. The last directors were Mr John Tuttle (Chairman and Managing Director) and my grandmother Mrs Dorothy May Eyre (Company Secretary).

Debenhams operated the store as "Tuttles" for a further 30 years or so. Following its closure as a store the building became something of a blot on the landscape, run down with parts occupied by various businesses, including a nightclub. However in recent years the area has undergone a transformation. There is an attractive pedestrian area, Station Square, with an interesting modern sculpture designed by Charles Normandale known as "The Spirits of Lowestoft", and part of the Tuttles building has been developed by Wetherspoons as a public house and restaurant named "The Joseph Conrad". The author Joseph Conrad was Polish and he landed at Lowestoft when he first came to England in 1878 where he settled and changed his name from Jozef Teodor Konrad Korzenioski – several of his voyages as a seaman, upon which some of his writings were based, were from Lowestoft. He subsequently settled in Kent. The area where the store was situated is known as "Tuttles Corner" and there is a restaurant of that name at the opposite end of the building to "The Joseph Conrad".

The Tuttles Building in 2016 showing "The Joseph Conrad" Public House – features of the building can be compared with the earlier photograph of the same part of the building

Chapter 6: Air Marshal Sir Geoffrey Tuttle KBE CB DFC

Geoffrey William Tuttle was born on 2nd October 1906, the second son of Major Ernest Tuttle. Ebenezer Tuttle was his grandfather and Ernest Tuttle ran the family business in Lowestoft from 1937 to 1955, being succeeded by John Tuttle his eldest son and Geoffrey's brother, who was the last chairman and managing director of Tuttles. Geoffrey Tuttle was my first cousin once removed.

Air Marshal Sir Geoffrey Tuttle KBE CB DFC

He was educated at St. Paul's School in London and joined the Royal Air Force in 1925 on a short service commission after a period working in the family business in Lowestoft. He was attached to No. 19 Squadron at Duxford, flying Gloster Grebe and Armstrong-Whitworth Siskin single seat fighters. His keenness and exceptional flying abilities took him to the Central Flying School at Upavon in 1928 and on to the newly-formed No. 605 (County of Warwick) light bomber squadron of the Auxiliary Air Force stationed at Castle Bromwich as adjutant. This squadron was equipped with DH9As of 1918 vintage.

In 1930 he attended a two year engineering course at Henlow, and in 1931 was granted a permanent commission in the rank of Flight Lieutenant. From 1932 to 1937 he was stationed in India, seeing service on the North West Frontier. He received his Distinguished Flying Cross in 1937 *"For gallant and distinguished service in Waziristan during the period November 1936 to January 1937".* This is a rare example of the award of the DFC during peacetime. He described his experiences at this time in a typical understatement as "playing tag" with rebellious tribesmen round the mountain tops of the North West Frontier!

On his return to the United Kingdom in 1937 Geoffrey Tuttle was promoted to Squadron Leader and appointed to command No. 105 Squadron at Harwell which was equipped with Fairey Battles, the first of the new generation of low-wing monoplane bombers in the RAF. At the outbreak of the Second World War the squadron was in Reims as part of the Advanced Air Striking Force and saw early action in the course of low level photographic recognizance over the Siegfried Line. This experience led Geoffrey Tuttle into the part of his RAF career for which he is most famous, photographic recognizance.

The RAF photographic recognizance unit was commanded by Sir Sydney Cotton who was regarded as somewhat unorthodox by the Air Staff – by all accounts he was a swash-buckling character from Australia. The unit needed to be sorted out and in 1940 with acting rank of Wing Commander Geoffrey Tuttle was appointed to command the unit with the authority to select any pilot he wanted to join his team – at this time the only RAF commander to be so authorised. Geoffrey Tuttle restored good relations with Whitehall but continued the buccaneering tradition of the crews of the unit. This was particularly highly skilled and dangerous work. The aircraft were unarmed and of various types. There was a handful of dashing pink-painted Spitfires, so coloured to be less easily observed against the setting sun. Many planes were lost, including a plane carrying Simon Bowes a photographer attached to the unit, the fiancé of my mother Pamela, Geoffrey's cousin.

Geoffrey Tuttle and his pilots first made a name for the De Havilland Mosquito. Geoffrey Tuttle obtained the first "wooden wonder" from the production line in 1941 and attained hitherto unheard of results because the speed of the Mosquito gave it a considerable advantage in obtaining photographic intelligence. In order to obtain more Mosquitos Geoffrey Tuttle organised a mock dogfight between a Spitfire and a Mosquito before King George VI and Queen Elizabeth to demonstrate the superior speed and manoeuvrability of the newer plane.

In 1940 Geoffrey Tuttle was made an Officer of the Order of the British Empire (OBE). In 1941 he was fortunate to survive when the Hornet Moth he was flying suffered an engine failure on take-off and crashed from fifty feet.

Confirmed as Wing Commander in 1942 and promoted to Group Captain in 1946 Geoffrey Tuttle held acting ranks above these substantive ranks for most of the remainder of the war, being Acting Air Commodore in several posts. His success in photographic recognizance led him to Coastal Command in 1943 and from bases in Tyree and Leuchars he supervised anti-submarine patrol duties.

His next postings were to the Mediterranean firstly to the command of No. 328, a general recognizance wing based in Algiers to cover operations in North West Africa. In March 1944 he became the senior Air Staff Officer at HQ Mediterranean Allied Coastal Air Force. He was involved in campaigns in Corsica, Sardinia and Italy and the liberation of Greece and took charge of the RAF there and the Royal Hellenic Air Force. For his service to Greece he was made a Grand Officer of the Order of the Phoenix. Another foreign decoration was the award of the Order of the Patriotic War (2nd Class) by the Soviet Union. France awarded him the Croix du Guerre and he was appointed a Commandeur du Legion d'Honeur.

Acting Air Commodore Geoffrey Tuttle in Greece - 1944

Geoffrey Tuttle was thrice mentioned in despatches and at the conclusion of the war he was made a Companion of the Order of the Bath (CB), and continued as a Group Captain but with the acting rank of Air Commodore which was confirmed as a substantive rank in 1948. He held various Staff and operational posts, and was promoted to Air Vice-Marshal on 1st January 1952 and Air Marshal on 1st July 1957. He was knighted as a Knight Commander of the Order of the British Empire (KBE) in 1957. From 1951 to 1954 he was Assistant Chief of the Air Staff (Operational Requirements) In 1954 he was appointed Air Officer Commanding No. 19 Group RAF, in 1955 leading No.28 Squadron on an extended goodwill tour of South America setting a pattern which continued for the next ten years. This was known as Operation Suntan, and a film of the tour can be viewed on the British Pathe News website, which includes shots of Air Vice Marshal Tuttle performing a "crossing the line ceremony" in the cockpit of a Shackleton aircraft. Geoffrey Tuttle named various of his boats "Suntan" recalling the considerable success of the operation.

Sir Geoffrey Tuttle's last post in the RAF was that of Deputy Chief of Air Staff from July 1956 until his retirement from the Service in 1959. During these years he was involved in important decisions involving procurement to ensure that the RAF moved with the times and took on board the new developments in rocket science which blew holes in the fighting theories which had relied upon machine guns and cannon. When Deputy Chief of Air Staff he was closely involved with the USAF in developing co-ordinated strategic plans and the deployment of Thor Intermediate Range Ballistic Missiles in the UK. This was a period of great change for the RAF, but the modern force that resulted acquired an enhanced role and secured future.

Sir Geoffrey Tuttle at a Ceremony in 1968 to mark the 50th Anniversary of the Founding of the RAF

Upon retirement from the RAF Sir Geoffrey remained in aviation but in connection with commercial aircraft rather than military. He became a Fellow of the Royal Aeronautical Society in 1960, the year he joined Vickers which subsequently became the British Aircraft Corporation (BAC) as general manager of its Weybridge plant. At this time the company was developing the VC10 and BAC 111 – the former, a magnificent aircraft, never achieved its full potential, but the BAC 111 did achieve excellent sales. In 1965 Sir Geoffrey was appointed Vice-Chairman of the Commercial Aircraft Division of BAC and became involved with the development and promotion of Concorde. He was on board for some of its earliest flights and devoted much of the remainder of his career to the aeroplane which despite its noisiness became a much loved icon of the late 20th century and a great example of international co-operation between Britain and France. Now of course the main European commercial aircraft, such as the Airbus family, are developed and manufactured by several countries in co-operation. Sir Geoffrey is reputed to have been one of the aircraft industry's most travelled executives (for example he visited China in the early 1960s when it was almost closed to foreigners) and was well known for his ability to travel light, swearing by his disposable paper underpants.

Sir Geoffrey handing over a VC10 to Ghana Airways

Sartorially he was an interesting mix. For formal occasions he was always dressed immaculately, in beautifully tailored suits (usually pale grey, lightweight, often made abroad) RAF or club tie and hand-made shoes. He had several pairs of crocodile shoes hand-made in Hong Kong. When my father admired these he was asked to provide an outline of his foot which resulted in two pairs of crocodile shoes, black and brown, which my father treasured and which I now have and still wear half a century after they were manufactured. However when dressing down he favoured canvas sailing trousers, deck shoes and polo shirts or polo-necked sweaters, depending upon the season. The décor of the lavatory at hia home at Kingswood Creek, Wraysbury will never be forgotten by those who entered it. The fittings were pale blue and the walls and all the paintwork black, with a photograph of Sir Geoffrey in the full dress uniform of an Air Marshal framed in a pale blue lavatory seat! The bathroom next door was pink, perhaps to remind him of his fleet of Spitfires when he commanded Photographic Recognizance!

When he retired from the British Aircraft Corporation in 1977, at the age of 71, he was said to have flown 103 different types of aircraft from biplanes to jets. Over the years he met many leading politicians – he once said to me that the two he most admired with whom he had dealings when he was working for BAC were Tony Benn (then known as Anthony Wedgwood Benn) and Michael Heseltine – quite a contrast!

Sir Geoffrey Tuttle had numerous other interests. He was a keen sailor, flying his own design of "Tuttle House Flag" on his various boats which members of the family and his many friends crewed with him. He took part in the London to Brighton Veteran and Vintage Car Rally on many occasions, preceding the run with an excellent lunch party at his home in Wraysbury the day before the event, to which some of the family were from time to time invited. He was President of the British Motor Cycling Racing Club for many years.

In an addendum to the best obituary of Sir Geoffrey Tuttle (in the Independent, 16th January 1989) his good friend Sir George Edwards, sometime Chairman of BAC, wrote "His family and those of us who were lucky enough to be his close friends knew of his uncanny ability to offer help before one knew that it was really needed." When I was a child suffering from a serious spinal illness in the 1960s "Uncle G" sent me some wonderfully comforting letters which I still have and treasure. He would turn up to visit his relations and friends who were ill, finding the time to do so however pressing his work commitments. The author of the obituary in the Independent, Sir Peter Masefield, concluded with these words:

"Quietly and competently enthusiastic about everything he undertook Geoffrey Tuttle was...the most companionable of men"

He died at the age of 82 after a sad decline into illness (having suffered several bouts of ill health during his life fought with customary strength of character) on 11th January 1989.

Chapter 7: The Berretts of Orford

I was able to start my researches into my Tuttle ancestors with a considerable amount of information at my disposal, from family papers, photographs and most importantly my memory of many conversations and continuing contact with my Tuttle relatives. It was possible to use the searching facilities now available to discover further detail and plug a few gaps, and to go back a couple more generations, but primarily my knowledge of the Tuttles revealed in this part comes from other sources available to me.

This was not so with the other families of which a member married a Tuttle. Apart from her maiden name and her life when married to my great grandfather Ebenezer I knew nothing of Mary Jane Berrett's origins and family history other than that she came from Orford. To discover more my first move was to search her name on the Ancestry.co.uk website.

Mary Jane Tuttle (nee Berrett) in the garden of Cliff House, Lowestoft

The starting point was various family trees compiled by others and I was able without difficulty to discover that Mary Jane was the eldest child of the unusually named Friston Berrett and his wife Celia Jane whose maiden name was Langmaid. The name Friston caused much confusion. It was often recorded in the family trees as Tristan or Tristram, presumably because no-one had heard of another Friston, and hand-written records were not always easy to read – similarly in some indexes the same errors occurred. He <u>was</u> named Friston – Friston is a small village between Saxmundham (where Friston stated in census records he was born) and Aldeburgh in Suffolk. Perhaps it was the actual birthplace of Friston Berrett.

By using the family trees and corroborating as much information as possible from the census records, parish records and trade directories it was possible to build up a picture of the Berretts and trace them back to the middle of the 18th century. Although I have entitled this chapter "The Berretts of Orford" it was the marriage of Friston to Celia Jane Langmaid, who was born in Orford, which commenced the connection of the Berretts with that delightful coastal town.

Friston Berrett (1819-1892) was baptised on 24th September 1819 at Saxmundham, Suffolk, the son of Henry and Mary Berrett. In the index records of his baptism his name is recorded correctly as Friston. By the time of the 1841 census he had moved away from his family home and in July 1850 he married Celia Jane Langmaid (1826-1915) at Orford – in the handwritten index of marriages his name is recorded as Triston and Tryston.

The story can then be taken up from the census returns.

At the time of the 1851 census the Berretts were living together in Orford with no children. Friston Berrett's occupation is given as butcher and farmer and that of his wife, dressmaker.

At the date of the 1861 census there were four children of the family, Mary Jane (b. 1852), Thomas Henry (b. 1853), Robert Samuel (b. 1857) and Celia Jane Berrett who was just 7 days old and there was a midwife resident with the family. Mary Jane Berrett, then 9, was staying nearby with her grandfather Thomas Langmaid and her unmarried aunt Mary Ann Langmaid, aged 33, who was the Postmistress at Orford.

A further child, Willie Francis Berrett was born in 1864. In the 1871 census the family, including all five children, was living at Berrett's Corner, Orford and Friston Berrett remained a butcher. Also living in the household at Berrett's Corner, Orford was the 71 year old Thomas Langmaid, the father of Celia Jane Berrett, described as an annuitant, i.e. living off an annuity. This was presumably a pension resulting from his retirement as a customs officer. He died later that year. [See Chapter 9 for more information about the Langmaids]

By 1881 only Robert, now 22 and described as a painter, was living with his mother and father. In 1891 Friston Berrett and Celia Jane Berrett, aged 71 and 65 respectively, were living in Church Street, Orford with no other members of the household.

Examination of trade directories on line provided confirmation of the census returns. White's Directory for 1855 lists Friston Berrett as a butcher and farmer in Orford. White's Directory for 1874 and the Suffolk Post Office Directory for 1875 list him among the tradesmen as a butcher.

Friston's wife Celia Jane Langmaid was the daughter of Thomas Langmaid (1798-1871) and Jane Butcher (1796-1848) who were my 3rd Great Grandparents. For the last few years of her life she lived at Cliff House, Lowestoft with her daughter and son-in-law and there is a photograph of her in my possession which I have been able to identify from a family tree on line. [See Chapter 9] She is recorded in every census record currently available, which shows that when the census was taken in 1901 she was staying in Saxmundham with a spinster called Jane Wade, presumably a friend, described as being of independent means.

Orford

Of the children other than Mary Jane Berrett who married Ebenezer Tuttle, two, Thomas Henry (1853-1920) and Robert Samuel (1857-1927) remained living in Orford. Thomas Henry took over the family butcher business from his father but he was also a sailor and general dealer in such items as coal and corn. His son, Frank Willie (1884-1951), continued the family's butcher business and he also owned a bakery in Market Square in the town centre. Frank Willie Berrett's son Lance Corporal Thomas

George Donald Berrett is the first person recorded on the Orford War Memorial for World War II – he died in October 1945 after hostilities had ended and he is buried in Cologne. Robert Samuel Berrett became a painter glazier and plumber – he and his wife, Caroline, had six children, one of whom, Evelyn (who married Alfred Searle) lived to be over a hundred years old.

The third son, Willie Francis Berrett (1864-1936), married Elizabeth Worboys and moved away from Suffolk. He worked for the Post Office, rising to become Chief Clerk and then Superintendent at Luton. He and his family were regular visitors to Cliff House, and the tone of Mary Jane Tuttle's entries in her journal seems to indicate that she was particularly close to her brother Willie, her youngest brother.

Mary Jane's sister, Celia Jane Berrett (1861-1891), remained unmarried. For the last few years of her life she lived with the Tuttle family in Lowestoft, and in the 1891 census, recorded shortly before her death, she is described as a companion.

I have been able to trace the Berretts back two further generations before Friston. His father was Henry Berrett (1776-1845) who married Mary Newson (1779-1826) – they were my 3rd great grandparents. In the 1841 census Henry Berrett is recorded living in Saxmundham, "at east side of Turnpike Road" with a daughter Harriott, aged 35. His occupation was stated as being a farmer.

Henry Berrett is also mentioned in a number of Trade Directories for Saxmundham as a "glover and breeches maker, shopkeeper, fellmonger, and glass, china etc. dealer". (Pigot's Directory 1830 and 1839, White's Directory 1844). He was also registered on the electoral roll for 1841 which is indicative of some means and status, because the electoral qualification, notwithstanding the

1832 Reform Act, was still quite restrictive. He was apprenticed to Jno Clark as an apprentice glover in 1791 and registered as a master of an apprentice called Chas English in 1806.

Henry Berrett's parents were James Berrett (1735-1786) and Mary Sallows (1744-1826). It has not been possible to trace any earlier ancestors, one possible explanation for which may be that the name Berrett is recorded as Barrett or another similar spelling.

Chapter 8: The Duckers of Great Yarmouth

Henry Tuttle, my great great grandfather married Mary Ann Ducker (1818-1870). They married in 1845. By using family trees and in particular the parish records for the parish church of St. Nicholas, Great Yarmouth, it has been possible to trace the Duckers back to the early 18th century. St. Nicholas is a fine minster church, the largest parish church in England, which has been substantially rebuilt following bombing in the Second World War. Many churches in ports are dedicated to St. Nicholas, the patron saint of sailors.

The birth of Mary Ann Ducker in 1818 reveals a sad story. Her parents, Francis William Ducker (1792-1861) and Mary Ann Patrick (1791-1818), married on 16th April 1817 at St. Nicholas's, Great Yarmouth. Mary Ann Ducker was baptised at the same church the following year, on 9th October. Nine days later on 18th October 1818 her mother, Mary Ann Ducker (nee Patrick) was buried at the same church. So within days of the birth of her daughter, at the age of 27, Mary Ann Ducker died. Mary Ann Patrick's baptismal record for 6th March 1791 at the Parish Church of Twyford, Norfolk, states that she was the baseborn daughter of Elizabeth Patrick – the use of the term "baseborn" indicates that she was born out of wedlock.

Francis William Ducker married his second wife, Rebecca Thompson, the following year and had three further children. The census returns for 1841 and 1851 indicate that he was a master mariner. A Master Mariner held a Master's Certificate which was required for any commander of a merchant vessel.

Such vessels could not sail except under the command of a Master Mariner, with the appropriate certification, who would be known as "Captain". Great Yarmouth was an important port, but most of the traffic would be coastal, although it was also a port for Holland. The likelihood is that Francis Ducker was the captain of a small commercial sailing ship, such as a brig, plying the coasts of Britain carrying cargo and possibly passengers. His will was registered on 18th February 1861 describing him as a gentleman. At the time of his death he and his wife were living at 19, Duke Street, Lowestoft, close to where Henry Tuttle, Francis's son-in-law by his first marriage, was residing with his family. Francis's widow then moved to live with her daughter, Rebecca, who had married John Pain who farmed 120 acres employing five men in Mundesley.

Francis William Ducker was the son of William Ducker (1767-1818) and the grandson of William Ducker (b. 1739). They also lived in Great Yarmouth or nearby and appear to have been seafarers, as seems likely to be the case with previous generations. In The Treasury Books of 1682 there is a record of the appointment of Rowland Ducker as a tidesman at Yarmouth in place of someone who had died. A tidesman was a Customs officer who boarded merchant ships to collect customs dues.

William Ducker (1767-1818), my 4th great grandfather, married Hannah Gaze (b. 1767). She came from an old-established Norfolk family and family trees on line list nine generations of Gaze ancestors back to Richard of Ridlington Gaze Gaze (1500-1526) my 13th great grandfather.

Chapter 9: The Langmaids of Polperro

It is possible to trace the Langmaid family, from which Celia Jane Langmaid (1826-1915), the wife of Friston Berrett, was descended, back to 1600, and the Wilton family into which an early Langmaid married back to the early 1400s. Researching the Langmaid family led to some interesting discoveries.

Celia Jane Berrett (nee Langmaid) – my great great grandmother

Celia Jane Langmaid was the daughter of Thomas Langmaid (1798-1871) and Jane Butcher (1796-1848), who were my 3rd great grandparents. From the 1841 census it was possible to discover no more than that Thomas Langmaid was an Excise officer, living in Orford, that he was born in a county other than Suffolk and the names of his wife and three children including Celia Jane were recorded. Subsequent census returns revealed that he was born in 1800, in Cornwall, which was an interesting piece of information indicating Cornish ancestry which was previously unknown. There was no mention of him in the 1851 census, but it is possible he was serving in the Royal Navy because there is a record of a Thomas Langmaid (who may be his nephew, also Thomas Langmaid) serving on board the HMS Princess Royal at this time, or perhaps he was elsewhere in connection with his duties as an Excise Officer at the time of the census. White's Directory for 1855 names him as the Commander of the Revenue Cruiser at Orford. His wife, Jane Langmaid (1796-1848), is listed in Pigot's Directory for 1830 as the Post Mistress at Orford. The entry states: "Letters from all parts arrive every morning at ten and are despatched every afternoon at four." It seems that their daughter, Mary Ann Langmaid, took over running the Post Office after the death of her mother for she is named as Post Mistress in Pigot's Directory for 1851. Later census records show Thomas Langmaid living in Orford with members of the Berrett family, described as an annuitant.

It has been possible by searching the parish records to discover Thomas Langmaid's antecedents which are remarkable for someone who became an officer of the Customs and Excise. The Langmaid family was a Cornish family. They lived in Polperro, in particular in the parishes of Talland and Lansallos. During the 18th century several of the Langmaids were involved in the smuggling trade which flourished in the area and which was a highly organised and successful business. Together with members of the Quiller family (from which family Sir Arthur Quiller-Couch who compiled the Oxford Book of English Verse is descended) the Langmaids appear to have been the leading smugglers of the area. Most of the brandy, gin, tea and tobacco was shipped across the Channel from Guernsey where these goods were readily available at much lower prices than in England where they were subject to heavy duty.

St Ildierna's Church, Lansallos where many members of the Langmaid family are buried

Thomas Langmaid was born in Cornwall and baptised at St Ildierna's Lansallos on 16th June 1798, the son of John and Celior (*sic*) Langmaid. By the time of his marriage in 1820 he had moved to Orford, Suffolk, where his marriage to Jane Butcher is recorded. Jane Butcher came from a Suffolk family. Thomas Langmaid's parents John Langmaid (1770-1810) and his wife Cecilia Scott, or Scaff, were my 4th great grandparents.

John Langmaid is well recorded in the parish records. He was baptised on 26th August 1770 at Lansallos and married on 1st August 1791 at Lansallos – to Cecilia Scott – some family trees say the bride's maiden name was Scaff. However the note of the parish entry gives the name Scott. Some records give her Christian name as Silya or Celior. The most detailed note of the parish record of the marriage (Cornwall On Line Parish Clerks) gives John Langmaid's occupation as mariner.

John Langmaid was involved in an attack upon Excise Officers on 5th March 1794 when they were carrying out a raid and recovering contraband in Polperro. A large mob, armed with firearms and other weapons, successfully prevented the Excise officers from removing most of the 100 gallons of foreign geneva (gin) and 100 gallons of foreign brandy which had been seized from the houses where it had been stored by the local smugglers. John Langmaid was one of those arrested and sent for trial for unlawful assembly at the Old Bailey. Cornish juries were reluctant to convict anyone connected with smuggling which may be the explanation for the trial not being heard at the local Assizes – however the most serious criminal cases have for many years been tried at the Old Bailey, now properly known as the Central Criminal Court, and an attack upon a Crown Officer would be regarded as a particularly serious offence.

The trial took place on 28th October 1795 and was prosecuted by the Attorney General, Sir John Scott, subsequently Lord Chancellor from 1801-1806 and 1807-1827 as Lord Eldon. Smuggling in Polperro was well-organised and managed by a man named Zephaniah Job, who acted as advisor, accountant and banker to the inhabitants including the smugglers. He even paid for lawyers to represent Polperro smugglers when they appeared in court and John Langmaid was represented in his trial by a barrister called Shepherd who effectively cross-examined some of the witnesses, making the point that John Langmaid was not arrested until 18 months after the incident to challenge the identification evidence, and he attacked the character and integrity of some of the Excise Officers. Despite this spirited defence John Langmaid was convicted and sentenced to death. The jury will no doubt have been impressed by compelling evidence from Thomas Pinsent, the local customs officer who knew him well, identifying John Langmaid as being in possession of a bayonet and a firearm during the riot. An Excise Officer said he was threatened by John Langmaid who "with a bayonet in one hand and a suzee in the other swore he would run me through if I did not desist."

However although he was convicted of a capital offence John Langmaid's death sentence was immediately respited by the judge (Mr Justice Heath) on condition that he served in the Royal Navy – this was, of course, during the French Revolutionary Wars when the Navy needed every able bodied man it could get. A Royal Pardon was subsequently issued.

It is interesting to wonder why John Langmaid became involved in such a grave crime. Smuggling was rife, but taking part in an armed attack upon the Excise Officers was much more serious. In the trial the local custom house officer at Polperro, Thomas Pinsent, after identifying John Langmaid as being armed with a gun with bayonet fixed, said he had known the prisoner some time: "Before this time he had a very excellent character; I have known him from a child, he has always borne a good character." Another witness, Thomas Roberts, called as a character witness, said: "I have known him these twelve years; he bears a very good character as far as I know, a very peaceable man, I suppose there were an hundred people of the parish that would have come and given him a good character, if they could have borne their expenses."

A full transcript of the trial is available from the Old Bailey Archives on line. John Langmaid's surname is misrecorded in the printed archive as John Longmead (probably as a result of a misreading of the manuscript when the record was printed) but it is definitely the same person.

Despite this criminal activity, the descendants of John Langmaid were able to put this notorious episode behind them. Thomas Langmaid, his son, moved to Suffolk and was an Officer of the Customs and Excise as is noted above. Another son, Reginald, joined the Revenue Service and eventually became a Chief Boatman at Plymouth and Reginald's son, Thomas Stap Langmaid also joined the Revenue Service and subsequently the Royal Navy. I sometimes wonder what John Langmaid would have made of the fact that his 4th great grandson became a senior circuit judge!

The parish records for Lansallos detail five previous generations of Langmaids all from the same area, commencing with Reginald Langmaid (1600-1645), who would have been my 9th great grandfather. His son John Langmaid married Marian Willton on 13th February 1654, my 8th great grandparents. The Willton family (variously also spelt Wilton and Wylton) were an old Cornish family from the area of Lanreath, and they can be traced back a further two centuries to my 14th great grandfather, Maurice Wylton de Fursden (born about 1427) whose son, Sir John Wilton Wylton de Fursden, as recorded in some family trees (1480-1531), married Lady Joan de Tregwenneck (1454-1525) who would have been my 13th great grandparents. It must, however, be stressed that all the information about the Willton ancestry before about 1530 comes from family trees posted on line by others and that no original source material such as parish records has been identified to corroborate the assertions, although there are parish records to confirm three generations before Marian Willton, the wife of John Langmaid. As I note in Chapter 27 there is some evidence from the family trees on line that the Willtons were descended from the Plantagenet Kings.

Part II – Tracing the Eyres

Chapter 10: Beginnings

The origins of the Eyre family, from which I descend, appear to be firmly rooted in Cornwall. There is a well-known family named Eyre in Derbyshire which can trace its roots back to the Norman Conquest and who have as their emblem a severed leg in armour said to derive from a knight called "Heyr" who lost a leg in battle. The Eyres of Derbyshire were wealthy landowners and it is believed that Charlotte Bronte chose the name Jane Eyre as a result of coming across them. There are several public houses called "The Eyre Arms" in Derbyshire, and Hassop Hall was one of several seats of this family. Unless there is an ancient link before the mid-17th century there appears to be no connection between the Eyres of Cornwall and Derbyshire.

The name Eyre (and its alternate spellings) was sometimes given to a person known to be the heir to a title or significant inheritance. One family of Eyres from Wiltshire (which is not that far from Cornwall from where my Eyre descendants hail) is said to be able to trace its origins to a crusader, Humphrey Le Heyr, although to what or to whom he was the heir is not known. He may be the same knight called Heyr from whom the Derbyshire Eyres claim descent. There are other spellings of Eyre, such as Ayre, Eyres, Eare (see below) and possibly, given the origins mentioned above, names such as Hare may have the same derivation, and although the name Eyre is relatively uncommon there are probably other parts of the country where families called Eyre became established.

The Eyre Legend

There is a romantic legend about the origin of the Eyre families which appears in some genealogies. The legend is that a knight by the name "Truelove" accompanied William the Conqueror and fought alongside him at the Battle of Hastings in 1066. William was thrown from his horse and his helmet was driven in to his face, suffocating him. Truelove was able to remove the helmet and save William's life, but in the process Truelove sustained an injury which necessitated the amputation of his leg.

After the battle William told Truelove: "Thou shalt hereafter instead of Truelove be called Eyre because thou hast given me the air I breathe". He was granted land in Derbyshire (where there are Eyres still living) and a coat of arms which featured as the crest a severed leg in armour. The arms also incorporate gold quatrefoils.

An alternative variation of the story is that Humphrey le Heyr of Bromham rescued Richard the Lionheart at the siege of Ascalon losing his leg in the process and the use of the severed leg in his coat of arms was granted to him in remembrance of the occasion.

> There is yet another legend relating to Truelove, namely that he was a grandson of King Edmund II and thus a second cousin of William the Conqueror, and that he was called "Heyr" because he was the rightful heir to the English throne.

It was, however, only when my researches were well under way that I discovered that my Eyre ancestors originated from Cornwall. My mother did not know a great deal about her ancestry, although she knew that her father had been brought up in Plymouth and it was always thought that the family's origins were in Devon. In fact it was her great grandfather, my 2nd great grandfather, George Booth Eyre who made the move from Cornwall to Devon when he established his furniture and cabinet making business in the 1840s. My mother, Pamela Russell, born Pamela Eyre in 1920, was the only daughter of George William Booth Eyre (1886-1935) and Dorothy May Tuttle (1889-1970). George Eyre, who was a bank manager employed by the National Provincial Bank, died in 1935 from septicaemia as a result of shrapnel which remained in his body after being wounded in World War I. George Eyre was brought up by relatives following the death of his mother when he was five, and although his father outlived him George's contact with his father, my great grandfather, Thomas Southwood Eyre (1857-1944), was only very sporadic – Thomas Eyre had suffered a breakdown after the death of his wife from which he never really recovered. Further, my mother's home in Purley, Surrey, was bombed in the Second World War resulting in the loss of nearly all their possessions and the return of my grandmother to Suffolk.

My mother and grandmother were fortunate to survive the bombing of their home in Purley. Both of them were in bed when the air raid siren sounded the alarm, but they decided to stay put rather than take refuge in the bomb shelter under the stairs. The bomb demolished the stair case and had they been sheltering there they would have been killed or seriously injured. As it was both of them fell in their beds to the floor below and survived uninjured. The next morning when they were surveying the destruction the telephone rang and my mother answered it by reaching through a broken window from outside. It was an enquiry from friends relieved to get a response, but the telephone was about the only item in the house which survived intact.

After this incident my grandmother moved to Lowestoft to live with her sisters and my mother went to live with the friends who had made the telephone enquiry. Shortly afterwards my mother was called up to join the Auxiliary Territorial Service. My grandmother had been driving an ambulance as a volunteer during the Blitz but when she returned to Lowestoft she commenced to work in the family business becoming the last company secretary of Tuttles.

Lieutenant George William Booth Eyre

As a consequence of these various events contact with the Eyre family was lost, with the exception of occasional correspondence between Florence Mabel Mortimer, whose mother was the sister of Thomas Southwood Eyre's wife, and my grandmother and later my mother. Florence Mabel Mortimer was the mother of Angela Mortimer, the Wimbledon Ladies Singles Champion of 1961.[6] Before her death, Mabs Mortimer, as she was known, wrote a letter to my mother setting out some of the history of the family of her mother, Florence Sarah Stephens, and that of Thomas Eyre's wife, Ellen Augusta Stephens (1862-1891), my great grandmother. This letter provided more clues, but not about the Eyres of whom there was no mention before Thomas Southwood Eyre.

Subaltern Pamela Eyre (ATS), my mother

---

[6] See Chapter 17 for a short biography of Angela Mortimer

My mother's brother, Anthony Eyre, after whom I am named, was a distinguished Battle of Britain pilot. His life deserves to be remembered and there is a separate chapter about him below.[7] My mother, Pamela Eyre (1920-2011), having worked for the Pearl Assurance Company in London until she joined the women's army, the Auxiliary Territorial Service, which she left with the rank of Subaltern (1st Lieutenant), met my father, Michael Hibberd Russell (1921-1987), after the war and married him in 1947. After two years in Canada they returned to England in 1950 where my father obtained a post as a general practitioner in the Wirral, where they settled and where my brother and I were brought up.

The information from Mabs Mortimer about my grandfather's upbringing was as follows. As a result of their mother's early death the two children George and his sister Emily Eyre were brought up by their grandmother, Ellen Stephens, who died in 1907. However, their aunt (Emily Eyre, wife of George William Eyre, their uncle, the elder brother of Thomas Eyre) thought that Emily was being spoiled so she was sent away to school at the age of five. From this time George and Emily spent only their holidays together with their uncle George William Eyre and his wife Emily. These guardians were very strict and the two children were significant support for each other. George Eyre was also sent to boarding school, but locally in Plymouth, and an examination of the census return for 1901 shows him to be a boarder at Plymouth College and his sister boarding with four other teenagers at the home of a schoolmistress also in Plymouth.

George Eyre worked for the National Provincial Bank and served in the Great War. As with any ancestor who served in the British Forces in the First World War it was possible to trace some

---

[7] See Chapter 14 for a biography of Anthony Eyre

records from the available on line sites, but I also had access to a diary of his mother-in-law, my great grandmother Mary Jane Tuttle, who noted the receipt of letters from her family and the locations from where they were sent, which enabled a picture of his army career to be built up. He enlisted as a Private in the West Kent Yeomanry in the summer of 1915. Conscription was not introduced until 1916, so he was a volunteer. He served initially at Gallipoli and then in Egypt and Palestine. He was commissioned into the Royal Field Artillery on 26th May 1917. He married Dorothy Tuttle on 1st August 1917 at Lowestoft. Thereafter he saw service in France and was wounded in action in late April or early May 1918, possibly at the Battle of the Lys which took place at the end of April. Given the huge loss of life in the Great War it is a remarkable fact that his three Tuttle brothers-in-law (Arthur, Ernest and Stanley) and the husband of his sister-in-law, Violet, Arthur Reynolds, who also served in the First World War, all survived although Stanley was, like George Eyre, wounded. All of them except Stanley Tuttle were commissioned as officers, the highest ranking being Arthur and Ernest who both ended the war as Captains. There were times when some of this family quintet were serving in the same fields of conflict and were able to make contact with each other despite being in different regiments.

*George and Dorothy Eyre – photographed before
George was commissioned*

After the War George Eyre resumed working for the bank and became the Manager of the Croydon branch of the National Provincial Bank. In 1935 he was promoted to a post in Leicester. Shortly after this he was taken ill with septicaemia, as a result of the shrapnel which had remained in his body, and he died in 1935 – at this time antibiotics had only recently been discovered and they were not in wide use. At the time of his death the family still lived at Kinlough, Purley Downs Road, Sanderstead, Surrey, and employed a servant, Edith Simmonds, who had previously been in service in Lowestoft with the Tuttle family. Despite relatively comfortable circumstances the death of George Eyre at an early age meant that the family's income was greatly reduced, with the result that Tony Eyre could not go to university as had been planned and his sister, my mother, left school early and went to work as an insurance clerk in the City of London.

George Eyre had a sister, Emily Augusta Eyre (1889-1986), who married William Ewart Appleton (1889-1943). The Appletons had a son and a daughter, Leslie and Peggy, the first cousins of my mother. After the death of George Eyre and the destruction of the family home in the war all contact with the Appletons had been lost until in 2000 I spotted the obituary of Leslie Appleton (who was an aircraft designer) in The Times and contacted his widow[8]. This led to my being able to arrange a meeting between my mother and her cousin Peggy Appleton, who is still living at the time of writing – they had not seen each other for over sixty years since they had been bridesmaids at the wedding of the parents of Angela Mortimer. Peggy Appleton has given me more information about the Stephens family of which her grandmother (and my great grandmother) Ellen Stephens (1862-1891), who married Thomas Southwood Eyre, was a member.

Peggy Appleton was also able to give me some more information about my great grandfather Thomas Eyre which filled in some gaps in my knowledge of him, derived from my mother.

Thomas Southwood Eyre was the younger of two sons of George Booth Eyre (1826-1885) a successful cabinet and furniture maker in Plymouth. In his will, which was proved on January 20th 1886, George Booth Eyre left £4,449 7s. 1d., what was in those days a sizeable fortune (over £1 million at today's values), to his two sons. Thomas Eyre invested his share of the estate in an annuity from which he lived off the income. Thomas Eyre had married Ellen Augusta Stephens in 1884. Ellen Eyre died in premature child birth in 1891 and she was buried on her 29th birthday. Following this Thomas Eyre went to South Africa for a time. The Stephens family blamed him for his wife's death so he may have been glad to get away. However all was later forgiven and he

---

[8] See Chapter 15 for a biography of Leslie Appleton

became great friends with Florence, his sister-in-law, who married Charles Beard and whose daughter, Mabel (Mabs), married Stuart Mortimer, parents of Angela Mortimer [Wimbledon Ladies' Singles Champion in 1961 – see Chapter 17]. He lived in various places, including in London in 1929-30 with his daughter Emily Appleton and her family. Thomas Eyre then returned to Plymouth. The house in Portland Square where he was living was bombed in 1940. He died in a nursing home on 5th December 1944 leaving his estate to his daughter Emily Appleton. He was estranged from his son's family, but why this was so is not entirely clear. From the membership records of the Freemasons, which are available on line, I was able to discover that Thomas Southwood Eyre was a member of the St. John's Lodge, Plymouth.

Thomas Southwood Eyre's elder brother, George William Eyre (1856-1921) and his wife, Emily Elizabeth Edgecombe (1856-1937), emerge from this tale in the guise of the unkind guardians, so often found in fiction. They had no children of their own. George William Eyre continued the cabinet making business of his father, George Booth Eyre, in Plymouth and became a magistrate and councillor. My grandfather, George William Booth Eyre, was a devoted father, adored by my mother, who did not like to celebrate her own birthday because it was on her fifteenth birthday shortly before he was taken fatally ill that she had last spoken to her father on the telephone, and it may be that his difficult and unhappy childhood determined him that his own children should not suffer similarly.

Chapter 11: Further Discoveries from the Census Returns

With the information from the family set out in the previous chapter I was armed with a number of starting points, and my first action was to research the census returns thoroughly. These confirmed that my grandfather, George, lived with his parents and sister, Emily, at the time of the 1891 census at 29, Staddon Terrace, Plymouth. The occupation of Thomas Southwood Eyre, his father, was given as upholsterer. Also living at the address was a general domestic servant. It was shortly after this that Ellen Eyre died in premature childbirth. Staddon Terrace still exists, consisting of reasonably substantial mid-Victorian terraced houses with bow-fronted ground floor windows.

In the 1901 census Thomas Southwood Eyre is shown living in The Salisbury Hotel, Plymouth, as a boarder. He was the only boarder so it must have been a very small hotel, perhaps a pub – it no longer exists but it was at 6, Clarendon Place close to where his father George Booth Eyre had last lived. This area, close to The Hoe, appears to have been substantially redeveloped, probably as a consequence of the major destruction of the centre of Plymouth in the Second World War. He is described as retired upholsterer (at the age of 44). In the 1911 census Thomas Southwood Eyre is shown as one of four boarders at 6, Clarendon Place, Plymouth. He is still described as a retired upholsterer.

Tracing further back it was possible by using the census returns to learn quite a lot about Thomas Southwood Eyre's father,

George Booth Eyre (1826-1885), my great great grandfather. He was born in Truro, the son of Thomas and Elizabeth Eyre and he married Emma Jane Southwood (1828-1881) on 24th August 1848 in Plymouth. Thomas Eyre, his father and my 3rd great grandfather, is someone about whom it has been possible to discover a great deal of information which will be explored in the next chapter.

At the time of the 1841 census, when George Booth Eyre was aged 15, he was living with his father and mother, Thomas and Elizabeth Eyre, in Truro, Cornwall together with five brothers and sisters who are named in the next chapter. His occupation is shown as carpenter.

By the date of the 1851 census George B Eyre was living at 56, Exeter Street, Plymouth with his wife Emma and their one year old daughter, Emma. His occupation is shown as cabinet maker employing ten men. Nearby at 57, Exeter Street, lived the Southwoods, his wife's family. Exeter Street is in the centre of Plymouth and it has been extensively redeveloped for commercial use – there is no longer any housing on the street.

William H Southwood (1786-1857) married Ann Milton (1795-1858) and they were my 3rd great grandparents. Their daughter, Emma Jane, the youngest of four children, married George Booth Eyre in 1848. William Southwood was a butcher trading from Exeter Street and Plymouth Market.

In the 1861 census George Booth Eyre is described as Cabinet Maker employing twelve men and five boys – residing in Bedford Street, Plymouth. George and Thomas Eyre, his two sons, were residing in the household at the date of the census, but not Emma, who would have been eleven years old. There was a house servant called Mary Harvey. Bedford Street still exists and some of the old houses are still there – these comprise average to large-sized terraced houses, and the area appears to have been a decent Victorian suburb not far from the centre of Plymouth.

In the 1871 census, George Booth Eyre is described as a cabinet maker. He was also an undertaker. Residing in the house, 24 Bedford Street, Plymouth, were his wife, Emma, George Eyre (son, cabinet maker's apprentice), Emma Birtwell (daughter, described as iron merchant's wife – she had married Joseph Birtwell) and Thomas Eyre (son, scholar).

At the time of the 1881 census, George B Eyre, now a widower (Emma Jane Eyre died in March 1881) was living at 1, Clarendon Place, Plymouth, described as cabinet maker employing two boys and seven men. The only other member of the household is Thomas S. Eyre, his son and my great grandfather, also described as cabinet maker.

George Booth Eyre died on 24th December 1885 leaving £4450 which using the assessment of the economic power of that value of wealth today would equate to approximately £1.2 million.

The discovery that George Booth Eyre was born in Cornwall was an interesting development which led to tracing several generations of Eyres with the assistance of some well-researched family trees on line, all well-corroborated by parish records, which were particularly complete and well-recorded. Thomas Eyre, my 3rd great grandfather and George Booth's Eyre's father, was an interesting and strong-willed character and his children led interesting lives as set out in the next chapter – researches into him by some of his descendants led to my making contact with a distant cousin in New Zealand who shares my interest in family history and who has done a considerable amount of research into his family's origins. I was able to give him a lot of information about the Eyre branch which remained in England of which he was unaware.

Chapter 12: Thomas Eyre and his family

My 3rd great grandparents Thomas Eyre (1791-1861) and his wife Elizabeth Isabell Eyre, born Elizabeth Isabell Murphy, (1796-1878) had a total of ten children, five of whom migrated to Australia or New Zealand. Some of their descendants have researched their ancestry and on the various ancestry websites will be found details of their family trees and requests for further information about their ancestors. Having come across these I realised that there was plenty of interesting material available, and I was fortunate to find that there were reliable sources to draw upon. As will be seen, Thomas Eyre turned out to be an interesting character about whom quite a lot could be discovered.

The entries in the census returns of 1841, 1851 and 1861 revealed considerable information about Thomas Eyre. I was able to discover the names of his wife, Elizabeth, and several brothers and sisters of my great great grandfather George Booth Eyre, the fact that Thomas was born in Bodmin, his wife was born in Southwark and his children were all born in Truro, where the family lived, and that Thomas was a collector of taxes and a house and estate agent. There was always a house servant living with the family.

Thomas Eyre was the fourth son of Joseph and Mary Robins Eyre, who were second cousins [see Chapter 13 below]. He had two further younger brothers and two sisters. His father, Joseph Eyre (1756-1808), appears to have been a successful merchant in Bodmin whose name appears in the 1784 edition of Bailey's

British Directory, together with Thomas Eyre (probably Joseph's younger brother born in 1758), as a yarn and textile merchant in Bodmin and in a later Directory (Universal British Directory 1791) as a grocer and linen draper. Two of the six sons of Joseph Eyre went to Oxford University, and subsequently took Holy Orders becoming Church of England clergymen. So it seems likely that my 3rd great grandfather Thomas Eyre enjoyed a comfortable upbringing. Some further details about the lives of his siblings and ancestors are set out in the next chapter.

Searches of parish records revealed that Thomas Eyre and Elizabeth Isabell Murphy were married at the church of St. George the Martyr in Southwark on 3rd October 1815. Copies of the marriage entry and the three readings of the Banns are all available to be viewed on line. Thomas was living in Southwark at the time of his marriage, but what took him there is not clear. I was intrigued by this discovery and I decided to visit the church when I was next in London. The church is located at the western end of the Roman Road from Dover to London, Watling Street, a few hundred yards south of London Bridge (opposite Borough Tube Station). Rebuilt in the mid-18th century there has been a church on the site since Norman times, and it has an interesting history. Some guidebooks claim that on the steps of the earlier church the Aldermen of the City of London assembled to welcome the triumphant King Henry V on his return from Agincourt in 1415. His procession will certainly have passed by the church. Dick Whittington, remembered in pantomime, was an Alderman at the time. The "Agincourt Song" was written for the celebrations which followed the victory. Buried in the churchyard was Nahum Tate, author of "While shepherds watched their flocks, by night" and the church is mentioned in Charles Dickens's "Little Dorrit" as the place where Little Dorrit is said to have slept with the Burial Register under her head.

Close by was the notorious Marshalsea prison, at that time a debtors prison, where Charles Dickens's father was imprisoned in 1824 for a debt owed to a baker.

The church today is little changed from the 18th century, and although I had been somewhat sceptical of the emotions displayed by celebrities visiting the places their ancestors lived on programmes such as "Who do you think you are?" I have to confess that I felt a shiver down my spine as I walked up the aisle to the altar where my 3rd great grandparents had been married two centuries earlier and saw the font where some of my ancestors were baptised. The experience decided me to try, whenever possible, to visit other places associated with my ancestors and I have found this an emotional and rewarding experience. As I recount in Chapter 23 I discovered the graves of some of my ancestors in such a visit, and discovered further information about the Potters as a result.

St. George the Martyr, Southwark in 2014

Interior – showing the altar at which Thomas Eyre and Elizabeth Isabell Murphy were married and the font at which various ancestors were baptised

Shortly after their marriage Thomas and Elizabeth Eyre moved to Truro – in 1816 Thomas Eyre appears in a local directory as a shopkeeper. It has been possible to trace his business career by examining the census returns and various trade directories available on line. By 1829 he had become a tea dealer and in 1833 a merchant's clerk. At about this time he is also recorded as a bookseller, stationer and printer. In the census returns for 1841 and 1851 his occupations are given as house and estate agent and later collector of taxes. His career is confirmed by entries in a number of trade directories including Pigot's directory for 1844 as an auctioneer with a printing business. In the Post Office Directory for 1856 he is recorded as a collector of taxes and house and estate agent. In the probate record he is stated to be an accountant. He was clearly a successful and enterprising man and subsequent researches into his forebears revealed various tradesmen, merchants and professional people.

Thomas and Elizabeth Eyre had a total of ten children, six girls and four boys. One boy, Andrew Robins Eyre (b. 1832) died aged one, and a daughter, Henrietta Olymphia Prudentia Eyre (1824-1842) was eighteen years old when she died, but the others all lived into adulthood and all but one of them married and had children. Several of them migrated to Australia and New Zealand. Because of the interest shown by their descendants there is a considerable amount of information available about these families which is summarised below.

The eldest child was Emma Matilda Eyre (1816-1857). She married Anthony Sara (1821-1854). In the 1851 census they were living in Falmouth and Anthony Sara's occupation was a miner (probably in the Cornish tin mining industry). They are mentioned in a letter Thomas Eyre wrote to his daughter Maria in Australia in 1850 – Thomas says of Emma *"she is as usual not very well"*. They both died young and appear to have had no children.

Next came William Thomas Eyre (1818-1879). In the 1851 census William Thomas Eyre and his first wife, Eliza Sarah Bishop (b. 1822), are recorded living in Great New Street, London (off Holborn in the centre of the legal and printing district) where William Thomas Eyre worked as a compositor in the printing trade. William migrated to Australia, probably following the death of his first wife. He married his second wife, Sara Story, in Melbourne in 1866. William died in Melbourne after a long illness. It is not known whether he left any children. Some family trees on line have conflated William's first and second wives as Eliza Sarah Story born in 1822, but careful analysis of all the available records shows that what is set out above is correct as well as making better sense, reinforcing what I have said elsewhere about the importance of consulting and analysing all available records before drawing a conclusion.

Maria Louisa Eyre (1820-1908) married Abraham Jacka (1825-1890) who also came from Cornwall. In 1849 both of them migrated to Australia on the ship "Nelson". In April 1850 she and Abraham Jacka married in Melbourne – they had seven children. Thomas Eyre wrote a long letter to Maria, dated 18th May 1850, after her wedding, of which he may not have been aware at the time of writing. It is a moving and revealing letter which emphasises the dangers of travel at such a time and the enormous break with home created by travelling to live at the other side of the world.

The letter, which was kept by Maria's descendants and which has been published attached to various family trees on line, commences in this way:

"I am now going to write you a long letter about a month since I received a letter from you informing us of your having safely arrived out after a very rough and unpleasant voyage. However it gave us much pleasure to find that you got out safe although when I think on it you are completely lost to the family for there is not the slightest prospect of ever seeing you again. But do write often. We were anxiously waiting the letter for as you say the vessel did not touch any port nor spoke with

no vessel on her passage accounts for our not seeing any account of her in our way whatever."

It is possible to work out from the letter that Maria had departed from England in about July 1849 and that it was only in mid-April of 1850, about nine months later, that her parents learnt that she had arrived safely. Maria's younger brother, John, had also migrated to Australia on a later voyage. The voyage to Australia was a long and hazardous one, which at this time could take between three and four months and sometimes significantly longer. The letter goes on to say that John had departed for Australia a few weeks after Maria, leaving for Sydney on 24th August 1849, and that his passage took fifteen weeks, having encountered a heavy storm and put in for a week at the Cape Colony in South Africa and that his ship had arrived earlier than Maria's which means that her voyage must have taken twenty weeks or so. Thomas Eyre had heard from his son John before receiving Maria's letter, hence his obvious relief at learning that she had arrived safely. It was only after these journeys that the clipper ships, which commenced to operate in the 1850s, resulted in a halving of the average voyage to about two months. In this modern age of instant communication it is difficult to comprehend the effect of not knowing the fate of a close family member for nine months.

The letter gives news of various members of the family including Maria's brother George Booth Eyre, my great great grandfather, saying that his business was doing very well (the cabinet and furniture business in Plymouth) and that he employed *"14 journeymen besides boys and apprentices"*. He also said that he feared *"he and his wife don't agree altho' I said nothing about it to him."*

The letter concludes:

"Your mother sends her kind love to you wishing you health and prosperity and so my dear Maria look at yourself. Remember the distance you are from either your mother sisters and myself, the only persons you have to look to this side of the grave. Isabel and Ellen likewise send their love and ? wishes with mine. May every blessing such a person can enjoy under the canopy of heaven attend you. May the almighty protect you from ill insult and oppression is the ardent wish of

Your Affectionate Father Thos Eyre"

The next daughter was Laura Olivia Violetta Eyre (1822-1906). Laura Olivia Violetta Eyre's death was reported in the West Britain and Cornwall Advertiser. After leaving school she had worked in a drapery establishment in Truro, but she became filled with the excitement of the gold fever and migrated to Australia and settled in Melbourne where she amassed a considerable fortune augmented by what the newspaper report describes as judicious investments in gas companies and banking institutions. She returned to England several times to visit her family and friends in Truro, finally returning at the end of the century and settling first in Brighton and then in Teignmouth where she died. She left most of her considerable fortune (over £6,000, at today's values in excess of five million pounds) to the Royal Cornwall Infirmary and William's Hospital in Truro and she is buried in St. Mary's burial ground where her parents and other family members were buried. She was unmarried.

Henrietta Olymphia Prudentia Eyre (1824-1842) came next, followed by my great great grandfather George Booth Eyre (1826-1885) mentioned above in Chapter 11. I wonder whether Thomas and Elizabeth Eyre had a sense of humour when choosing their children's' names? Laura Olivia Violetta Eyre's initials spell LOVE and her sister Henrietta Olymphia Prudentia Eyre's spell HOPE.

John Charles Eyre (1829-1912) also migrated to Australia in 1849, departing a few weeks after his sister Maria, on the "Sarah". In 1855 he married Rebecca Richards who also came from Cornwall. They subsequently moved to New Zealand where many of their descendants still live. They had a total of ten children, 6 daughters and 4 sons.

Andrew Robins Eyre (1832-1833) did not survive infancy. The next child was Isabell Andrew Eyre (1834-1861) who married Richard Huxtable (1824-1913) in 1856. They had two children and lived in Corfe. Following Isabell's death in 1861 Richard Huxtable married Emma Grover by whom he had four further children. Richard Huxtable was a gardener.

Thomas and Elizabeth Eyre's youngest child was Ellen Ashtead Eyre (1837-1904). She married James Dawson in Islington in 1862 and the family resided in Fetter Lane, St Dunstan in the West, London, until 1873 when they migrated to New Zealand on the "Cardigan Castle" settling in Dunedin. Ellen Ashtead Eyre was a teacher of dancing. James Dawson's origins were also in the West Country and he was a professional photographer, described as a photographic artist, with a studio in Fetter Lane, London which is in the vicinity of the Temple and the other Inns of Court. They had 8 children. One of those was Percy Dawson (1877-1965). His grandson, John Leslie Dawson (b. 1947), a retired teacher, living in New Zealand, my 3rd cousin once removed, and I made contact as a result of our interest in and descent from Thomas Eyre and we have been able to exchange information about our respective branches of the Eyre family.

Thomas Eyre's house at 3, Ferris Town, Truro

Thomas Eyre died on 12th December 1861 and was buried in the graveyard of St. Mary's Church, later incorporated into Truro Cathedral, where his children Andrew Robins Eyre (1832-1833) and Henrietta Olymphia Prudentia Eyre (1824-1842) were buried with many others of their forebears. Although his effects were valued for Probate at £300, which using the assessment of the economic power of that value of wealth today would equate to approximately £550,000, the family seems to have been of relatively substantial means because in 1862 there was a sale of furniture from the family home occasioned by Elizabeth Eyre's moving to Devonport and the advertisement describes the house as consisting of two parlours, kitchen, back kitchen and four bedrooms, and the furnishings included mahogany chairs, sofa, dining and drawing room tables, paintings and prints, a pianoforte, a long case clock, a four-post bed and other beds and many other items indicating a well-equipped middle class home. The Probate Records describe Thomas Eyre as an accountant.

Number 3, Ferris Town, Truro, the last home of Thomas Eyre, still stands. As the illustration shows, it is an attractive Georgian townhouse, situated on a corner, quite close to where Truro railway station is situated. The house is now divided into flats.

Useful and Modern Household Furniture, *At No. 3, Ferris Town, Truro, to be Sold by Public Auction.*

ROBERT JULIAN begs to announce that he has been instructed to SELL by PUBLIC AUCTION, on TUESDAY, the 17th day of June next, and the following day if required, the entire

HOUSEHOLD FURNITURE and Effects, of the representatives of Mr. Thomas Eyre, deceased, at his late Residence, No. 3, Ferris Town, Truro: consisting of the Furniture and Appendages of Two Parlours, Kitchen, Back Kitchen, Passages, Landing, &c., and also of Four Bedrooms.

Parlours. — The furniture consists in mahogany, of drawing and other chairs, sofa, dining and drawing-room tables, Brussels and other carpeting, hearth rugs, fender and fire-sets, bookcase, sideboard, paintings, prints, some old china, chimney glasses, and ornaments, piano-forte by Collard, several volumes of books, together with a variety of other articles.

Passages and Landing. — The several furniture, eight-day clock in mahogany case.

Kitchens. — Consisting of chairs, tables, earthenware, china, tea and coffee sets, glass, also the various other useful articles and culinary requisites, together with a revolver, nearly new.

Bedrooms. — Four-post and other bedsteads, feather beds, bolsters and pillows, hair, and wool mattresses, carpeting, toilet glasses and sets, dressing tables, washstands, some bedding, &c., &c.

GREENHOUSE, VALUABLE PLANTS, &c.

The Auctioneer respectfully invites attention to the foregoing furniture and effects, which will be found in every respect desirable, and are to be sold only in consequence of the proprietors leaving the county.

On view Monday preceding the day of sale, from twelve a.m. to four p.m.

Sale to commence punctually at eleven o'clock p.m.

ROBERT JULIAN, Auctioneer.

Dated Offices, Prince's-street, Truro, May 28, 1862.

Advertisement re the sale of Thomas Eyre's effects

It is interesting to ponder why it was that of the eight children of Thomas Eyre who survived into adulthood five chose to migrate to Australia and New Zealand. This was a relatively prosperous middle class family. The Australian Gold Rush commenced in 1851, so this cannot be the explanation for the departures in 1849. However at this time the Cornish tin industry was in decline, and much of the Cornish economy relied upon the tin industry. Although only one member of the family, Anthony Sara, the husband of the eldest daughter Emma Matilda Eyre, appears to have had any connection with mining, the decline of the industry will have had a knock on effect and resulted in unemployment in other types of work and will also have had an adverse effect on trade and business, so the likelihood is that prospects of living a prosperous life in Cornwall at the time were somewhat diminished. The Australian gold rushes caused a huge influx of people from overseas. Australia's total population more than tripled from 430,000 in 1851 to 1.7 million in 1871. Between 1852 and 1860, 290,000 people migrated to Victoria from the British Isles. Only one of the brothers and sisters who migrated to Australia, Laura Eyre, appears to have prospered from the Gold Rush itself by her investments in banking and utilities.

At the time of the 1871 census, Elizabeth Eyre, now widowed, was living alone at 74, Carhouse Street, Devonport, not far from where her son, George Booth Eyre my great great grandfather, and his family were living. Elizabeth Eyre died in 1878 and like her husband was buried in Truro at the graveyard of St. Mary's Church where her daughter, Laura Olivia Violetta Eyre was later buried.

The Murphy family from which Elizabeth Eyre came was well established in London. It has been possible to trace her ancestors back a further three generations. Many of them are recorded in the parish records of the church of St. George the Martyr in Southwark. Her father, Charles Murphy (1775-1819), appears in various London trade directories as a law stationer operating from premises in Bream's Building, Chancery Lane. Earlier members of the Murphy family are also recorded as stationers in various London directories. The letter from Thomas Eyre to his daughter Maria referred to earlier contains references to two of his wife's sisters coming to visit them for a holiday in Truro.

Chapter 13: Earlier Eyre ancestors – cordwainers, peruke makers and clergy

With the family trees on line as a starting point and the confirmation of details as to dates of baptism, marriage and deaths from the parish records it has been possible to trace direct Eyre ancestors back four generations from Thomas Eyre, to my 7th great grandparents who were Thomas Eyre's great great grandparents. Thomas Eyre's parents were second cousins, each with the surname Eyre (Joseph Eyre and Mary Robins Eyre). Until I worked it out this caused considerable confusion and I doubted the accuracy of some of the family trees. However once it was established that this was the case everything else fell into place. Discovering information about the Eyre family was quite easy because the family was a prosperous middle class family, so there are numerous entries relating to them in trade directories which helped to build up a picture. Also they remained in the same part of Cornwall until the middle of the 19th century where the parish records are complete, well recorded and readily available on line. To follow the Eyres it is probably easier to start with the earliest generation rather than work backwards as I have done up until now.

In the 17th century records the name Eyre is spelt Eare and the first ancestors of whom accurate records exist were my 7th great grandparents John Eare (1664-1704) and his wife Christian Robarts (1665-1722).

John Eare was baptised at Kenwyn, Cornwall on 23rd August 1664 and buried at St Clement, Truro, Cornwall on 28th April

1704. His baptismal record states that his father was Frances (sic) Eare, but there is no record of a Francis or Frances Eare in any available records. He would be likely to have been born in about 1630-40 and a possible candidate is Francis Eurey (which may be the result of difficulty in deciphering handwriting) baptised in Braddock, Cornwall in 1632, his father being named John. There is a record of the burial of a Frances Eyrie (whether male or female is not stated) at St. Mary Magdalene, Launceston in 1684.

The marriage of John Eare and Christian Robarts is recorded at St. Clement, Cornwall on 15th November 1687. Christian Eyre was buried at St. Clement, Truro in 1722

The village of St. Clement, near Truro

The attractive village of St. Clement, southeast of Truro, is in the valley of the Tresillian River. This is the first place where known direct Eyre ancestors of mine lived and some of their descendants remained in the parish for several generations.

The children of John and Christian Eare include Francis Eare (1688-1750), the eldest son of the marriage, and Thomas Eare (1694-1750). Both of these brothers are my 6th great grandparents by reason of the marriage between a grandchild of each of them [Joseph Eyre (1756-1808) whose grandfather was Francis Eare, and Mary Robins Eyre (1758-1817) whose grandfather was Thomas Eare]. Joseph and Mary Robins Eyre were the parents of Thomas Eyre, the subject of the last chapter.

The elder of these two brothers, Francis Eare (Eyre) (1688-1758), married twice. His first wife, Elizabeth Pascoe, died in 1726, and it is by virtue of his second marriage to Mary Robins (d.1757) that my ancestry is established. It also appears that it was during Francis Eare's life that the spelling of the surname Eyre became adopted, before the date of his first marriage for so the name is spelt in the marriage record. Francis and Mary Eyre were my 6th great grandparents.

Francis Eyre was baptised as Francis Eare on 23rd October 1688 at St. Clement, Truro. Francis Eyre's first marriage to Elizabeth Pascoe took place at St. Mary's Church, Truro, now part of Truro Cathedral, in 1714. They had 5 children, Christian (b.1714), John (b. 1715), Richard (b. 1717), Elizabeth (b. 1719) and Francis (1722-1792). All were baptised at St. Mary's Truro. Francis Eyre (1722-1792), the youngest son of this marriage, became an attorney and died in London.

In 1727, following the death of his first wife the previous year, Francis Eyre married, secondly, Mary Robins. They married in Philleigh, Cornwall, which was probably Mary Robins's home. They appear to have had the one son, Joseph (1732-1761), who was also baptised at St. Mary's Truro, who is my fifth great grandfather.

Francis Eyre was a cordwainer – i.e. a maker of fine quality bespoke shoes. The term comes from cordwan, a soft goatskin leather of the highest quality from Cordova in Spain, used for the best shoes throughout Europe in the Middle Ages. The Worshipful Company of Cordwainers is one of the oldest livery companies in the City of London with roots dating back to 1272. Cobblers made much cheaper and inferior shoes. Mary Eyre's burial is recorded in 1757 at St. Mary's, Truro and Francis Eyre's burial is recorded in 1758 at St. Mary's, Truro. St. Mary's Church was the parish church for Truro where many Eyre ancestors were baptised, married or buried: it is now incorporated into Truro Cathedral.

Another younger son of John and Christian Eare was Thomas Eare (Eyre) (1694-1750) who married Elizabeth Philip (d. 1753). They were also my 6th great grandparents.

Thomas Eare (Eyre) appears to have remained in the parish of St. Clement, Truro. Three children are recorded baptised at St Clement as the children of his marriage to Elizabeth Philip, Elizabeth (b. 1724), John (b. 1726) and Jacob (b.1730). Of these children John is my ancestor. However it appears that at some time later Thomas Eyre and his wife moved to Bodmin where Thomas is recorded as buried in 1750 and Elizabeth in 1753.

The next generation, my 5th great grandparents, comprised Joseph Eyre (the son of Francis and Mary Robins Eyre) and his first cousin John Eyre (the son of Thomas Eyre and his wife Elizabeth) and their respective wives.

Joseph Eyre (1732-1761) was married to Mary Bailey (1733-1770). He was baptised at St. Mary's Truro in 1732. Joseph Eyre and Mary Bailey (spelt Baley in the record) married at St. Mary's Truro in 1756. They had three children, Francis (b. 1757) who died aged 2 months, Mary Robins (b. 1758) and Joanna (b. 1761) all of whom were baptised at St. Mary's Truro.

Joseph Eyre was a Peruke maker. A Peruke is a man's wig usually gathered at the back with a ribbon, similar to the short wigs worn in court by barristers and judges today. Joseph Eyre was buried at St. Mary's Truro in 1761 and his wife was buried at St. Clement, Truro in 1770. Their children included Mary Robins Eyre (1758-1817) who married her second cousin, Joseph Eyre (1756-1808).

Joseph Eyre's cousin John Eyre (1726-1793) was married to Grace White (d. 1782). He was baptised on 16th October 1726 at St. Clement, Truro, Cornwall. His name is spelt Eyer in the baptismal record. John Eyre and Grace White married in 1750 at St. Stephen by Launceston, Cornwall (probably Grace White's home). They appear to have moved to Bodmin after their marriage since all their children were baptised there.

Their six children were: Richard (b. 1751), Elizabeth (b. 1753), John (b. 1754 – see note below on The Revd. John Eyre), Joseph (b. 1756) my 4th great grandfather, who married his second cousin Mary Robins Eyre, Thomas (b. 1758) and Francis (b. 1760). There are several Grace Eyres whose burials are recorded in Cornwall in the late 18th century, but the most likely candidate was buried at Bodmin in 1782. John Eyre was a fellmonger, i.e. a dealer in hides and skins, also recorded in later trade directories as a merchant of textiles and yarns and as a grocer.

The Revd. John Eyre (1754-1803)

John Eyre had an elder son, John Eyre (1754-1803), my 5th great uncle (and elder brother of my 4th great grandfather, Joseph Eyre) who became an evangelical minister who helped establish some of the major national evangelical institutions. He was born in Bodmin and educated in a private school in Forrabury. At the age of fifteen he was apprenticed to a clothier and mercer in Tavistock (James Oliver) and after a life of revelry underwent a religious conversion and began preaching in the town. At the end of his apprenticeship he returned to his father's business in Bodmin and preached in the Town Hall to large crowds who flocked to hear him preach. His father disapproved and expelled him from home when he refused to give up preaching.

John Eyre then commenced to work amongst the dissenters ministering in Cornwall, Lincoln and London. In 1778 he matriculated at Emmanuel College, Cambridge and took Holy Orders in 1779, and was ordained deacon by the Bishop of London and priest by the Bishop of Lincoln in the same year. He served as curate in Lewes, Reading and Chelsea.

The Revd John Eyre

In 1785 The Revd. John Eyre was appointed minister of Homerton, Hackney, and he opened a school at Well Street, Hackney. He contributed regularly to the Evangelical Magazine which he planned and helped to found. He was a founder of the London Missionary Society in 1794/5. He was involved in establishing what became Hackney Theological College which opened in 1803, the year of his death, and he was buried in a vault on the south side of the communion table in Homerton Chapel Hackney. The college evolved into Homerton College, Cambridge. He married Mary Keene from near Reading in 1785.

This brings us to my 4th great grandparents Joseph Eyre (1756-1808) and Mary Robins Eyre (1758-1817) who were second cousins. The family tree below indicates this relationship. Joseph Eyre had an elder brother, John, whose story is set out above.

Joseph Eyre was baptised in Bodmin on 18th February 1756. He and Mary Robins Eyre were married at Bodmin in 1781, and all of their children were baptised at Bodmin. Joseph Eyre's burial took place at St. Mary's Truro in 1808, and Mary Robins Eyre's burial, also at St. Mary's Truro, was in 1817. Joseph Eyre and his brother Thomas continued the business of their father dealing in hides, textiles and yarns, and in the Oxford University List of Alumni which records the names of two of his sons, Joseph Eyre is described as a gentleman of Bodmin.

Joseph and Mary Robins Eyre had at least eight children. The eldest was Francis Eyre (b. 1783). In 1804 Francis Eyre was named as the prospective father of an illegitimate child to be born to a woman of the parish of St Mary Truro named Elizabeth Annear. The care of bastard children was the responsibility of the Parish into which they were born, and the law permitted the Parish to require a father, if his identity could be established, to enter into a Bastardy Bond to indemnify the Parish. In this case Francis Eyre and his brother, Joseph, voluntarily entered into such a bond in the sum of £20 on 25th February 1804, which would be enforced only if they failed to provide for the child's maintenance, education and welfare by other means.

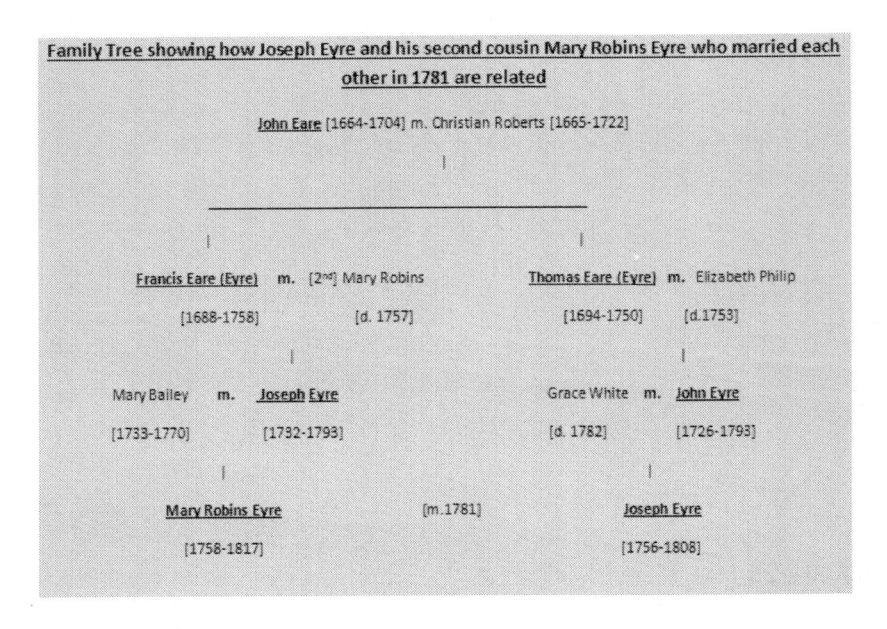

Family Tree showing how Joseph Eyre and his second cousin Mary Robins Eyre who married each other in 1781 are related

John Eare [1664-1704] m. Christian Roberts [1665-1722]

Francis Eare (Eyre) m. [2nd] Mary Robins	Thomas Eare (Eyre) m. Elizabeth Philip
[1688-1758]　　　　[d. 1757]	[1694-1750]　　　　[d.1753]
Mary Bailey m. Joseph Eyre	Grace White m. John Eyre
[1733-1770]　　　　[1732-1793]	[d. 1782]　　　　[1726-1793]
Mary Robins Eyre　　[m.1781]	Joseph Eyre
[1758-1817]	[1756-1808]

The second son was Joseph Eyre (b. 1786) who became a clergyman, one of two of Thomas Eyre's brothers to do so. The next two children were John Eyre (1788-1791) and Sarah Maria Eyre (b. 1790). Then came Thomas Eyre (1791-1861) who married Elizabeth Isabell Murphy (1796-1878) – my 3rd great grandparents [see the previous chapters]. After them came Humphrey Robins Eyre (b. 1795) and finally William Eyre (1797-1841) and Mary Bailey Eyre (1802-1817).

Thomas Eyre's youngest brother, The Revd. William Eyre, (1797-1841) married Grace Mahala Magor (1798-1873) – the Magors were a Truro family. They had several children. At the time of his death in 1841 William Eyre was Headmaster and Librarian of Archbishop Tenison's Grammar School in central London, which originally operated in the crypt of St. Martin in the Fields. It was still located nearby and the record of The Revd. William Eyre's burial states that he resided in the Parish of St. Martin in the Field and the address of the school at this time was off Leicester Square. Founded in 1685 the school moved to a site at The Oval in 1928 and it now operates as a voluntary-aided school. The list of Oxford University Alumni reveals that William Eyre was also Chaplain to St. Martin's Workhouse.

Both clergymen, Joseph and William Eyre (my 4th great uncles), were educated at Oxford University, at Exeter College and Magdalen Hall (subsequently refounded as Hertford College) respectively – they are recorded in the published lists of alumni of the university. They appear to have been the first of the Eyres to be educated at Oxford University, an unusual event in any family at this time, given that there were only the two universities in England. Their uncle, the Revd John Eyre, of the previous generation, had been educated at Cambridge University. This and all other information about the Eyre family in the latter part of the 18th century and the early part of the 19th century point to it being a relatively prosperous and successful middle class family in Cornwall.

It has not been possible to trace the Eyre family back beyond John Eare, born in the middle of the 17th century, other than to note that he was the son of a Frances Eare. However there are some earlier records of a family called Ayre in Cornwall, and although what is set out below cannot be corroborated there is obviously a possibility that these records refer to earlier members of the Eyre family from which I am descended.

In the College of Heralds' Visitation of Cornwall of 1620 there is a reference to John Ayre als (alias) Eyre who had sons, Will'm, Phillip and Francis and a daughter Margaret. Given the coincidence of the names, John and Francis (see above), because it was common for names to be passed down successive generations and sometimes alternating, a son being named not after his father, but his grandfather, it is not beyond the realms of possibility that these are earlier ancestors. If this is the case there is an interesting and distinguished connection because John Ayre's grandfather, Robert Arundell was the bastard son of Sir John Arundell of Trerice (1495-1561). John Ayre's father was William Arundell and it seems that the name of Ayre was adopted at some stage, possibly to conceal the illegitimate lineage. The use of the name Ayre or Eyre to indicate that a person was an heir entitled to an inheritance [referred to in Chapter 10] may be an explanation for this. Sir John Arundell was twice Sheriff of Cornwall, Vice-Admiral of the West under Henry VIII, was knighted at the Battle of the Spurs in 1513, and served in various offices under Edward VI and Mary I. He bore the nickname "Jack of Tilbury", possibly reflecting his naval connections. His grandson, also called Sir John Arundell, nicknamed "Jack for the King", was a prominent leader of the Royalist Cause in Cornwall in the English Civil War. Other members of the Arundell family, one of Cornwall's leading families and one of the few with Norman origins, served both locally and nationally, and include a Bishop of Exeter, a judge, various soldiers and members of Parliament. The family was strongly Catholic and so their influence declined after the Reformation.

Trerice House, near Newquay, now a National Trust property open to the public, was from the 14th to the 18th centuries the seat of the Arundell family whose line died out in 1768 when the house passed to the Wentworth and then the Acland families. The house was considerably extended in the early 16th century and is a fine example of an early Tudor manor house.

In the documents held by the Cornish Record Office recorded by the St Keverne Local History Society (St Keverne is a large parish on the Lizard peninsula, south of Truro) is a document recording the grant of land in the St Keverne parish to a Robert Eyre, with references to Peter Eyre and Ralph Eyre. This document is dated 1469, which indicates that there were Eyres in Cornwall in the 15th Century, and it is possible that my Eyre ancestors are descended from these people.

Chapter 14: Wing Commander Anthony Eyre DFC

Anthony Eyre was my uncle, the brother of my mother, Pamela, and first cousin of Geoffrey Tuttle [Chapter 6] and Leslie Appleton [Chapter 15]. He was usually known as Tony, and my grandmother consented to my being named after him, but on condition that I was never known as "Tony".

He was born on 12th November 1918, the day after the Armistice, the only son of George William Booth Eyre and Dorothy (nee Tuttle). The family lived in Purley in Surrey where Tony and his sister were brought up, and Tony was educated at Whitgift School in Croydon.

Various articles about Tony state that on leaving school he commenced to train as a lawyer, but my mother did not recall this. Her recollection was that on leaving school he went into banking. In any event in 1938, at the age of nineteen, Tony was commissioned as a pilot officer in the Auxiliary Air Force with 615 (County of Surrey) Squadron. The pilots of the Auxiliary Air Force were known as "weekend fliers", but at the outbreak of the Second World War the 21 squadrons of the Auxiliary Air Force were incorporated into the Royal Air Force and provided some of the most courageous and distinguished pilots of the war. 615 Squadron was known as Churchill's Squadron because Winston Churchill was its Honorary Commodore.

In November 1939, two months after the outbreak of the Second World War 615 Squadron was moved from its base in Kenley to northern France as part of the British Expeditionary Force and was based at Vitry-en-Artois, between Arras and Douai. Tony was promoted to Flying Officer in January 1940. He was flying fifty hours a month or more (the equivalent of a mission a day) in Gloucester Gladiators (the biplane with which the squadron was then equipped).

On 10th May 1940 the German Blitz-Krieg swept into northern France and the Battle of France began. 615 Squadron switched airfields four times in ten days. Between 10th and 20th May Anthony Eyre shot down three enemy aircraft and he is widely credited with having shot down the Kommandeur of II/JG26 Luftwaffe, Hauptmann Herwig Knuppel, near Tournai on 19th May. As the British Army was forced to retreat to the channel coast 615 Squadron destroyed the aircraft that could not be evacuated and on 21st May its members sailed home on the

Southern Railway steamer "Biarritz" a few days before the evacuation at Dunkirk.

Meanwhile Tony was entrusted with a special mission. Because wireless telegraphy could not be trusted for communications, Anthony Eyre was charged with carrying important information from London to France ahead of the German advance. He eventually got home to Redhill in one of the last Gladiators left in France on 22nd May. In the citation to his DFC awarded in August 1940 is recorded:

"During the evacuation from France Flying Officer Eyre was entrusted with an important message from England to France and successfully completed this mission which required great coolness and presence of mind. He has at all times shown great devotion to duty".

His actions are regarded as having contributed to the saving of many lives at Dunkirk.

Flying Officer Anthony Eyre DFC with the Hurricane he flew in the Battle of Britain

615 Squadron was now equipped with Hurricanes and returned to Kenley from where its pilots became heavily engaged in the Battle of Britain as part of 11 Group, Fighter Command, commanded by the charismatic Australian, Air Vice-Marshal Keith Park. On his first mission in a Hurricane on 11th June 1940 Tony is believed to have destroyed a Messerschmitt Bf 109 and followed this up with 2 Bf 110s. On 20th July as a Convoy BOSOM made its way up the channel it was the subject of a ferocious attack by the Luftwaffe. Anthony Eyre was one of a trio of 615 pilots who together downed 3 Bf 109s. A total of about 150 aircraft were engaged in the battle surrounding this convoy which, despite the efforts to protect it was badly damaged, and HMS Brazen was sunk. During August Tony brought down another five German aircraft.

On 18th August Kenley was the subject of a daring low level raid by the Luftwaffe which caused considerable damage and 615 Squadron moved to nearby Croydon. Tony Eyre and eight colleagues took on a formation of eighteen enemy Dorniers and thirty escorting German fighters on 28th August. The following day the squadron was posted to Prestwick for rest and to re-equip. Tony Eyre's DFC was announced in the London Gazette the following day.

As the Battle of Britain was coming to its conclusion 615 Squadron returned south to Northolt in October and then to Kenley just before Christmas.

A photograph of members of RAF 615 Squadron when Flight Lieutenant Anthony Eyre DFC (standing, third from the right) was its commanding officer

In January 1941 Tony was promoted to Flight Lieutenant and from 23rd February he became the Commanding Officer of 615 Squadron when its CO, Raymond Holmwood, was killed. In the short time that he was CO he set about restoring the morale and confidence of the squadron following the loss of a popular and inspirational CO. Tony Eyre left 615 Squadron on 21st April 1941 and was posted to the headquarters of 12 Group Fighter Command (Midlands).

However he returned to more front line duties in December 1941, promoted to Squadron Leader and later in the month to Acting Wing Commander, to lead 132 Spitfire Wing at RAF North Weald. On 30th December 1941 Tony Eyre married Jean Spence, the daughter of Lieutenant Colonel Patrick Spence, at Sidlow

Bridge in Surrey. In February and March he flew various missions over northern Belgium and France, but on 8th March 1942 when leading a raid over France his Spitfire was damaged and crashed near to Mardyck Aerodrome, west of Dunkirk.

The remainder of the war was spent as a prisoner of war at Stalag Luft III, the newly established prisoner of war camp at Sagan in Silesia (now in Poland and known as Zagan). Tony Eyre was one of the first prisoners to be incarcerated at this camp built for the purpose of imprisoning captured air force officers – his POW number was 4. Whilst there his acting rank of Wing Commander was confirmed and made substantive.

Prisoners of War at Stalag Luft III

L to R - Lt Col McNicholl (USAAF), Wing Commander Robert Stanford Tuck DSO DFC, Wing Commander Joseph Kayll DSO DFC, Wing Commander Anthony Eyre DFC and Wing Commander Richard Milne DFC. This photograph, inscribed on the reverse with the names of the subjects, together with the negative, was in the possession of my grandmother and has been passed on to me. The reason for the photograph and the circumstances in which it was taken are not known.

Stalag Luft III was the camp from which the famous "Wooden Horse" and "Great Escape" breakouts were made and which have become the stuff of legend in popular films. Fifty of the seventy-three captured escapers who took part in the "Great Escape" were summarily executed by the Gestapo, an atrocity which caused considerable anxiety in the family when the news reached England only to be eased when the news that Tony had not been involved eventually reached home.

In January 1945 as the Russians moved further westwards the Germans moved the ten thousand or so prisoners from Sagan and marched them in appalling conditions around the country as Germany crumbled. The extent of this terrible ordeal has only recently been fully appreciated. When Anthony Eyre got home he was suffering from frostbite.

A further photograph of Anthony Eyre at Stalag Luft III

In August 1945, confirmed as a regular RAF officer, Anthony Eyre was appointed CO of RAF Fairwood Common, now Swansea Airport. He and Jean settled at Pennard in the beautiful Gower peninsula. Fairwood Common was a busy centre where squadrons passed through before being disbanded, redeployed or in the case of Empire and Commonwealth Squadrons returning home.

On 16th February 1946 Tony Eyre took up a Hawker Tempest on a routine flight. The plane developed an engine fault, the engine cut out and as he tried to reach RAF St Athan the plane crashed into a tree and Tony was killed instantly.

On 20th February 1946 Wing Commander Anthony Eyre DFC, aged 27, was buried with full military honours at Llangennith near where he and Jean had made their home in Gower. His grave remains beautifully tended and I was privileged to visit it with his sister, Pamela, my mother, sixty years later in 2006.

Tony's daughter, Penny, was born posthumously in July 1946. His widow Jean subsequently married Barry Frentzel, who had served in the RAF with Tony, and bore another child, David. After Barry's death Jean married Tony Pickford who died some years ago. Thus Jean, who died in 2014 aged 95, was thrice widowed. Penny married Peter Birts, a barrister who has become a QC and a Circuit Judge, but they are now divorced. They have three children, Melanie who married an Army Officer, Charlotte, also married, and William, a doctor who has also recently married.

On Remembrance Sunday 2010 the church at Llangennith marked the occasion of the 70th anniversary of the Battle of Britain by concentrating on the pilot whose grave is of considerable prominence in the churchyard. A memorial booklet was produced (from which I was able to obtain some information which was previously not known by me) and Penny was invited to attend the event, which she did with her brother David and son William. Penny met three people there who had known her father.

Tony Eyre's funeral at Llangennith

Tony Eyre was one of "The Few" to whom we all owe our lives and liberty and is a relative of whom my family is rightly very proud. He was a true hero – a term frequently misused these days. His name is recorded on the Battle of Britain Memorial erected a few years ago on the Embankment in London.

Winston Churchill summed up the debt owed to Anthony Eyre and his comrades in the well-known words:

"The gratitude of every home in our island, in our Empire, and indeed throughout the world, except in the abodes of the guilty, goes out to the British airmen who, undaunted by the odds, unwearied in their constant challenge and mortal danger, are

turning the tide of the war by their prowess and their devotion. Never in the field of human conflict was so much owed by so many to so few."

Chapter 15: Leslie Appleton OBE

Leslie Richard Eyre Appleton was my first cousin once removed. His mother was Emily Eyre the sister of my grandfather George Eyre and thus Leslie Appleton was the first cousin of my mother and Tony Eyre, which is of particular interest because of the connection with the Hurricane aircraft. All contact with this branch of my family was lost, following the death of my grandfather and the subsequent bombing of my grandmother's home in the Second World War until I spotted the obituary notice of Leslie's death in 2000 and was able to make contact with his sister Peggy.

Leslie Appleton was born on 24th April 1914, the son of William Ewart Appleton (1889-1943) and Emily Augusta Appleton (nee Eyre, 1889 - 1986). He was born in Birkenhead where his father worked as an electrical engineer, but most of his childhood was spent in Bermondsey. He was educated at St. Olave's School and Downing College, Cambridge where he read mechanical sciences.

He went to work for Hawker Aircraft at Kingston-on-Thames working under Sir Sydney Camm (designer of the Hurricane) on various assignments including the Hurricane and Typhoon aircraft and also the design of the mast for Sir Tommy Sopwith's yacht which raced in the 1937 America's Cup.

Throughout the Second World War he worked on armaments and was largely responsible for gun and rocket installation on aircraft such as Hurricane, Tempest and Typhoon. He left Hawker in 1946 and briefly teamed up with an architect who was designing a new kind of catamaran, but in 1947 he was recruited by Fairey Aviation. It was with this company that he made his name as an aircraft designer.

The Fairey Delta 2

Leslie Appleton's principal claim to fame was as leader of the team which designed the Fairey Delta 2 (FD2) which shattered the world airspeed record in March 1956 by flying at 1,132 mph, more than 300 mph faster than the previous record held by an American plane, the Super Sabre.

As Chief Technician at Fairey Leslie Appleton had been given the task of conceiving an aircraft which could make up ground on the Americans, who were thought to be seven years ahead of the British in aerospace research. The result was the FD2 whose revolutionary delta wing and drooping nose are widely seen as a forerunner to Concorde. Despite its outstanding success and revolutionary design the FD2 was never developed for the RAF and was the victim of defence cuts in the late 1950s. However the idea was seized upon by the French and the plane-maker Marcel

Dassault, using information passed on by Fairey, based the hugely successful Mirage aircraft on it.

Meanwhile Leslie Appleton became the chief engineer of Fairey's new guided missile plant and was responsible for the production of the Fairey Fireflash, Britain's first air-to-air guided missile for which in 1958 he was awarded the OBE.

Following the sale of Fairey Aviation to Westland in 1960 he became the managing director of Fairey Engineering where amongst other things he was involved in equipping the nuclear power station at Trawsfynydd in North Wales. Later he rejoined what had become Hawker Siddeley as general manager of its subsidiary Allied Systems which was responsible for trying to sell equipment to the Americans which included the successful sale of the Harrier aircraft to the US Marine Corps. He moved to the British Manufacture and Research Company, part of the Oerlikon-Buhle Group, in 1976, becoming chairman, and in 1979 he also became chairman of another company in the group, Pilatus-Britten-Norman, which manufactured aircraft. He retired from business at the age of 75 in 1989.

Leslie Appleton married his first wife, Christina Matilda Schwart in 1937, by whom he had a daughter, Jillian. Christina died of cancer in 1956 and three years later Leslie married Gillian Hatton by whom he had two further children - Richard and Elizabeth.

Leslie Appleton died on 15th September 2000 aged 86. It is quite remarkable that my family should have produced three members who made a considerable contribution to aviation in such different respects.

Chapter 16: The Stephens Family

My great grandmother Ellen Augusta Stephens, Thomas Southwood Eyre's wife, who died in premature childbirth aged a few days short of her 29th birthday in June 1891, came from a Cornish family. She was one of the seven children of William John Stephens (1823-1885) and Ellen Thomas (1836-1907). Something of her story was known to me from information from Mabel Mortimer, the mother of Angela Mortimer[9]. It is probably best to set out the information revealed in a letter to my mother verbatim.

"Ellen Thomas was the Cornish-born daughter of a civil engineer. William John Stephens and Ellen Thomas met in India where William was serving in the Royal Navy and they married at Bishop's College, Calcutta in 1858. Later they lived in South Africa where William was serving in H.M. Dockyard, Cape Town. When living there Ellen Stephens travelled from Cape Town to Johannesburg in a milk wagon, the journey taking four days. In 1862 their daughter Ellen [my great grandmother] was sleeping in a pram in their garden in Cape Town when a huge ape crept towards the pram and it was chased off by the gardener."

The letter went on to say that William John Stephens was the son of John Stephens and Jenefer Henwood Hill. Jenefer was the daughter of William Hill of Budock in Cornwall, known as Squire Hill. Squire Hill is said to have been an autocratic man

---

[9] See Chapter 17 for a short biography of Angela Mortimer

who disapproved of his daughter Jenefer eloping with one of his tenant farmers, John Stephens. He never forgave his daughter.

This tale obviously had some interesting aspects. Who was Squire Hill? Was it possible to find out about William John Stephens's career in the Royal Navy? From what family did Ellen Thomas hail? As with other researches my first port of call was the census records and from these it was possible to discover a considerable amount about the life of William John Stephens.

Other researches established that William John Stephens was born in 1823, baptised on 16th November in Budock. He was the eldest child of John Stephens (1798-1871) and Jenefer Henwood Hill (1800-1885) and he had two brothers and three sisters.

In the 1841 census return, William John Stephens was living with his parents and siblings in Budock. In the 1851 census William John Stephens is shown living in Budock with his parents, John and Jenefer Stephens. He is described as "Mariner (Navy)". He is said to have been a boatswain in family records, which is confirmed by other information. The boatswain was an important non-commissioned officer on a Royal Navy vessel responsible for overseeing the deck crew.

Some naval records survive. Service was not always continuous and sailors could be paid off when a ship was decommissioned and then re-enter the service at a later date. There is a record of a William J Stevens (*sic*) born in 1823 who first joined the Royal Navy in 1840 and who served on three ships between 1840 and 1846, namely HMS Persian, a sloop, HMS Helena, also a sloop launched in 1843 when HMS Persian was scrapped, and HMS Cleopatra, a frigate. All three ships were involved in suppressing the slave trade off West Africa. This seems likely to be part of William J Stephens's early Royal Navy career.

There is no entry for William John Stephens in the 1861 census records. This is because he was serving overseas in the Royal Navy. He was at Calcutta in 1858, where he married – this was shortly after the Indian Mutiny had been suppressed. The birth places of some of his children, including my great grandmother, Ellen Augusta Stephens, in South Africa between 1859 and 1865 indicate that he was stationed there, as the known family history revealed, stationed in H.M. Dockyard, Cape Town.

HMS Tamar at Alexandria in 1882

Unusually William John Stephens appears in two entries in the 1871 Census. He and his family are recorded as resident at 12, Cambridge Street, Devonport. However at the date of the 1871 census (2nd April 1871) William John Stephens was serving as boatswain on HMS Tamar, which was berthed at Devonport, and his name is recorded in the Census Return for the ship as "On the ship's books, but not on board". The Captain and many other officers and crew were not on board either. HMS Tamar was a troopship, described on the Census return as on "Special

Service". Launched in 1863, she regularly took troops to the Cape and China. In 1874 she formed part of the Naval Brigade that helped to defeat the Ashanti in West Africa during the Ashanti War. In 1882 she took part in the bombardment of Alexandria, but by this time William John Stephens had retired from the Royal Navy. In 1897 HMS Tamar became a base ship in Hong Kong, and the shore base was named HMS Tamar after her. The ship met a sad end in the Second World War when she was scuttled and blown up on 12th December 1941 to prevent the invading Japanese from using her.

1871 was an important year in European History. Following defeat in the Franco-Prussian War France was in turmoil. Paris had been under siege and its population had suffered considerably. The French Third Republic was established and there was a revolutionary government controlling Paris for some weeks in the spring (The Paris Commune). It was in connection with this situation that HMS Tamar was deployed on "Special Service". Naval records indicate that on 25th January 1871 HMS Tamar arrived at Spithead from the West Indies. On 1st February she took the 97th Regiment from Dover to Ireland (to Queenstown now known as Cobh). She returned from Ireland and on 12th February she was loaded with provisions for France. On 13th February she sailed from Portsmouth to Dieppe with a full cargo of Navy biscuit and flour from the Government Victualing Yards at Plymouth and Portsmouth to be used towards the re-victualing of Paris. Days after this the National Guard rebelled against the new government of France and took control of Paris and the red flag flew over the city. The Paris Commune was suppressed and Paris was retaken by troops of the Third Republic at the end of May following a bloody conflict with considerable loss of life. Having returned to Plymouth, and being there on 2nd April when the census took place, when it appears that William John Stephens spent some leave on shore with his family, HMS Tamar set sail on 6th April with passengers (troops) and stores for the Cape of Good Hope, Mauritius, Hong Kong and Japan.

By the time of the 1881 census William John Stephens, now retired from the Royal Navy, was living in Plymouth with his wife Ellen and five of their children – Ellen A (aged 18, born Cape of Good Hope), milliner, Gertrude H (16, born Cape of Good Hope), drapers assistant, Henry M (12, born Pembroke), Florence S (9, born Devonport) and Ethel M (6, born Devonport). The birthplaces of the children are indicative of William John Stephens's naval career. The family address was the Hoe Park Hotel, Saltram Place, Plymouth and William is described as licensed victualler, so it would appear that like many mariners when he left the Royal Navy he became a publican. The Hoe Park Hotel appears to have ceased operating as an hotel in the 1920s.

William John Stephens and his wife Ellen had a total of seven children. Their names were known to me from family records. The eldest was Fanny Stephens (1859-1944) who was born in South Africa. She married William Goad and had four daughters, Augusta, Florence, Hilda and Edna. The next child was a son, William, born in 1861, also in South Africa. My great grandmother, Ellen Augusta Stephens (1862-1891), came next – she was also born in South Africa, as was her sister Gertrude (born 1865). Henry Stephens was born in 1869 in Pembroke – he married a lady named Olivia and had three children, Harry, William and Frederick. Then came Florence Sarah Stephens (1871-1969), who was born in Devonport after 2nd April when the census took place, because she is not recorded in the 1871 census. She married Charles Stephen Beard and had a daughter, Mabel (Mabs), who married John Stuart Mortimer – they were the parents of Angela Mortimer [See Chapter 17]. The final child was Ethel Maude Mary Stephens (1874-1962) who married Ernest James Dunning who was a shop owner – they had a daughter, Edna.

William John Stephens died on 25th September 1885 – his effects were valued at £837, a not inconsiderable sum in those days which using the assessment of the economic power of that value of wealth today would amount to approximately £1 million.

Following the death of William John Stephens his widow Ellen continued to live in Devonport (Plymouth) until her death in 1907. In the 1891 census Ellen Stephens was living at 2 Albany Place, Plymouth with her daughters Florence and Ethel. She is described as a licenced victualler.

In the 1901 census she was recorded as living at 23, Marlborough Street, Devonport, running a confectionery business. Living with her were her daughter Ethel Maude Dunning, her granddaughter Edna Dunning (16) and another granddaughter Fanny Goad (3).

It was possible to trace William John Stephens's parents in the census returns for 1841, 1851 and 1861 to their home in Budock where the census return for 1841 revealed them living with a total of six children. John Stephens is described as a farmer farming four acres with no labourers in his employ.

It has not been possible to trace further back beyond John Stephens, William John's father (1798-1871). However it has been possible to trace the ancestry of his wife, Jenefer Henwood Hill (1800-1885) who was one of seven children of William Hill, the autocratic Squire Hill referred to in family papers (1764-1844). Squire Hill was born in Penryn, Cornwall, baptised on 10th December 1764. He married Elizabeth Henwood (1762-1807) at

St. Enoder, Cornwall. Squire Hill and Elizabeth Henwood were my 4th great grandparents.

In the marriage record William Hill is described as a victualler. The 1841 census reveals William Hill living in Budock St, Budock, Cornwall with his daughters Temperance Hill and Mary Hill, aged 35 and 30 respectively. William Hill is described as a merchant. In Pigot's Directory of 1840 he is listed as a corn and flour merchant. He was also a landowner and a man of some means.

William Hill was the son of another William Hill (b. 1740) who married Elizabeth Truscott (b.1743). They married in 1762 at St. Winnow, Cornwall. They were my 5th great grandparents. It has been possible to trace the Truscott ancestors back five further generations to my 10th great grandparents, Nicholas Truscott (1573-1610) and Alison Skantilbew (b. 1575), and the Skantilbews can be traced even further back to my 14th great grandfather John Skantilbew, born in 1460. Other than their identification from the parish records it has not been possible to discover anything about the lives of these people, but it is interesting to note that the Truscott and Skantilbew families came from Lanreath in Cornwall a small village where the Wilton family also lived into which an early Langmaid ancestor of mine married - John Langmaid (1631-1697) and Marian Wilton (1634-1685) were my 8th great grandparents [See Chapter 9]. It seems highly likely that ancestors of mine through each of my mother's parents, the Tuttle and Eyre lines, would have been acquainted with each other.

Pronounced Lanreth, the Parish of Lanreath can trace its existence back at least to the Domesday Book of 1086, when it was known as Lanredoch. The present version is a derivation of the "church site (Lann) of Raydhogh". Lanreath is well steeped in legend, including the alleged sighting on numerous occasions of a ghost dressed in black driving a coach pulled by headless horses. In 1620, the Punch Bowl Inn at Lanreath is said to have become the very first licensed public house in the land. Parts of the building date back even earlier. The building has served variously as a courthouse, coaching inn and smugglers den, but closed on the 1st May 2012. The present day Lanreath has a population of around 500, its economy sustained by farming and tourism.

It took a considerable amount of research to discover information about the antecedents of William John Stephens's wife, Ellen Thomas (1836-1907), about whom nothing was known other than the fact that her father was an engineer. However a careful examination of the census records and the local parish records established that she was born in St. Austell in 1836, the daughter of James and Agatha Thomas (3rd great grandparents). The fact that it was known from family records that her father was an engineer led to the identification of her father as James Thomas (1794-1867) and her mother as Agatha Harris (1794-1845) who married in Redruth in 1815. It was also possible to confirm that Ellen Thomas married William John Stephens in Calcutta in 1858, something stated in the letter from Mabel Mortimer to my mother referred to earlier.

James Thomas was an engineer with a large engineering business, the Charlestown Ironworks in St. Austell which employed 107 labourers at the time of the 1851 census. The family is recorded in the 1851 census, living at 45, Charlestown, St. Austell, which is now occupied by an architect's practice. In the household were sons and daughters Elizabeth (34), James (25), Emma (21) Edwin (18) and Ellen (16). Also living in the household was a servant. Ellen is described as a scholar. The two sons were working in the family engineering business. Charlestown Iron Foundry and Ironworks Co was situated further up the hill from Charlestown Harbour, on Charlestown Road, St. Austell, Cornwall. The business had been founded in about 1827 by James Thomas.

Charlestown Foundry made heavy machinery for the Cornish mining and clay industries including an enormous 35ft pitchback water wheel, which operated at what is now a Clay Museum at Wheal Martin by 1884 (after the death of James Thomas). It was used to pump clay slurry up to the surface from the bottom of the china clay pits. The power from the wheel had to travel large distances via the ingenious system of connecting rods made of iron called flat rods. They travelled uphill for over half a mile and through narrow tunnels on a system of pulleys. The wheel still exists and is on display at the China Clay Country Park.

The business remains in operation today as a blacksmith and forge producing mainly wrought iron products such as gates, fencing and railings. It is known as Charlestown Forge but no longer operating from the original site which has been developed for housing.

Chapter 17: Angela Mortimer

Angela Mortimer – Wimbledon Ladies Singles Champion

Angela Mortimer was the Wimbledon Ladies Singles Champion in 1961. She is my second cousin once removed, through my descent from the Stephens family as set out in the previous chapter. Ellen Augusta Stephens (1862-1891), the wife of Thomas Southwood Eyre and my great grandmother, had a younger sister, Florence Sarah Stephens (1871-1969). Florence Stephens married Charles Stephen Beard in 1900 and they had a daughter, Florence Mabel Beard (1902-1987), who married John Stuart Mortimer in 1929, the bridesmaids being my mother and Peggy Appleton as previously stated. Angela Mortimer was one of their three children born on 21st April 1932 at Plymouth.

Aged seven at the outbreak of World War II, Angela Mortimer's family was living in Plymouth, which suffered many air-raids because of the naval base. So the family moved to a farm near Totnes for the duration of the War. As hostilities ended the family returned to Plymouth and Angela continued her education at Moorfields School. It was as a teenager that she developed a passion for tennis, and in her last year at school, 1948, she captained her school's first tennis team to victory in the Plymouth Inter-schools Championship. Spotting an announcement in the local newspaper that a tennis coach was giving free coaching at the Palace Hotel in Torquay she decided to go by bus to the event. The result was not encouraging because the coach, a Mr. Arthur Roberts, told her that she hadn't a clue how to play the game and that she should forget tennis. Fortunately Angela was not put off by this experience and indeed she returned for more free tuition to the only coach available in the area and in the end Mr. Roberts was prepared for his very enthusiastic pupil (who he conceded had guts, even if he did not think much of her tennis) to enter her first tournament at Sutton. She won the handicap singles event (in a match which lasted three hours) and reached the third round of the junior singles competition and her career had begun.

In 1949 she played at Wimbledon for the first time in the Junior Wimbledon competition and reached the semi-finals of the singles and with her partner from Torquay, Ross Bulleid, won the junior girls' doubles finals. This secured them an entry to the

Wimbledon Championships proper that year, but they were knocked out in the first round.

Angela Mortimer made steady progress and played in the Ladies Singles at Wimbledon for the first time in 1951 and played in the next eleven championships. She also played in all the major championships abroad winning the French Championship in 1955 and the Australian Championship in 1958.

At Wimbledon she reached the quarter finals in 1953 (as fifth seed) and 1954 (sixth seed). In 1955 when she was seeded Number 4 she was knocked out in the second round, but reached the quarter finals again in 1956 (third seed). She lost in the third round when seeded Number 7 in 1957, and was unseeded in 1958 when she reached the final to be beaten 8-6 6-1 by the Number 1 seed Althea Gibson of the USA. She was seeded Number 2 in 1959 and again was knocked out in the quarter finals. Similarly in 1960, seeded Number 7, she was knocked out in the quarter finals by that year's champion, Maria Bueno of Brazil.

In 1961 Angela Mortimer was again the seventh seed. Also seeded were two other British players, Christine Trueman at Number 6 and Ann Haydon at Number 3, the rising star of British tennis. Ann Haydon was knocked out in the fourth round, but Angela Mortimer and Christine Trueman reached the final, the first all-British final since 1914. Christine Trueman led until well into the second set but Angela was able to take control and win a hard fought match 4-6 6-4 7-5.

An indication of how over the last half century things have changed in the sporting world (and not in my view for the better in every respect) is that Angela Mortimer drove herself to Wimbledon from her Aunt's home in Kingston in her Austin A35, and that her only financial reward for victory was a £20 voucher to be spent on tennis equipment. The Wimbledon Championship was only open to amateurs until the late 1960s. Rod Laver, one of the greatest tennis players of all time, was the Men's Champion in 1961.

Angela Mortimer played one more time at Wimbledon the following year, seeded Number 6, and lost to an unseeded player in the fourth round.

Regarded as a sound and controlled player rather than a spectacular one, to paraphrase her husband's assessment of her in his history of the Wimbledon Championships, there is no doubt that strength of character played a major part in Angela Mortimer's success. She battled against adversity, persevering against the gloomy prognostications of her first coach with whom despite his disparagement of her abilities she stayed for a long time, and suffered significant periods of ill-health. During her career she became progressively deaf, being told at the age of 22 that she might be totally deaf by the age of 30. In fact this did not occur but her deafness did worsen over the years.

Following her tennis career Angela Mortimer worked for the fashion designer Teddy Tinling, best known for his ladies' tennis outfits.

In April 1967 Angela Mortimer married John Barrett another tennis player who became better known for his writing and broadcasting. For many years he was the principal BBC tennis commentator, succeeding Dan Maskell as the voice of Wimbledon. He is the author of many books on racquet sports, including "Wimbledon: The Official History of the Championships" published by Collins Willow in 2001. They have two children and live in Kingston-on-Thames, not far from Wimbledon.

Angela Mortimer published her autobiography "My Waiting Game" in 1962.

Part III – Tracing the Russells

Chapter 18: The Starting Point

The name Russell was originally used as a nickname for someone with red hair or a red face.

Of my four grandparental families that which gives me my surname has been by far the most difficult to research. Although I had a number of pieces of information about my mother's family to start from, the same was not so in respect of my father. My father, Michael Hibberd Russell (1921-1987) was the second of three brothers. He was a medical practitioner who married my mother in 1947 and after two years living in Canada, where my father worked in a team of doctors setting up the Canadian Blood Transfusion Service, my parents returned to the United Kingdom and settled in the Wirral where my father practised as a general practitioner. The eldest brother, Peter Byrom Russell (1918-1996), was a chemist who lived in the USA for most of his adult life, and the youngest of the trio was Thomas Patrick Russell (1926-2002) who was a barrister, Queen's

Counsel, subsequently a High Court Judge and finally a Lord Justice of Appeal - The Right Honourable Sir Patrick Russell[10].

My father, Dr Michael Hibberd Russell

My grandfather was Sidney Arthur Russell (1884-1953) who married Elsie Potter (1888-1948). Sidney Russell was an electrical engineer of some note, having been the Chief Engineer of The Manchester Tramway Company and a number of power stations in the Manchester area and elsewhere. His family came from the Southampton area. Elsie Potter came from a Lancashire family [see Part IV]. Apart from two cousins, one being always referred to as Cousin Jim, the other being Lena Lloyd, the daughter of Sidney's sister Maud, there was no contact between my father and his brothers and any other member of the Russell family and such contact as there was between them and these two cousins was very limited and occasional.

---

[10] See Chapter 21 for a short biography of Sir Patrick Russell

My father, Michael Hibberd Russell MB ChB, and his elder brother, Peter Byrom Russell PhD, after receiving their degrees at Manchester University c. 1945

My father knew that his second name, Hibberd, had some family significance but he did not know from where or from whom the name came. He also knew that a number of members of the Russell family had been teachers in Southampton, but other than this there was not a great deal of information available to me.

It was not difficult to discover that Sidney Arthur Russell was born in 1884, his birth being registered in South Stoneham, Southampton. His parents were Henry and Mary Russell, and Henry was indeed a schoolmaster. Sidney Arthur Russell lived with his parents, latterly at 40, Carlton Road, Shirley, Southampton, until at least 1901. He trained as an electrical engineer and at the time of the 1911 census he was living in Leicester working as an electrical engineer for the municipal tramways. When the census return for 1911 was indexed for the website I was using his first name was misread and in the index he appears as Binney Arthur Russell. This meant that for some time I wondered whether he had gone abroad for some time as there appeared to be no trace of him in the census. This serves as a reminder that all information should be examined carefully and that errors can easily occur. Sidney Russell served in the First World War in the Royal Army Service Corps as a private, which included service in France.

Sidney Russell married Elsie Potter in June 1916 at Prestwich (Manchester). He worked in the electricity industry for the whole of his working life, mainly in the Manchester area but also for a time in the 1920s at Portishead, Somerset. Following the Allied victory in the Second World War he was given the task of supervising the restoration of the electricity supply in Berlin. During this time he lived in the officers' mess and was given the status of a Lieutenant Colonel. Berlin was in ruins and until the opening of the new power station in December 1949 the British, American and French sectors of Berlin were dependent upon the Russians for the supply of electricity. The Russians controlled the remaining sector of Berlin, which was located in the Russian controlled part of Germany which became East Germany. In the crisis in 1949 which led to the Berlin Air Lift, the supply of electricity to the Western sectors was cut off for a time by the Russians.

Sidney Russell (3rd from left) in Berlin with the Electricity Committee

Sidney Russell was an Associate Member of the Institute of Electrical Engineers (A.M.I.E.E.).

From this information it was possible to trace back from Sidney Russell two further generations to his Russell grandparents (my great great grandparents) in the early 19th century but using all the links available from the genealogy websites I was accustomed to rely upon I reached a dead end. When I had completed the text of this book I had written that it had been a source of some regret that I had not been able to discover more about my Russell ancestors from whom I derived my name.

However when checking my work I decided that I would see whether by other researches I could tie up some loose ends, one of which was to pin down the birth of Henry Russell senior, my 2nd great grandfather, who, according to the 1841 census return had been born in Bath in 1819. Initially all my researches had drawn blanks – there were very few records for Bath available on any of the websites I regularly used. So, everything else having failed, I entered a general search for "Somerset parish records" in a search engine and came across a website which is itself basically a searching facility with a huge database of parish records of births marriages and deaths from which it was possible not only to identify the most probable candidate for Henry Russell and his parents, but because the family had remained in the same parish in Bath for many years it was also possible to identify three further generations of Russells. The website, rightly, warns that it is only a search facility and that an entry should not be regarded as proof, but in this case the continuity and the fact that some of the entries were, once discovered, corroborated by other evidence, provided sufficient proof that my balance of probability test could be satisfied. However, I sound a note of caution. There is another possibility for the identification of Henry Russell which I discuss in the next chapter.

This experience serves as a reminder of the importance of searching for as many sources of information as possible. It also illustrates the point that researching never ends – more and more information is published on the Internet as research is carried out. This discovery of the parish records emphasised how reliance upon the family trees prepared by others can result in serious errors. There were some family trees on line which purported to trace Henry Russell's ancestry back for several generations. However I had already discovered serious anomalies in these lines of descent and had discounted them, so my more recent researches reminded me that the researches of others should not be taken at face value as will be seen again in Chapter 25. In the following chapter I set out what was discovered about previous generations of Russells.

Chapter 19: The Russells of Somerset and Hampshire

From the census returns of 1881 and 1891 it was possible to identify Henry and Mary Russell (my great grandparents) as the parents of my grandfather Sidney Arthur Russell and seven further children: Henry H Russell (1876-1881); Florence M Russell (1877-1942) who married Albert Henry Brazier and had two sons; Maud Winifred Russell (1879-1953) who married Henry A Lloyd and had a daughter, Florence Lena Lloyd (1907-2002) the Cousin Lena referred to in the previous chapter; Charles Hibberd Russell (1880-1955) who married Elsa Maud Biggs and had two sons; Harold Henry Russell (b. 1882) who married Beatrice Findlow and had a son; after whom came my grandfather Sidney Arthur (1884-1953); then Ewart William Russell (1886-1951) who married May Hammond; and finally Reginald Russell (1887-1940) who married Ella Rowe and had a son.

It was interesting to discover my father's second name Hibberd cropping up again, and when I found the marriage record for Henry Russell, Sidney's father, in 1875, I realised why this was so, because Henry Russell (1851-1902) had married Mary Hibberd (1853-1920) in 1875 in Southampton.

From the census returns from 1871 to 1901 it is possible to discover quite a lot of information about Henry Russell's life. He was the only one of my ancestors whose birth certificate I felt it necessary to obtain in order to confirm his birth, established to be on 21st January 1851 at 2, York Street, Southampton, because of the fact that there were two Henry Russells born in 1851 in

Southampton appearing in the census returns and it was necessary to eliminate one of them as an ancestor. Careful analysis of all the information and cross-referencing enabled me to identify the correct Henry Russell as my great grandfather and to eliminate the other candidate, and thus also identify other family members. An important clue was the fact that Henry Russell's father, also named Henry, was stated to be a carpenter and joiner in the census returns and this occupation (stated on the birth certificate) was the consistent factor which linked all the documentation enabling other possible candidates for ancestry to be discounted.

Henry Russell appears in the 1871 census as a student at St. John's College, Vicarage Road, Battersea. This was the first British teacher training college, founded in 1838 by James Kay-Shuttleworth, a famous social reformer, who also established the first schools inspection system. St. John's College has undergone several transformations since Henry Russell studied there, amalgamating with other colleges, then becoming a constituent part of the University of Exeter and its present day successor is the University of St. Mark and St. John based in Plymouth.

As part of my researches to satisfy myself as to the proper identification of Henry Russell in addition to his birth certificate I also obtained a copy of his marriage certificate for 5th January 1875, which confirmed that Henry Russell was the son of Henry Russell, a carpenter, that he was a schoolmaster aged 23 and that he married Mary Hibberd, aged 21, the daughter of William Hibberd, a dairyman. They were married at the Independent Northam Chapel in Southampton near to where both of them lived.

At the time of the 1881 census Henry Russell was living in Carlton Road, Shirley, Southampton with his wife Mary and the four eldest children listed above and a general servant (Eliza Ann West). Henry is described as schoolmaster (Board School). The Board Schools were set up in 1870 under the Elementary Education Act 1870 to provide compulsory elementary education for children under twelve years of age.

At the time of the 1891 census the Russell family was living at 40, Carlton Road, Shirley, Southampton. Henry was still a schoolmaster (Board School) and the fourteen year old Florence is described as a pupil-teacher. My grandfather, Sidney Arthur Russell (aged six), was not at home when the census took place but he was staying with his uncle and aunt, Henry and Ellen Ransom (his aunt being his father's sister Ellen Mary Russell, 1844-1913) at 41, Alexandra Road, Southampton. Henry Ransom is described as a nurseryman – they also had a boarder and a servant living with them.

In 1901 census the family was still at 40, Carlton Road. All the seven surviving children listed above resided at the house. Henry Russell is still described as a Board Schoolmaster, Florence, his daughter, as a Board Schoolteacher, and sons Charles as an office clerk and Harold as a pupil teacher.

Henry Russell died on 13th July 1902 leaving estate valued at £982 which using the assessment of the economic power of that value of wealth today would equate to approximately £800,000.

Shirley is a suburb of Southampton quite close to the city centre. Carlton Road still exists and it is likely that No 40 is still there.

At the time of the 1911 census Mary Russell, widow, was residing at 89, Atherley Road, Southampton with her widowed daughter Maud Lloyd (a singing teacher), and granddaughter Florence L M Lloyd, aged three (born in Portsmouth) - Cousin Lena - and sons Harold H. Russell, aged 29, single (an elementary school teacher) and Reginald Russell, aged 23, (a clerk in the Civil Service working for the Ordnance Survey). Mary Russell died in 1920 and it was the following year that my father, her grandson, was born and given as his second name her maiden name, Hibberd.

It was possible, from the birth certificate for my great grandfather Henry Russell who was born on 21st January 1851, to identify his parents as Henry Russell (1819-1893), a carpenter, and Mary Ann Russell (formerly Lavey), living at 2, York Street, Southampton, and thus find the census record for 1851 which indicated that the elder Henry Russell was born in Bath, was aged 32, and that his occupation was "house and ships carpenter", later described as "joiner". Although the genealogy websites could not supply any reliable information to establish his birth, a general search for Somerset parish records revealed that a Henry Russell was baptised on 9th January 1820 (born in 1819) at the church of St. Swithin, Walcot, Bath. In 1841 Henry Russell was living in St. Mary, Southampton as a lodger and thereafter in York St, St. Mary, Southampton. Mary Ann Lavey (1820-1892) was born in Ropley, Hampshire, the daughter of Thomas and Ann Lavey (3rd great grandparents) of whom so far no further details have been discovered.

There is a record of a Henry Russell born 1819 (who may be this Henry Russell) being apprenticed in the Merchant Navy in November 1835 at Portsmouth to Messrs Burrell and Company on the ship "Camilla". This would fit with the reference to him in the census records as a ships carpenter and the fact that he ended up living in Southampton. He is listed as a carpenter and builder in various trade directories for Southampton.

Henry Russell and Mary Ann Lavey married in 1843 in Southampton. In addition to their son, Henry, they had five daughters, Ellen Mary (1844-1913) who married Henry Ransom, Emily Jane (b. 1848), Harriet Eliza (b.1849), Kate Taylor Russell (1855-1911) who married William Henry Noice (1857-1937) and Mary Ann (b. 1860).

In 1871 Henry and Mary Ann Russell's daughter Ellen was a dressmaker and Harriet a domestic servant. The family was living at 2, York Street, Southampton in 1851 and had moved to 24, Belvedere Terrace by 1861. These addresses are in the centre of Southampton, close to the River Itchen. York Street no longer exists, but Belvedere Terrace does, but as part of an industrial area. Both streets feature strongly as locations where crew members of the liner "Titanic" lived.

In the 1861 census Mary Ann Russell is described as a schoolmistress (the first of several schoolteachers in the Russell family) and daughter Ellen a dressmaker, and daughter Emily a silver polisher. This all fits in with what was passed down by word of mouth that the Russells were schoolteachers in the Southampton area. In 1871 Ellen was still a dressmaker and Harriet now was a domestic servant. Henry, the son, was at this time a student at a college in Battersea – see above. In 1881 all the children had left home and Henry and Mary Ann Russell, now in their early sixties, lived at Nichols Terrace, 72, Brinton Road, Southampton, where they were still living in 1891 two years before the death of Henry Russell Senior. The Royal South Hants Hospital now occupies the area surrounding Brinton Road, which is in the same part of Southampton as the other addresses where the Russell family lived and which also was a location where several crew members of "Titanic" resided.

By careful research I had been able to identify Henry Russell Senior and discover what appeared to be the likely record of his baptism in Bath in 1820. The baptismal record for the church of St. Swithin, Walcot, Bath indicated that he was baptised on 9th January 1820, so he was probably born in late 1819, as declared in the census returns. He was the son of Thomas and Mary Ann Russell and his father's occupation was noted as stonemason. An address of Pleasant Place was noted in the record. The fact that the son of a stonemason became a joiner and carpenter also seems a likely event.

Because of the difficulties I had encountered in tracing the Russells, I checked all the available records on the website for Russells born in Bath at around the relevant time and there was one other Henry Russell baptised in Bath, also at St. Swithin Walcot, who could have been my ancestor. However, the circumstances of his baptism are somewhat unusual. Three children of Henry and Ellen Russell were baptised on the same day in 1823. The eldest was Henry and the record states that he was born on 6th June 1818, so he would have been five at the date of his baptism. Also baptised at the same time was his sister Matilda, born on 16th December 1819, and their brother Charles, whose date of birth is not recorded, probably because he was a babe in arms. For this Henry to be my great grandfather his age was wrongly recorded in all subsequent documentation, although the difference of one year is not that great. There is no further record of Henry and Ellen Russell, the parents of these three children. It seems likely that this family was visiting Bath and left after a short time. I have come to the conclusion, applying my balance of probability test, that the most likely ancestry establishes Thomas and Mary Ann Russell as my 3rd great grandparents and that it was their son Henry who was my 2nd great grandfather. However, of all the ancestry I have been able to trace I am least sure of this and I hope that further material may come to light which assists in establishing the position more clearly, particularly as it is my Russell ancestors who give me my name. This reinforces the point I have previously made that this sort of research is a continual exploration and new evidence may be discovered which can affect one's conclusions. It was the publication on line of many parish records for Somerset as this book was being written which enabled me to make the discoveries about the Russell family of Bath set out below.

Based upon my conclusion that Henry Russell was the son of Thomas and Mary Russell, it was possible to trace the ancestry further back. Thomas Russell (1793-1853) was baptised on 7th July 1793. He married Mary Ann Atkins (1794-1871) on 13th September 1815. All these events are recorded in the parish records of the same church, St. Swithin, Walcot, Bath. Mary Ann Atkins was the daughter of Thomas and Joyce Atkins. Thomas and Mary Ann Russell are found in the 1851 census living in Bristol. Thomas Russell is described as a mason and Mary Ann Russell as a launderess. Thomas Russell is noted as a marble mason in some records and it may be that it was his work which took him to Bristol. Following the death of her husband Mary Ann Russell is recorded in the 1861 census return as living back in Bath with Edwin Russell, a younger son born in 1822. Edwin Russell died in 1869 and in the 1871 census Mary Ann Russell is listed as a pauper residing in the Bath Union Workhouse where she was buried, at the age of 77, on 12th September 1871. This is a sad end, but not uncommon in those days. She had probably lost contact with her son Henry, my 2nd great grandfather, who was living in Southampton, something which we find difficult to comprehend but which undoubtedly occurred regularly when communication was more difficult than is the case today.[11]

Thomas Russell's father was also named Thomas. Thomas Russell senior (1761-1826) was recorded in the baptismal records of St. Swithin, Walcot, Bath on 14th November 1761. The record states that his parents were George and Mary Russell, about whom no more is currently known. He married Sarah East on 24th June 1788 at St. James's Church, Bath. Thomas and Sarah Russell were my 4th great grandparents. The fortunate discovery of these records and the fact that several generations of Russells lived in the same parish in Bath for at least 60 years enabled three further generations of ancestors to be traced.

A search on the Internet for the church of St. Swithin, Walcot, Bath revealed an interesting history. There was a Saxon church on the site which was badly damaged by storms in 1739. A new church in the Georgian style was built on the site, which was soon found to be too small, so a further larger Georgian church was built, later in the 18th century. It was a fashionable church and in 1764 the Revd George Austen married Cassandra Leigh there – they were the parents of Jane Austen, and George Austen was the curate of the parish for a time, although by the time of Jane's birth in 1775 her father was the Rector of Steventon, Hampshire. In 1797 William Wilberforce, the MP and social reformer, married Barbara Spooner (who he had met only 6 weeks previously) at the church of St. Swithin, Walcot.

So from at least 1760 to 1820 it would appear that my Russell ancestors were living in Bath and from about 1840 to the early

---

[11] See Chapter 24 for the fate of Samuel "Beau" Byrom who, coming from a wealthy family, having squandered his inheritance, died a pauper in circumstances which are not known.

20th century, when my grandfather Sidney Arthur Russell moved to the Manchester area, they were living in Southampton.

Chapter 20: The Hibberds of Hampshire and Dorset and related families

The discovery that my great grandmother was born into a family called Hibberd, thus explaining my father's unusual second name, was an exciting one and led to my unearthing ancestors who lived in the county of Dorset as far back as the early 1500s. Initially the information came from family trees on line, but many of the details have been corroborated from parish records available on line. The name Hibberd is sometimes spelt Hibbard or Hebbard in these records and in the process I found ancestors with even more unusual names, namely Sweetapple and Meatyard.

The name Hibberd is probably derived from the Anglo-Saxon Hyge, the same derivation as the name Hugh, which means "mind, courage". The Hibberds were a Dorset family. The family originates from a number of villages to the north and east of Blandford Forum in the area known as Crichel Down from where the remaining families noted in this part also originate. These were old established Dorset families, confirming how unusual it was before the 19th century for people to move far from where they were born. They seem to have been country folk living in small rural communities, most of whom were probably engaged in farming.

The earliest Hibberd it has been possible to trace is James Hibberd (b. about 1750) who was married to Melior Hart (b.1753), my 5th great grandparents. The marriage record of James Hibberd and Melior Hart states that James Hibberd was from

Witchampton, Dorset. This seems highly likely to have been his birthplace but there is no record of his baptism currently available to confirm this and no other Dorset record which might correspond to him. Witchampton is one of the villages in the Crichel Down area near Blandford Forum.

The marriage of James Hibberd and Melior Hart (spelt two different ways in the parish register as Mellyear Hart and Milyear Hart) took place on 2nd February 1779 at Tarrant Rushton. The witnesses were James and Ann Hart, the bride's mother and father. Melior Hart, was baptised on 6th December 1753 at Moore Crichel. The baptismal record spells her name as Melior Heart, the daughter of James and Ann Heart. James Hart's marriage to Ann Whitlock, in the parish of Moore Crichel, Dorset is recorded on 5th July 1752. His burial is recorded on 11th July 1791 at Nether Compton, Dorset. James Hart (1730 - 1791) and Ann Hart were my sixth great grandparents who had a total of nine children of whom Melior was the eldest.

James and Melior Hibberd had three children, James (b.1780), John (1781-1850) my 4th great grandfather, and Hannah (b. 1782). Initially they lived in Moore Crichel but at some stage they moved to Christchurch. There is no record of the death of either James Hibberd or Melior Hibberd in any of the records available nor have any of the compilers of the family trees on line been able to find any information. Given that they lived in parishes where the records appear to be well kept and the fact that there are records available for their Hibberd descendants perhaps they emigrated. It is odd that both of them appear to have disappeared without trace. A James Hibberd served as an ordinary seaman on board HMS Africa during the Battle of Trafalgar 1805 – this is unlikely to have been my fifth great grandfather who would have been aged about 50 or more, but it is likely to be his son James who was born in 1780, my fifth great uncle. HMS Africa was under the command of Captain Henry Digby (later Admisal Sir Henry Digby GCB) and as a small elderly ship of the line was ordered by Lord Nelson to pull back from the battle to avoid being overwhelmed. However Captain Digby deliberately misinterpreted the order and weaved between the advancing enemy exchanging broadsides, eventually sending a boarding party onto the Santissima Trinidad, the Spanish flagship, in the mistaken belief that she had surrendered. However, in an act of chivalry, the Spanish admiral allowed the boarding party to return to their boat unharmed. HMS Africa continued to take part in the battle engaging with the French ship Intrepide for 40 minutes until joined by HMS Orion and the two ships secured the surrender of the Intrepide. HMS Africa lost 62 men killed or wounded.

John Hibberd (1781-1850) married twice. His first wife, my 4th great grandmother, was Ann Sweetapple (1779-1811) and their eldest son, Ambrose Hibberd was my 3rd great grandfather. John Hibberd and Ann Sweetapple had four further children: Anthony (1803-1858), Maria (b. 1805), William (1807-1887) who married Eliza Dymock (1807-1888) and Ann (b. 1809). Following the death of his wife Ann, John Hibberd was married a second time to Mary Troke by whom he had seven further children. The discovery of an ancestor called Sweetapple was charming and led to tracing several generations of Sweetapples in Dorset and some particularly well recorded parish records.

But, back to John Hibberd. The parish records for Moor Crichel, Dorset, record the baptism of John Hibbard (*sic*) on 15th March 1781, the child of James and Melior Hibbard. John Hibbard married Ann Sweetapple at Christchurch, Hampshire on 2nd August 1800. Ambrose Hibberd was baptised at Christchurch on

1st January 1801, which means that Ann Sweetapple was pregnant with him when the marriage took place.

John Hibberd and his second wife, Mary, were living in Christchurch, Hants at the time of the 1841 census. He was an agricultural labourer. Living nearby was a son by his first marriage, William, also an agricultural labourer. William was living with his wife Eliza and their six year old son, George. William Hibberd subsequently became a grocer.

John and Ann Hibberd's eldest son Ambrose Hibberd (1800-1862) was my 3rd great grandfather. He, like his father, was married twice. His first wife, my 3rd great grandmother, was Sarah Mew (1793-1851). They had six sons of whom the second, William, was my 2nd great grandfather. The other sons were John (1827-1851), George (b. 1830), James (1834-1917), Ambrose (1834-1919) and Stephen (1835-1859). Following the death of his first wife Ambrose Hibberd married Elizabeth Bailey and a seventh child, a daughter, Sarah Louise (1863-1939) was born shortly after her father had died.

Ambrose Hibberd was born in Christchurch. He was a gardener. In the 1841 census he and his family are shown living in South Stoneham, Southampton. In the 1851 census he was living at Willow Cottage, Highfield, South Stoneham, Southampton with sons George (garden labourer), Ambrose (apprentice carpenter and joiner) and Stephen (servant). In 1861 he and his second wife, Elizabeth were living at Fir Grove (described as "back of lodge") in South Stoneham.

The South Stoneham area of Southampton was an area dominated by large houses including Highfield House. This area is now known as Highfield and The University of Southampton Campus dominates the area. There is a Bed and Breakfast concern called Willow Cottage in the area which may be Ambrose Hibberd's home.

Ambrose and Sarah Hibberd's son William Hibberd (1828-1886), my great great grandfather, who was born in South Stoneham, like his father and grandfather was married twice. His first wife was Elizabeth Martin (1814-1875), my great great grandmother. It has been possible to trace her ancestors back for several generations which revealed some interesting parish records summarised below. They had four children: Sarah (b. 1850) who married Ernest Veal and had seven children, William (1852-1891), Mary Hibberd (1853-1920) my great grandmother who married Henry Russell, and Fred (1859-1881) who married Mary Joy and had two children. Two years after the death of his wife in 1875 William Hibberd married Fanny Trim by whom he had a further son.

The 1851 census shows William Hibberd and his wife and daughter Sarah living in Prince Street, Southampton. His occupation is dairyman, confirmed in various trade directories. By 1861 they had moved to Northam Road, with the four children named above and William Hibberd's occupation is given as toll collector. In 1871 the family was living at 6, Union Street, Southampton. William Hibberd had reverted to being a dairyman, as was his son William. Sarah Hibberd is described as a dressmaker and Mary Hibberd as a draper's assistant.

William Hibberd died in 1886 leaving an estate valued at £1223 – a considerable sum, worth approximately £1 million today. His brother Ambrose (a carpenter) was the executor.

Ann Sweetapple (1779-1811) who married John Hibberd (1781-1850) came from an old Dorset family and I was able to trace Sweetapples back to the early 16th century. The line was recorded in a number of family trees on line which were well corroborated by extensive parish records for Dorset which were informative. For several generations the Sweetapples lived in the village of Hinton Martell. The records of this parish are particularly well kept, in beautiful handwriting, very easy to read. It must have been a very small parish because on the two pages of records of baptisms from 1695-1701, a total of 36 baptisms are recorded, an average of one every two months, and of these four were the children of Thomas and Elizabeth Fiford, one of whom was Mary Fiford who married Giles Sweetapple in 1737, my 6th great grandparents. The village is situated about three miles north of Wimborne and today has a population of fewer than 400 people.

Working back from my 4th great grandmother, Ann Sweetapple, who married John Hibberd in 1800, she was baptised at Christchurch on 21st February 1779, one of nine brothers and sisters, the children of William Sweetapple (1738-1810) and Mary Lockyear (1740-1808) who came from another Dorset family about which some information follows below. William and Mary Sweetapple were my 5th great grandparents. Another of their nine children was William Sweetapple (1781-1858), my 5th great uncle, who married Sarah Rodgers and emigrated to Newfoundland where he settled on Gooseberry Island. There are a number of families with the name Sweetapple in that area today who are descended from him and his wife.

The church at Hinton Martell

William Sweetapple, my 5th great grandfather was born in Hinton Martel, Dorset and baptised on 22nd June 1738, the son of Giles and Mary Sweetapple. The marriage of William Sweeetapple and Mary Lockyear is recorded at Christchurch on 26th May 1763 – their two first children may have been illegitimate if the details of their dates of birth taken from family trees on line are correctly noted. William Sweetapple died in Christchurch. His father, my 6th great grandfather, Giles Sweetapple (1710-1771), was baptised on 22nd October 1710 at Hinton Martell, the record stating that he was the son of Willm Sweetapple. He married Mary Fiford on 12th April 1737 at Hinton Martell – the record reads "1737 Giles SweetApple & Mary Fiford both of this Parish (by Banns) April ye 12th" The only other marriage that year took place on 26th December between Richard Sweetapple and Eve Burt, and there are records of numerous Sweetapples on the parish registers for Hinton Martell. Mary Fiford (1699-1780) was baptised at Hinton Martell on 20th January 1698 (under the old calendar which ran from 25th March to 24th March, so 1699 in modern usage), the daughter of Thomas and Elizabeth Fiford – the entry states that Thomas Fiford was a labourer. Giles Sweetapple was buried at Hinton Martell on 25th May 1771 and Mary Sweetapple, his wife, on 17th March 1780, also at Hinton Martell.

Giles Sweetapple was the son of William Sweetapple (1680-1736) and Mary Mortimer (d. 1715). William Sweetapple was baptised on 8th June 1681 at Hinton Martell, the son of Giles and Ann Sweetapple. As an example of a parish record a copy of the baptismal record of William Sweetapple is illustrated below. The marriage of William Sweetapple and Mary Mortimer took place on 17th April 1704 at Hinton Martell. Mary Sweetapple was buried at Hinton Martell on 12th July 1715. William Sweetapple was buried at Hinton Martell on 13th July 1736.

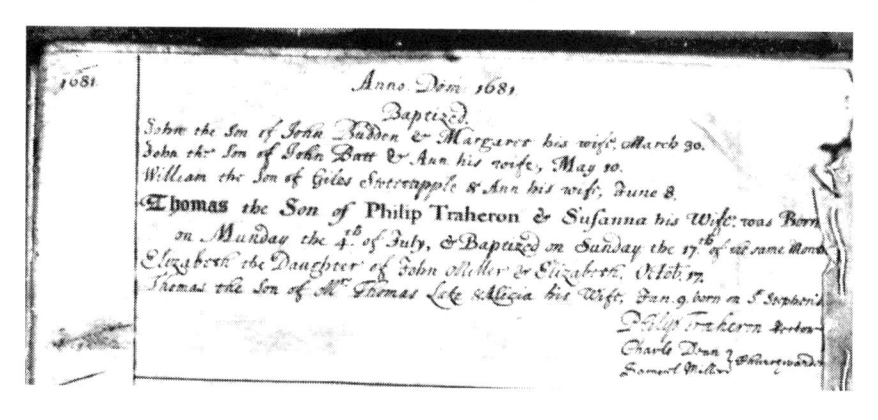

Extract from the parish records for Hinton Martell, Dorset showing the record of the baptism of William Sweetapple on 8th June 1681

William Sweetapple's parents were Giles Sweetapple (1630-1704) and Ann (d. 1695) whose maiden surname is not known. Giles Sweetapple was born in Edmondsham, Cranborne, Dorset, baptised on 10 September 1630 – in the baptismal record his name is spelt Gyles. He was buried on 13th January 1704 in

Hinton Martell, Dorset and the parish record states that he was a husbandman. A husbandman was a free tenant farmer or small landowner. The social status of a husbandman was below that of a yeoman. The meaning of "husband" in this term is "master of house" rather than "married man". This meticulously kept parish record shows what information can sometimes be obtained from such records, should the minister have chosen to record more than the fact of the date of burial. On the same page is the record of the burial of Amy Frampton, "a poor maid". The occupations of all the deceased males are noted, usually yeoman, husbandman or labourer, indicative of the fact that this was a farming community, although in the extract illustrated there are also a carpenter and a tailor. The ages of the deceased are not recorded, but if they were infants is noted. On the opposite page is recorded the death of Ann Sweetapple, the wife of Giles Sweetapple on October 10th 1695. A final column for each entry is headed "Affidavit brought" with a date, usually a few days after the burial.

Extract from the parish records for Hinton Martell, Dorset showing the record of the burial of Giles Sweetapple on January 13th 1704

The baptismal record from Edmondsham, Dorset for Gyles Sweetaple (sic) states that he was the son of Robert Sweetaple

(1585-1638). Robert Sweetapple was born in Damerham, Wiltshire and died in Edmondsham, Cranborne, Dorset where his wife, Frances Bremble (1590-1633) was born. They were my 9th great grandparents. Their marriage is recorded in the parish records for Edmondsham on 1st November 1614. It is perhaps appropriate that a Sweetapple should have married a Bremble, because Frances Bremble's ancestors' name was also sometimes spelt Bramble! Her father Roger Bremble (1570-1641) married Mildred Gould (1570-1615) – my 10th great grandparents. Roger Bremble's father was William Bramble (b. 1548) my 11th great grandfather.

Robert Sweetapple was the son of Christopher Sweetapple (1565-1608) and his wife Tamsyn (1565-1612) and the grandson of Robertus Sweetapple (1520-1591). Robertus Sweetapple, my 11th great grandfather, was buried at Edmondsham on 8th November 1591, and Christopher Sweetapple, my 10th great grandfather died in Damerham, Wiltshire in 1608.

There is another Sweetapple ancestor who probably comes from the same family. Mary Lockyear (1740-1808), my fifth great grandmother who married William Sweetapple (1738-1810), was the daughter of Joseph Lockyear (1704-1746) and Hannah Sweetapple (b. 1701), who were my 6th great grandparents. Mary Lockyear (spelt Lockyer in some records) was baptised at Christchurch on 16th November 1740. Her father, Joseph Lockyear (b.1704), sometimes spelt Lockyer or Lockier, came from a Dorset family. He was baptised on 10th October 1704 at Edmondsham, the son of William and Elizabeth Lockier. He married Hannah Sweetapple in August 1731 at Warblington, Hampshire. Many family trees state he died on 1 April 1746, but there is no parish record available to confirm this.

Hannah Sweetapple, Joseph Lockyear's wife and Mary Lockyear's mother, does not appear in any of the family trees on line which set out the Sweetapple family noted earlier. With such an unusual name it is likely that she came from the same family and further researches into available records revealed that Hannah was the daughter of James and Mary Sweetapple (7th great grandparents) and that they were Quakers – her birth is recorded in the Quakers Quarterly Meeting records for Dorset and Hampshire on 16th April 1701.

Hannah Sweetapple's mother and father were James Sweetapple and Mary Hatcher. The record of their marriage according to the Quaker tradition is recorded in a most interesting document recording their taking each other by the hand in a public and solemn assembly of witnesses. The text of the document is set out below.

Text of the marriage record of James Sweetapple and Mary Hatcher

Whereas James Sweetaple of the parish of Havant in ye County of Southton, Shoemaker & Mary Hatcher, daughter of John Hatcher of Reigate in ye County of Surray, Spinster, having declared their intentions of taking each other as husband and wife before several public meetings of the people of God called Quakers in Reigate aforesaid, whose proceedings therein after a deliberate consideration thereof & consent of parties & relations connected backing they appearing clear of all others on that view: were approved by the said meeting: Now for ye full accomplishing of their said intentions the one and thirtieth day of ye 10th month 1690. They the said James Sweetaple & Mary Hatcher appeared in a public and solemne assembly of ye aforesaid people met together for that end & purpose in their public meeting house in Reigate aforesaid and in a solemne manner according to ye practice of the holly man of God Recorded in Scripture of truth; He the said James Sweetaple taking the said Mary Hatcher by the hand: did openly declare as followeth viz.: I James Sweetaple do in ye presence of God & you his people, take this my friend Mary Hatcher to be my Wife promising by ye assistance of God to be to her a faithfull loving Husband till death separate us; And then & there in the said assembly & manner by the said Mary Hatcher did in like manner declare as follows viz.: I Mary Hatcher do in ye presence of God & you his people take this my friend James Sweetaple to be my Husband promising by ye assistance of God to be to him a loving and faithfull Wife till death separate us: & the said James Sweetaple & Mary Hatcher, now Sweetaple, as a further confirmation thereof did to these escribe their names: And those whose names are underwritten being present at ye solemnizing of ye said Marriage & Subscription as Witnesses thereunto have also & to these presents subscribed our names the day & year above written.

John Hatcher
    {James Sweetaple}
Edward Sweetaple
    {Mary Sweetaple }
Richard Hatcher
Samuel Hatcher
Jonathan Hatcher   Rachel Lillington
Benjamin Hatcher   Sarah Hatcher
Joseph Lyss   Mary Sweetaple
John Young   & Severall others
Tho: Ingram

The marriage took place on 31st December 1690, December being the tenth month of the year in the old calendar – "decem" being Latin for ten. James Sweetapple, a shoemaker, came from Havant and Mary Hatcher came from Reigate and the marriage is recorded in the Quakers Quarterly Meeting records for Surrey and Sussex. Family trees on line suggest that James Sweetapple may have died in Newfoundland, which is interesting because it was to Newfoundland that a later Sweetapple, William, the brother of Ann who married John Hibberd, definitely did emigrate about a century later.

The Quakers were persecuted during the 17th century. James II was instrumental in ending the persecution and in the first year of the joint reign of William and Mary the Tolerance Act 1689 repealed earlier legislation which had restricted the activities of the Quakers. Quaker Marriage was not recognised as lawful until the passing of the Marriage Act of 1753 which also stated that Common Law marriages would no longer be recognised. Mary Hatcher's birth in 1658 is recorded in the Quaker records for Reigate. She was the daughter of John and Rachell Hatcher – John Hatcher, my 9th great grandfather, was baptised at St. Mary's, Reigate, in 1625.

Elizabeth Martin (1814-1875), my great great grandmother who married William Hibberd (1828-1886), came from another long-established Dorset family which is of particular interest because of the parish records. It is possible to trace the family back through the generations to John Martin (b.1636), my 7th great grandfather. His grandson, my 5th great grandfather was also named John Martin (1704-1786). He married Ann Lane (1713-1788).

John Martin was baptised on 10th September 1704 in the parish of Gillingham, Dorset. The vicar was obviously a learned man because all the parish records are in Latin, so John Martin is referred to as "Johannes, filius Gulielmi Martin" – John son of William Martin. Ann Lane was from the same parish and her baptism is recorded in Latin as Anne, daughter of William Lane, on 21st October 1713. The full record reads: "Anna, filia Gulielmi Lane baptizala erat 21 October 1713". The marriage between John Martin and Ann Lane (spelt Ane Lane in the record) took place at Gillingham on 27th December 1730. There was a different clergyman in post at Gillingham now and the somewhat brief record of the marriage is recorded in English. John Martin was buried at Gillingham on 21st May 1786 and Ann Martin was buried on 9th April 1788 at the same church.

Extract from the parish register for Gillingham 1704 relating to John Martin's baptism

Their son, William Martin (1735-1810) married Sarah Meatyard (1756-1810) on 24th October 1773 at the parish church of East Stour. Sarah Meatyard was twenty years younger than her husband who had been previously married to Bethiah Samways (1736-1771). They had a son, Edward Martin (1785-1837), baptised at East Stour on 2nd October 1785, who they both lived long enough to see married on 25th September 1808 to Elizabeth Francis (1789-1847), my 3rd great grandparents. In the parish register, while Edward Martin signed his name, his wife placed her mark in the form of an "X". William Martin was buried at East Stour on 12th December 1810, about six months after the death of his wife, Sarah, buried at the same church on 29th May 1810.

Christ Church, East Stour, Dorset

Edward Martin and Elizabeth Francis were the parents of Elizabeth Martin (1814-1875) who married William Hibberd (1828-1886). Edward Martin's death was recorded at Lyndhurst, Hampshire on 16th January 1837.

Elizabeth Francis came from another local family, and it has been possible to trace them back three further generations to Matthew Francis (b.1690) who married Elizabeth Axon (1690-1743) on 14th November 1715 at Shaftesbury. They are my 6th great grandparents. The family lived at East Stour, the next generation being Joseph Francis (1717-1795) who married Margaret Plowman (b. 1720) at Motcombe, Dorset on 10th November 1740. Their son John Francis (1758-1824) married Esther Davidge (1755-1835) also from East Stour.

The Davidge family is worthy of mention because of the information which can be gathered from the parish records. Esther Davidge was baptised on Christmas Day 1755 at East Stour, Dorset, the last entry in the parish record for the year. The next entry, the first for 1756, is Sarah Meatyard, who was the second wife of William Martin (1735-1818) – see above – baptised on January 5th 1756. Esther Davidge was married to John Francis on 30th October 1783 at East Stour – in the marriage record Esther Davidge is referred to as Hester. She was buried on 10th September 1835 at East Stour.

Esther Davidge's father was John Davidge (1729-1788) who married Jane Hayward (1729-1774). John Davidge was baptised on 19th November 1729 at Melbury Abbas, Dorset. His marriage to Jane Hayward is recorded on 13th April 1755 at East Stour and his occupation is given as labourer. There is also a record of the reading of the Banns of Marriage at East Stour on 2nd February, 9th February and 23rd March 1755. He was buried at East Stour on 26th October 1788. Jane Davidge was buried at East Stour on 27th March 1774. John Davidge's parents, my 6th great grandparents, were Richard Davidge (1704-1765) and Rachel Horder (1705-1757).

Richard Davidge was baptised at Marnhull, Dorset on 11th February 1702. He married Rachel Horder at Melbury Abbas Dorset on 10th September 1724. He was buried at Melbury Abbas on 30th December 1765.

Rachel Horder's family origins are something of a mystery. The Horders were a Dorset family living in the area around Compton Abbas. The parish records reveal many Horders in the area, some of whom will be direct ancestors of Rachel Horder who is definitely recorded as marrying Richard Davidge at Melbury Abbas on 10th September 1724.

In February 1667 five people named Horder were buried within the space of a few days at Compton Abbas. This implies something of a tragedy which may be The Great Plague which started in London in 1665 and spread throughout the country only subsiding in the Autumn of 1667.

In the family trees on line there are various anomalies in relation to Rachel Horder's dates and the dates I have selected (1705-1757) seem to me, on analysis of the available evidence, to be the most likely. Various family trees on line give different birth dates for her, some as late as 1745 which is impossible for her to have been the mother of John Davidge. There is no record of a baptism at an appropriate date in the available records, however a number of children were born to Richard and Eliza Horder in the years 1700 to 1710 in Melbury Abbas where Rachel Horder was married to Richard Davidge, including Repentance Horder – is it possible she subsequently used the name Rachel rather than Repentance? There is a record of the burial of a Rachel Davidge in September 1757 at Yarlington, Wiltshire, not too far away, which may be her, but insufficient details are available to make a definite identification. There is also a record of the burial of a Rachel Davidge in Melbury Abbas in 1779 but other researchers have identified this as the Rachel Davidge born in 1745, who may be a daughter of the older Rachel.

The final ancestors traced in this section of my researches are the Meatyard family, also from Dorset. The unusual name is sometimes spelt Meteyard, and the family can be traced back in parish records to William Meteyard (1680-1746) and his wife Mary (1685-1711), my 7th great grandparents. They are identified in the parish records for Stour Provost, Dorset, as the parents of Joseph Meteyard (1716-1764) who married Sarah Cassel (1731-1813) at Melbury Abbas on 23rd July 1751. Joseph and Sarah Meatyard were the parents of the Sarah Meatyard (1755-1810) who married William Martin (1735-1810). The younger Sarah Meatyard was baptised on 5th January 1756 at East Stour, she married William Martin there on 24th October 1773, and was buried there on 29th May 1810.

However there are what appear to be well-researched family trees on line which trace a direct line of male Meatyard ancestors back to the 14th century. There are some parish records and a probate record attached to some of these entries, although not for all of them. Further all the indications are that these ancestors lived in the same group of villages around East Stour in Dorset which adds a degree of corroboration to the assertions. It seems probable that these trees are correct. There are several references in the records to male members of the Meatyard family being yeomen which indicates ownership of land, almost certainly farmland, in Dorset for centuries.

The line provides an interesting example of how the recording of names can alter over the centuries. The earliest ancestor named, who would have been my 16th great grandfather, is Richard Metiarewe. His grandson was Thomas Metyer (1400-1465), and this remained the spelling (noted in some parish records of the 16th century) until Richard Metyer (1535-1616), my 11th great grandfather. From his son, Geoffrey (1570-1651), for a further 4 generations the name was usually spelt Metyard – however in the burial record of Geoffrey's wife Dorothy in 1655 the name is spelt Meatiard. The spelling of William Metyard's name as recorded in his baptismal record of 1680 as Metyard had changed to Meteyard by the time of the birth of his son, Joseph, in 1716. By 1751 the spelling Meatyard had become established as noted in the marriage record of Joseph to Mary Cassel (my 6th great grandparents) at Melbury Abbas on 23rd July 1751.

Researching the Meatyard family resulted in an interesting reference to the elder brother of my 6th great grandfather Joseph Meatyard (1716-1764). This was my 7th great uncle, William Meteyard (so spelt in the records discovered) who was born in 1713. His name appears in the Militia Lists for Dorset for the years 1763-1778 as a yeoman of Stour Provost for whom a Robert Wilders consented to serve as a substitute. Under the Militia Act of 1757 a national military reserve of county militia regiments was created. Men were selected by ballot but could pay substitutes to take their place. Uniforms and weapons were provided, and regiments were mobilised for training for short periods and occasionally to deal with civil disturbances.

Chapter 21: The Right Hon. Sir Patrick Russell

The Hon. Mr. Justice Russell

Without doubt the most distinguished member of the Russell family was Thomas Patrick Russell (1926-2002), my uncle, the youngest of three brothers, of whom the middle was my father, Dr. Michael Hibberd Russell (1921-1987). The eldest was Dr. Peter Byrom Russell (1918-1996). They were the sons of Sidney Arthur Russell (1884-1953), an electrical engineer, and Elsie (nee Potter – 1888-1948).

Known always by his second name and usually in its shortened form Pat was born on 30th July 1926 in Manchester. The family lived in Urmston where Pat had his home for the whole of his life. The three brothers were educated at Urmston Grammar School and all of them were very keen cricketers and enthusiastic members of Urmston Cricket Club. Pat however was the best cricketer of the three and he continued to play cricket for many years while the other two retained their interest more passively. The family led a comfortable yet modest existence in Urmston, with annual holidays taken in Nefyn. Pat was aged only 13 at the outbreak of the Second World War so his formative years were influenced by the conflict.

The three brothers, each of whom was very clever, followed very different careers. All went on to Manchester University. Peter, the eldest, studied chemistry, took a Ph.D and became part of an important team of researchers formed at Manchester by Professor Todd who he followed to Cambridge remaining in the team for the duration of the Second World War. Their research was into the component parts of DNA. Professor Todd was subsequently raised to the peerage. After the war Peter migrated to the USA where he continued to work in the chemical industry. His two children Timothy and Pamela, both became lawyers, Timothy in the USA; and Pamela became an English solicitor and married John Walford a barrister who became a Circuit Judge on the North Eastern Circuit. Michael, my father, studied dentistry and then medicine and became a much respected general practitioner in Little Sutton in the Wirral. My brother, Nicholas, followed our father into medicine and he has recently retired from being a consultant physician in Cumbria.

Called up in 1945 Patrick Russell served in the Intelligence Corps and subsequently the Royal Army Service Corps attaining the rank of Staff Sergeant. During his army days, which he thoroughly enjoyed, he took up boxing. It was during this time that he met my mother, who knew him for 56 years, at Addington House in Surrey, where my mother was living with the Still family and where my father was working as a locum GP, which is how my parents met. Pat was outraged when a member of the Still family told him that they allowed the soldiers from the local army barracks to use their swimming pool but that they always changed the water for the officers after the "other ranks" had been using the pool. However he kept his feelings to himself. Others weren't so lucky. Once when at church (having not attended for some time because of his Army service) the vicar preached a sermon, castigating those who were not regular worshippers. With the words "I can see we are not welcome here!" he led his party out of the church in the middle of the sermon. At a performance of a Joe Orton play "Loot" in the 1960s he announced to his companions: "I have seen enough of this tasteless rubbish, I will see you in the bar!" The Midland Bank suffered his wrath when the manager wrote to inform him that he had exceeded his overdraft by a few pounds (at a time when as a successful Queen's Counsel he received thousands of pounds in fees) – his response was a shirty letter concluding with the words: "I had always been under the impression that the Midland Bank Limited existed for my benefit rather than I for its".

However to return to the post-war years, after a curtailed two years reading law at Manchester University where Pat captained the University Cricket Team, he was called to the bar by the Honourable Society of the Middle Temple in 1949, wearing the wig worn by Gregory Peck in the film "The Paradine Case" because his wig had not been made in time by Ede and

Ravenscroft, the legal outfitters, so he had to go to a theatrical costumiers in Covent Garden to hire a wig.

He joined the chambers of Arthur Jalland in Manchester. Arthur Jalland subsequently became one of the last King's Counsel (before the death of King George VI) and then Queen's Counsel and Recorder of Preston (I was the Recorder of Preston from 2006 to 2015). Meanwhile Pat had met Janie Ireland and in 1951 they married – it was a happy and successful marriage between a couple who were devoted to each other. They had two children Susan (who became a teacher, thus following in the footsteps of several of her Russell ancestors who were teachers in Hampshire before our grandfather broke the mould and became an engineer and moved north to Manchester) and Helen.

Patrick became one of the greatest barristers on the Northern Circuit and subsequently one of the most respected and admired judges of his generation. However, as with all barristers in the 1950s, his early career was not easy. It was difficult to make a huge living at the junior bar and life was spent earning a few guineas in the magistrates' courts, quarter sessions and assizes, and by giving legal opinions and preparing pleadings for cases in the county and divorce courts. There was far less litigation in those days and limited legal aid. But despite these difficulties Pat made a reputation for himself as a hard-working barrister and sound advocate, acquiring in 1961 the then important office of Prosecuting Counsel for the Post Office on the Northern Circuit, and a large civil practice and many criminal briefs in the more serious cases. He also took the first step onto the judicial ladder in 1961 as an assistant recorder of Bolton. In 1970 he was appointed the last Recorder of Barrow-in-Furness, an office held until the last day of 1971 when the court system was reformed and the posts of recorders of boroughs where quarter sessions were held were abolished – certain honorary titular recorderships (such as my own at Preston) were retained. He was immediately appointed a Recorder of the Crown Court with effect from 1st January 1972.

The last Recorder of Barrow-in-Furness and his wife meeting HM The Queen at Barrow

By the end of the 1960s Pat Russell was one of the busiest barristers on the Northern Circuit and in the summer of 1970 he was summoned in to the chambers of Mr Justice Ashworth (then a very senior Queen's Bench judge) and told that he should apply for silk. He did so and in 1971 was appointed Queen's Counsel – also appointed from the Northern Circuit that year were George Carman (who became one of the country's most famous QCs), Geraint Morgan MP, David Waddington MP who subsequently became Home Secretary and later a peer, and Mark Carlisle MP, subsequently also a cabinet minister and a peer.

He left his chambers at Ship Canal House and joined what was regarded as the Northern Silks' set at 5, Essex Court, The Temple, but with a clerk and later premises in Manchester. His career in silk was outstanding. He appeared in many of the major cases in the northwest of England, criminal and civil. When the IRA began its campaign of bombing cities in England in the early 1970s Patrick Russell QC was selected to lead for the prosecution in all the cases heard on the Northern Circuit. In these cases he led Charles Mantell who himself subsequently became a Lord Justice of Appeal. The most famous case in which he appeared was that of the prosecution of the Birmingham Six who were accused of the Birmingham pub bombings in 1974. The trial took place in 1975 in Lancaster Castle and the prosecution team was led by Harry Skinner QC who was the Leader of the Midland and Oxford Circuit, with Pat as number two, and with Charles Mantell and John Maxwell (later a Circuit Judge in the Midlands) as juniors. Sixteen years later the verdict was overturned when new evidence was uncovered by a television programme and it was felt that the verdict was rendered unsafe because of unreliable police and scientific evidence in the trial. There was not the slightest criticism of the legal team.

In 1978 Patrick was elected a Master of the Bench ("Bencher") of his Inn of Court, The Middle Temple, and in the same year he was elected Leader of the Northern Circuit. A very popular leader, he always took the trouble to take the time to encourage others in their own careers. He was very approachable and a sympathetic listener. I benefited greatly from his encouragement and kindness. When I was ill in hospital as a teenager in 1965 he visited me many times in hospital in Liverpool despite his very busy career. His family were his first concern, but the Northern Circuit was also regarded by him as family and despite the fact that he last practised as a barrister in 1979 and died in 2002, he is still remembered with much affection by all who knew him. Whilst in practice on the circuit he was a keen member of the Manchester and District Medico-Legal Society of which he was President in 1978-9 and Patron from 1987 until his death.

In December of 1979 whilst in the midst of a long murder trial he was summoned to see the Lord Chancellor, Lord Hailsham. Remarking to the trial judge "I don't know what I have done wrong" he set off for London. He was appointed a Judge of the Queen's Bench Division with effect from the beginning of January 1980. The appointment carries with it an automatic knighthood and thus he became Sir Patrick Russell, known officially as The Honourable Mr Justice Russell.

As a High Court Judge he spent as much time as he could justify on the Northern Circuit even before he became its Presiding Judge in 1983. He loved the life in judges' lodgings and on circuit generally. It was at the Manchester lodgings that the reception was held following the marriage of his daughter Susan. His sittings in London included many in the Court of Appeal Criminal Division and so it was no surprise when in 1987 he was appointed a Lord Justice of Appeal. The Right Honourable Lord Justice Russell was one of the judges of the five-judge court which in 1991 gave a landmark ruling abolishing a husband's immunity from rape of his wife. His judgements were always short and to the point, described in one obituary as models of clarity, logic and decisiveness. Many felt that upon the retirement of Lord Lane he should have succeeded as Lord Chief Justice, but instead Lord Taylor of Gosforth was appointed. Manchester University marked his being their first graduate to be appointed a judge of the Court of Appeal by awarding him the honorary degree of Doctor of Laws.

In 1996, aged 70, he retired as a Lord Justice of Appeal but continued to sit for some time as a deputy. He was also for a short time a Justice of the Court of the Court of Appeal for Gibraltar, and continued to sit as a member of the Judicial Committee of the Privy Council (hearing appeals, including some where the death penalty still applied, from Commonwealth jurisdictions) having been sworn a Privy Councillor on his appointment as a Lord Justice of Appeal.

His love for the law and the courts was equalled only by his love of cricket. He played cricket for Urmston for many years and then became its President. In 1999 he was elected President of Lancashire County Cricket Club an honour which probably meant more to him than all the accolades which he acquired in the legal profession, and became a Vice-President on relinquishing the office in 2001.

His first love though was for his family. Sadly a succession of illnesses dogged the last few years of his life, as for many years ill-health had also affected Janie. Both of them bore their troubles with great fortitude. On 28th October 2002 after a further short illness Pat Russell died of heart failure.

His close friend, Sir Christopher Rose, then Vice President of the Court of Appeal Criminal Division, gave the eulogy at the funeral and concluded his address with the words: "We shall not see his like again."

Part IV – Tracing the Potters

Chapter 22: A Paucity of Information

When I embarked upon this project to trace my ancestors I knew less about the Potters than any of the others of my four grandparents' families. My grandmother's sister, Marion, who died in 1977, spoke a little of her family, but her father, Thomas, had died when she was a little girl and his occupation of Sanitary Superintendent was rather underplayed – my father and his brothers referred to him as the lavatory man! In fact the role was an important local public health office and today he would probably be called an environmental health officer, and the fact that he was a superintendent signifies managerial responsibilities. There were some clues about the status of the Potters derived from the inheritance of some high quality pieces of furniture from that family.

Having little to go on I began to work from the census returns, having found these a useful tool, and by this means I was able to discover some information about the family, particularly in the later part of the nineteenth century with the starting point of my knowledge that my grandmother, Elsie Potter (1888-1948, wife of Sidney Arthur Russell), and her sister Marion were two of three sisters and of their respective ages. Potter is a very common name in Lancashire where they lived, and although I was able to identify the family of Thomas and Mary Potter and their three daughters in 1901, living in Ashton-under-Lyne, and trace them back to the previous census year 1891, when they were living at the same address, going back further from the census returns was difficult because of the large numbers of people called Potter.

Elsie Potter, my grandmother

I also had a photograph of a portrait of my great grandmother, Mary Potter, but I did not know her maiden name. In this case the existence of some family trees on line were an invaluable aid, because this enabled me to discover that Mary Potter's maiden name was Oldham, and someone has done a lot of research into the Oldham family which is deep-rooted in the Longdendale area of Northeast Cheshire.

Portrait of Mary Potter (nee Oldham)

With this information it was possible to find the marriage record of Thomas Potter in 1886, the record stating that he was a sanitary superintendent, thus confirming beyond doubt his identity, and Mary Elizabeth Oldham. The record identified Thomas Potter's father as James Potter, deceased, draper and Mary Oldham's father as Charles Oldham, butcher. So the evidence was slowly building up and with more names and dates confirmed it was possible to use the census returns and parish records to trace this ancestry.

My father's elder brother was christened Peter Byrom Russell. It was always said that the name Byrom was given him because there was a connection with the Byrom family of Manchester of which John Byrom was the most famous member. However no-one knew how this came about, and the more cynical members of the family thought that the name was adopted simply because my grandparents liked it. However my discovery that my father's second name, Hibberd, was a family name made it much more likely that the first son's name Byrom was also a family name. I discovered that James Potter, the deceased draper mentioned in the marriage record of his son Thomas Potter, my great grandfather, was married to Ann Byrom by reason of the fact that her father Henry Byrom was living with the Potter family at the time of the 1851 census. It was then possible to discover that he was from the Wigan area and, as more evidence was uncovered, that he was indeed from the Byrom family which had lived in that area for centuries and that the Manchester Byrom family from which the famous John Byrom came was a collateral branch of the same family. My relationship to John Byrom is very distant indeed – he is my 7th cousin 10 times removed!

This discovery was rather like striking gold because the Byroms were a very distinguished and well-connected Lancashire family as will emerge, and it established a fascinating lineage for our family of which we knew nothing until recently. The Byrom family has been researched by various local historians and it has been possible to corroborate much of the information in family trees on line from parish records and various published articles about the Byrom family. There is also a published pedigree of which I have acquired a copy. Further researches into the Byroms led to the finding of a line of ancestry back to the Saxon Kings of Wessex and England, to the Plantagenets, to many distinguished Lancashire families and to European Royal families as will be seen.

One must guard against a risk of making a mistake particularly when the excitement of discovering a link to Royalty and the aristocracy has occurred. When examining various family trees on line which contained links to the Byrom family I discovered a serious error in most of the family trees confusing two women with the same name, Margaret Butler (or Boteler), in the 16th century. Both of them appear to have died in the same year, 1537. One of them, descended from the Irish de Botelers (hereditary chief butlers of Ireland, the family of the Earls of Ormonde), did not marry Sir Richard Bold as many family trees maintain. The other, descended from the English de Botelers of Warrington (hereditary chief butlers of England) did marry Sir Richard Bold. It was a descendant of this couple who married into the Byrom family. One persuasive factor was the fact that it was much more likely that a member of the Bold family from Lancashire would marry a member of the Butler family from Lancashire rather than a member of the Irish Butler family, and in fact there was other conclusive evidence to establish this and prove that the family trees were wrong. This shows how easy it is for mistakes to be made, that care must be taken to check the family trees of others on line, before relying upon them, and that every effort should be made to corroborate information. [12]

The link to the de Boteler family (Butler being merely the modern version of the name) is an important one because it is through the de Botelers that a direct link to the Plantagenet kings is established – see Chapter 26. Margaret Butler was my 14th great grandmother and she was the 5th great granddaughter of Elizabeth Plantagenet, daughter of King Edward I. Thus Elizabeth Plantagenet, who married Humphrey de Bohun, was my 21st great grandmother and King Edward I my 22nd great grandfather. This is not as surprising as may be thought. We each

---

[12] See Chapter 25 for more information about the error relating to Margaret Butler.

have over 16 million 22nd great grandparents because as one goes back each further generation, assuming no duplication, the total of direct ancestors doubles. What is unusual is to be able to trace the descent.

There can never be certainty, but all the evidence points to my definite descent from the Byroms of Lancashire, and since the Byrom name is not widespread even if there is an error in tracing the precise line of descent, all the Byroms of the Wigan/Winwick area from whom I am definitely descended appear to be members of the same family. However before exploring that in more detail there is much to learn about the Potter and Oldham families and some of the families connected with them.

Chapter 23: The Potters of Lancashire – inspecting nuisances

Having identified Thomas Potter (1847-1904) as my great grandfather it was possible to build up a picture of his life from a combination of census and parish records. The parish records for the Manchester Diocese are readily available on line and I was able to find the record of Thomas Potter's baptism which established that he was baptised on 13th May 1847, having been born on 12th April that year, along with his brother, James Ferdinand Potter, who had been born in 1845. The baptismal record for Oldham Parish Church named the boys' parents as James and Ann Potter, gave James Potter's occupation as draper and the family's address as Cheapside, Oldham. This document was the first evidence to be discovered which identified the previous generation of Potters.

The census returns from 1871 to 1901 gave a good account of how Thomas Potter's life and career progressed. At the time of the 1871 census he and his brother James Ferdinand were both boarders at an address in Ashton-under-Lyne each working as a "master cotton manufacturer". In 1881 Thomas was living as a lodger at the home of his brother, James Ferdinand Potter, who was now married with two children. The address was 55, Burlington Street, Ashton-under-Lyne. Thomas was now an "Inspector of Nuisances" and his brother's job is described as warehouseman. On 16th September 1886, Thomas Potter married Mary Elizabeth Oldham (1860-1931) at St. George's Church, Mossley. The parish record states that Thomas Potter was now a sanitary superintendent, confirmed that his father was James

Potter, deceased, a draper, and that Mary Oldham's father, Charles, was a butcher.

By the date of the 1891 census the family had two children, Elsie (my grandmother, 1888-1948) and Amy (1890-1923), and Thomas was still a sanitary superintendent – also living with the family was a housekeeper. They lived in Wellington Street, Ashton-under-Lyne. By the time of the 1901 census my great aunt Marion (1893-1977) had been born to the family. Thomas Potter's employment was now described as "Local Sanitary Superintendent". The office of Inspector of Nuisances, superseded by that of Sanitary Inspector, was an important public office. Inspectors were appointed by the local council as part of the council's obligations under the Public Health Acts to monitor all aspects of public health. Today they are usually referred to as environmental health officers. The use of the term superintendent implies that Thomas Potter was the head of a team. This was work which required a degree of specialist training.

The next task was to discover as much as possible about Thomas Potter's parents, James and Ann Potter. With some difficulty, because of the large number of James Potters in the index, it was possible to find them in the 1841 census, living in Oldham, with two daughters. The 1841 census records are not very informative although the fact that James Potter was a draper (as stated in the parish record of the marriage of his son, Thomas) was confirmation that the entry related to my great great grandparents. Tracing him was not helped by the fact that an important census entry, that for 1851, has been misread and the entry was indexed under the name James Patter, not Potter. However when this record was eventually discovered and read, it proved to be a most valuable document.

At the time of the 1851 census James and Ann Potter were living in North Chadderton, part of the Borough of Oldham. James Potter's occupation is given as linen and woollen draper. There were five children of the family including Thomas Potter, aged three, but also staying in the household was Henry Byrom, aged 74, born in Ashton in Makerfield, retired grocer, and identified as being the father-in-law of the head of the household, James Potter. This discovery, possibly arising from the pure chance that Henry Byrom was visiting his daughter and son-in-law and staying with them when the census took place, was a magnificent piece of good luck. In the first place it cleared up a mystery as to the second name of my uncle, Peter Byrom Russell, and confirmed that Byrom was indeed a family name, but it also enabled me to discover that my great great grandmother was born Ann Byrom which led to being able to trace her birth details and the marriage details of her and James Potter. It also led to my being able to trace the ancestry of the Byrom family back to the time of the Norman Conquest and to discover interesting links to Royalty and some famous people in English and European history. These discoveries will be explored in later chapters.

For now I will continue with the Potters and then trace the ancestry of Mary Elizabeth Oldham, the wife of Thomas Potter. James Potter was born on 25th March 1802 and baptised on 11th April 1802 at the Parish Church of All Saints, Wigan. The record is particularly complete and states that James was the first born son of William Potter, staymaker of Wigan Wallgate, and that Ann, his wife, was the daughter of John and Nancy Litler.

My great great grandparents, James Potter (1802-1851) and Ann Byrom (1802-1884), were married on 25th January 1827 at the parish church in Wigan. The marriage record states that James Potter was from Oldham. However in the census return for 1851 it is stated that he was born in Wigan and aged 49. The explanation is that he was born in Wigan but was living in Oldham at the time of his marriage. Ann Byrom was born on 13th June 1802 and baptised at Winwick on 11th July 1802.

The 1841 census indicates that the family was living in Curzon Street, Oldham (the centre of the town) and that James Potter was now a draper – which was the business his father had been engaged in. There were two children living in the household, Alice (3) and Agnes (1). There were at least four older children, William, John, Mary and Emma, who were not at home when the census was recorded. From examination of other census returns of the time it appears to have been quite usual for children to live with relatives other than their parents, so this may be the explanation. At least three other children of the marriage died in infancy. There is a record in the parish records for Winwick, the parish where most members of the Byrom family lived, near Wigan, of the burial of Charles Potter, aged one, the son of James and Ann Potter of Oldham. The little boy had died of measles and he was buried on 22nd June 1832. On the same day Mary Byrom, the wife of Henry Byrom of Wigan was also buried, aged 53, having died of apoplexy. She was the mother of Ann Potter and the little boy's grandmother. Although recorded in the parish records for Winwick the burial of Charles Potter took place at St. Thomas's Church Ashton (formerly known as Ashton Chapel, a chapel of ease for St. Oswald's Church Winwick). The gravestone still exists as I discovered by chance on a visit to the church to see if I could find any Byrom clues, and the infant Charles was buried alongside his grandmother Ann Potter, and uncle, John Potter, a younger brother of James Potter his father. Subsequently William Potter, his grandfather, and two further children of James and Ann Potter, Hannah Potter (1836-7) and Blanche Potter (1841-2) were laid to rest in the same grave.

By the time of the 1851 census the family was living in Chadderton (Oldham). James Potter is described as a Linen and Woollen Draper and his wife's occupation is stated as "domestic duty". There were five children living in the household: John, aged 21, linen draper's assistant; Mary, aged 18; Emma, aged 16, James, aged 5; and Thomas, aged 3. Alice and Agnes, who would have been 13 and 11, were not at home at the time of the census. Also recorded in the list of people resident at the address was Ann Potter's father, Henry Byrom aged 74, described as a retired grocer and specifically referred to as the father-in-law of James Potter, born in Ashton-in-Makerfield (i.e. the Wigan area, very close to Winwick). It is possible he was simply visiting his daughter – the census requires the naming of all people residing in the household on the night of the census, including visitors, without specifying whether the residency was permanent. Rail travel had by 1850 become commonplace, and the first passenger railway between Manchester and Liverpool passed through the parish of Winwick. James Potter died in late 1851.

In the 1861 census Ann Potter (described as widow, retired draper) is recorded as living at Frank Hill, Oldham (a district north of Oldham town centre) with two sons, William (33) and John (31) both of whom were linen and woollen drapers. Also living with them was a house servant, Ann Martin, aged 22. By 1871, according to the census, Ann Potter had moved to Southport where she lived on Manchester Road with her daughter, Agnes (29) and a servant. Her rank is stated as "annuitant" presumably indicating she was in receipt of an annuity. Ann Potter still lived with her daughter Agnes in Southport, and a servant, at the time of the 1881 census but she had moved to 78, Windsor Road. Ann Potter died in 1884 in Southport. Her daughter Agnes (my great great aunt) died, a spinster, in 1923 in Southport.

James Ferdinand Potter, Thomas Potter's brother and my great great uncle, is shown in the 1881 census as a warehouseman. He does not appear in any subsequent census records but Probate Records show that he died in 1893 at Palamcottah, Tinnevelly, India.

It has been possible to discover the identities of two further generations of Potters and to propose some possibilities for earlier generations. The parents of James Potter (1802-1851) could be identified from his baptismal record as William Potter (1778-1834) and Ann Litler (1780-1816). They were my 3rd great grandparents. William Potter was born on 1st March 1778 in Winwick, baptised at Ashton Chapel on 1st April. He married Ann Litler on 15th February 1801 at the Chapel of St Helen, Prescot, and is described as a "Stay Maker", i.e. manufacturer of corsets. He died on 17th August 1834 when living in Wigan. His occupation is given in the parish burial record as draper and it is stated that he died of a liver complaint. Both he and his wife, Ann, are buried at St. Thomas's church, Ashton-in-Makerfield, now a suburb of Wigan, where the gravestone which also records the burial of the three infant children of James and Ann Potter lies in a prominent position close to the gate leading into the churchyard.

The Potter gravestone at St. Thomas's Ashton

The Inscription reads:

        William and Ann Potter   Their two breadths

In memory of Ann Potter wife of William Potter of Wigan Who departed this life Novr 11th 1816 Aged 35 years

Since I could stay no longer here Farewell! Husband and Children I've left you in the care of Heaven Hoping through Christ to be forgiven

Also in memory of John Potter, son of William and Ann Potter, of Wigan, who departed this life June 18th 1828 Aged 24 years

Also in memory of Charles Potter Grandson to the above William and Ann Potter, who departed this life June 22nd 1832 Aged 13 months

Also in memory of William Potter who departed this life August 14th 1834 Aged 56 years

Also of Hannah Potter Grandaughter to the above William and Ann Potter who departed this life April 20th 1837 aged 1 year

Also of Blanche Potter Daughter of James and Ann Potter of Oldham who died September 26th 1842 Aged 15 months

From William Potter's baptismal record (at Newton Chapel, in the parish of Winwick) it was possible to identify his father as John Potter (b. 1747), my 4th great grandfather. So far it has not been possible to identify John Potter's wife, although there are records of the marriage of a John Potter to Izabel Merrick at Winwick in March 1772 and of an earlier marriage between a John Potter and Elizabeth Atherton at Wigan in April 1764.

John Potter's baptismal record of 1747 states that his father was William Potter. From the Winwick Parish records a possible candidate for William Potter is William Potter of Newton, born on 8th September 1712, and baptised at Winwick on 14th September. He was the son of John Potter, and as has been seen elsewhere it was common for sons to be named after their grandfathers in a pattern, in this case John-William-John-William for four generations. A probable candidate for this John Potter was baptised at Winwick on 24th May 1696, the son of Thomas Potter, although this would mean John was married at a young age (and there is no marriage record available – marriage records seem to be less well kept than baptisms in the parish records) and that his son, William, was born when he was sixteen. Until the mid-eighteenth century a male could marry at the age of fourteen and a female at the age of twelve.

Another possible candidate is William Potter, b. 4th April 1711, baptised at Ashton Chapel (in the Parish of Winwick) on 15th April. His father was Oliver Potter, born in 1687, baptised at Winwick on 5th June 1687. Oliver Potter was the son of Gerard Potter. In terms of dates this ancestry seems slightly more likely, but the coincidence of names must assist the claim of the other William Potter. There are no Olivers or Gerards in any subsequent Potter relatives whereas there are several Thomases, Williams and Johns. A family tree on line names this William

Potter's wife as Ann but the details are scant and unfortunately I have not discovered any marriage records.

Just as the Hibberd family into which my great grandfather Henry Russell married had deep roots in Dorset, so also did the Oldham family into which my great grandfather Thomas Potter married - but their roots were in a small region in the northeast of Cheshire known as Longdendale, the main village in the area being Mottram-in-Longdendale, a few miles northeast of Stockport.

The surname Oldham may have the obvious reference to the Lancashire town, but it can also refer to a long, formerly cultivated river flat, "holm" being a word for a river flat. On line is a family tree which traces the Oldham line back to Tudor England. In some records the name is spelt Ouldham. The family appears to have originated in the Stockport area and lived in Mottram-in-Longdendale, in the North East tip of Cheshire from the 18th century, although there are hints that the family may have originally been a Manchester family. In the records of Manchester Cathedral, which are available on line, there are records of various baptisms, marriages and burials of members of the Ouldham family including those noted below. This appears to have been a large family with strong connections to the Cathedral during the 17th Century, which was then the Collegiate Church of St Mary, St Denys and St George and the Parish Church for Manchester. Manchester was in the Diocese of Chester at this time and the Collegiate Church was in effect a pro-cathedral for this part of the diocese – its clergy consisted of the Warden and Fellows. The links of the Oldham family with the Collegiate Church make it likely that they were acquainted with the Manchester branch of the Byrom family [see Chapter 24].

The earliest ancestor traced is Raffe Ouldham (1550-1586) whose wife was named Alice (1552-1613), who were my 11th great grandparents. Each of their descendants can be identified and to name them all would be excessive, but their grandson Thomas Ouldham (1596-1678) is the first to be identified from the Manchester Cathedral records, being married to Alice Yates at the Collegiate Church of St. Mary, St. Denys and St. George on 25th May 1616. This record spells his name as Oldam. He is described as Thomas Ouldham of Crompsall (now Crumpsall, North Manchester) in the burial record for 3rd September 1678. He and his wife were my 9th great grandparents. Their son and grandson were both named Joshua, and it was the grandson, Joshua Oldham (1673-1756) who is the first recorded with the modern spelling of the name in the Collegiate Church record of his baptism on 24th August 1673. He and his second wife Martha Etches (b. 1676), my 7th great grandparents, lived in Hyde, Cheshire, in the Longdendale area northeast of Stockport. Joshua's first wife, Mary Birch, had died little more than a year after they were married in 1697 at the Collegiate Church in Manchester of which comprehensive records are readily available on line.

Their son, also Joshua Oldham (1700-1770), married Cecily Fullalove (1705-1767), who came from a family which had been living in Mottram-in-Longdendale for at least two centuries, because it has been possible to trace her direct ancestors to my 11th great grandparents, Stephen Fullalove (1549-1598) and his wife Alice Hadfield (1549-1606). Cecily Fullalove was baptised as Sicilie Fullalove at Mottram-in-Longdendale on 3rd February 1705. It appears that this branch of the Oldham family which had hitherto lived in Manchester moved to Mottram with this marriage and that the family became firmly based in this part of Cheshire from the early 18th century onwards. Of their nine children Thomas Oldham (1731-1761), who married Ellen Chatterton (b. 1743), was my 5th great grandfather. Thomas Oldham was baptised on 11th March 1739 at Mottram in Longdendale. His marriage to Ellen Chatterton took place at Mottram in Longdendale on 3rd January 1764. The next generation comprised their son William (1763-1837) who married Mary Shaw (1766-1837). William Oldham was baptised on 17th April 1765 at Mottram in Longdendale – his name is spelt Ouldham, the son of Thomas Ouldham. His marriage to Mary Shaw took place on 25th May 1787 at Mottram-in-Longdendale. He was buried at St. Mary's Stockport on 10th May 1837. They had nine children eight of whom were boys, one of whom was Joshua Oldham who was my 3rd great grandfather.

The census records enabled more information to be discovered about the Oldham family in the 19th century. Joshua Oldham (1799-1870) was baptised on 15th January 1799 at Mottram-in-Longdendale. He married Mary Moss (1801-1855) at Stockport on 16th July 1820. They had a total of five children – their son Charles was my great great grandfather. In the 1841 census the family was living in Mottram-in-Longdendale. Joshua Oldham's occupation is cotton spinner and the eldest son, Robert, was working as a cotton piecer

In the 1851 census the family was living in King Street, Mottram-in-Longdendale. Joshua's occupation is watchman. His wife's birthplace is stated as in Yorkshire. All the children save the youngest were working in the cotton industry.

In the 1861 census Joshua Oldham was living in Cooper St, Glossop, Derbyshire – Joshua was a widower and his occupation is given as labourer. Also living in the household were Robert Oldham, Wright Oldham and William Oldham and Hannah Hall (Hannah Oldham) and her twin children Marie and Joshua, aged seven, Mr Hall being elsewhere. All the adults worked in the cotton industry.

Charles Oldham (1833-1886), my great great grandfather, ended up as a butcher, although when young he worked in the cotton industry. He married Rebecca Ann Handford (1835-1895) who came from another local family (originally from Derbyshire) whose members were engaged in the cotton industry. Her father, William Handford, was the manager of a power loom. The 1861 census reveals Charles and Rebecca Oldham living at the home of Rebecca's parents in Mottram-in-Longdendale. Charles Oldham's occupation is shown as "butcher journeyman" and his place of birth Mottram. Rebecca, born in Mellor in Derbyshire, was working as a power cotton weaver, probably in the power looms of which her father William Handford was the manager. In the census records for 1871 and 1881 the Oldham family was living in Mossley, Ashton-under-Lyne where Charles Oldham was a butcher. Their daughter, Mary Elizabeth Oldham, who married Thomas Potter, was baptised on 13th May 1860 at Mottram-in-Longdendale.

Chapter 24: Discovering the Byrom Family

The chance discovery from the census return for 1851 that James Potter's father-in-law was Henry Byrom, and that therefore James's wife Ann's maiden name was Byrom, was most fortunate. In the first place it confirmed that my Uncle Peter's second name was given him for a reason rather than simply being chosen out of the blue. I doubt if it would have been possible to make this link without the census record, because Potter is such a common name, particularly in the northwest of England, and there would have been too many possibilities to come to any conclusions. With this knowledge it was possible to use the available parish records to uncover the marriage record of James and Ann Potter in 1827 at the parish church of Wigan, the baptismal records of both James Potter, who was born in the Wigan area, and Ann Byrom his wife, and the baptismal record of Henry Byrom, who was born in 1777 and baptised at Winwick. As I discovered later many members of the Byrom family were baptised, married and buried at this church and two associated churches within the same large parish, the chapels at Ashton and Newton (now known as Ashton-in-Makerfield and Newton-le-Willows).

The ancient Parish of Winwick was a very large parish in South Lancashire, about ten miles long by five miles wide, an area of approximately fifty square miles, with the towns of Wigan to the North and Warrington to the South, Leigh and Eccles to the East and St. Helens and Prescot to the West. In the 19th century with the industrialisation of the area the parish was divided up. Byrom Hall, the principal seat of the Byrom family, is in Lowton within the ancient parish of Winwick – see the map below. Until the Industrial Revolution this was a rural community of isolated villages. Half way between the cities of Manchester and Liverpool, the M6 motorway runs from North to South through the middle of the old Parish and the M62 crosses it from East to West approximately along the Southern boundary. St. Oswald's Church, Winwick, dates from the 14th century although there have been earlier churches on the site dating back to Saxon times. The present church has been extensively rebuilt and restored. The Chapel of St. Thomas at Ashton dates from the very end of the 17th century, the first baptismal record being dated 1698, and the current parish church was built in the late 19th century as the township of Ashton-in-Makerfield grew. Until it became a parish church the chapel was served by curates from Winwick. Newton Chapel has earlier origins, also being served by curates from Winwick until a parish church was consecrated. St. Peter's Church, Newton-le-Willows is the successor to this chapel, the current building dating from the late 19th century.

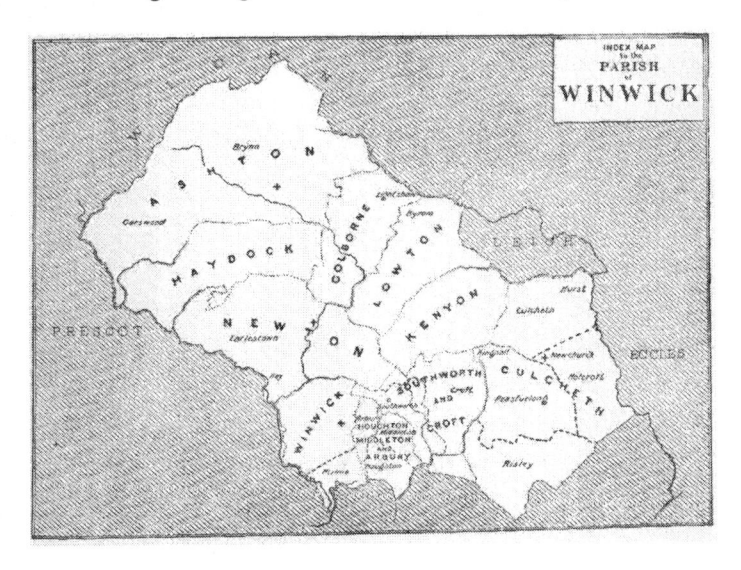

The Parish of Winwick before its division in the mid-19th century

Winwick is a place which today is usually overlooked and passed through on the motorways or on the East Lancs Road, but a detour off these routes reveals a district of flat farmland and one can spot old houses and cottages which give some idea of what the area must have been like before the Industrial Revolution. St. Oswald's Church, Winwick is a fine red sandstone building on a slight hillock, dominating the surrounding countryside.

I already knew that the Byrom family was an old-established Lancashire family from the Wigan and Winwick area with a branch in Manchester of which the well-known poet and polymath, John Byrom, was a member. On line were some family trees which included my 3rd great grandfather Henry Byrom and indicated a direct lineage back to the Norman Conquest, commencing with Michel de Bures (1010-1090) who if this line was correct (as it proved to appear to be) was my 28th great grandfather. Clearly this called for further research and checking for as much corroboration as possible. Because of where it was leading me I was particularly careful to check every piece of evidence and to cross-reference as much as possible. It is very unusual to be able to trace an unbroken line of 26 generations of direct male ancestors, but this is what the family trees revealed. When reading the names of the wives of this line of male Byroms from Michel de Bures in the 11th century to Henry Byrom in the 18th century I immediately recognised some of the names as representing important Lancashire families. This in turn led to following up their ancestry with interesting results as will be seen.

The son of Michel de Bures was called Ralph de Buron, who built Horestan Castle near Derby during the reign of King Henry I, and the name gradually developed into Byrom and Byron in different parts of the country. The family of Lord Byron, the poet, has the same roots. A useful piece of corroborative evidence in relation to the Lancashire and Manchester Byroms was "The Byrom Pedigrees" researched by The Revd. Francis Raines, a local historian in the 19th century, and published by the Chetham Society. This supplied independent support for information contained in the family trees on line from the 14th to the early 18th centuries, in particular confirming that the direct line of male ancestry was correct. Fortunately the 18th century parish records were well kept and available on line and so it was possible to establish Ann Byrom's direct line of descent from the Byroms of the 14th century (together with all the important connections I refer to later) to a high standard of proof, well in excess of the balance of probability standard I had set myself. After careful consideration I became absolutely sure that the links were as well-established as they could possibly be.

But before outlining these discoveries I shall begin with revealing what I could find about Henry Byrom, my 3rd great grandfather (1777-1862). Henry is a name given to many members of the Byrom family, other frequently given names being William and John. The parish record of his baptism is available. Henry Byrom was born in Ashton-in-Makerfield (now a suburb of Wigan), on 14th January 1777, the son of William Byrom, and he was baptised on 5th February 1777 at St Thomas, Ashton-in-Makerfield. St Thomas, Ashton, was a chapel of ease for the parish church at Winwick – in the 18th century most Byrom family members were baptised, married and buried at this church or the chapel at Newton, both of which were nearer to Byrom Hall and Lowton than the mother church at Winwick.

Ascertaining precisely to whom Henry Byrom was married has been difficult. The family trees on line were not consistent, some naming Mary Cundliff, others Anne Cunliffe. The similarity of surnames will not have helped researchers, a number of whom identify a further name, Mary Candliff. For a number of reasons I favour Mary Cundliff. First, there is a parish record of the marriage of Henry Byrom and Mary Cundliff, at Winwick, within the Byrom territory, on 15th May 1796. There is also a baptismal record for Mary Cundliff, at Winwick, on 5th November 1779, daughter of William Cundliff of Golborne within the parish of Winwick, whereas it is not possible to identify an Anne Cunliffe from any available records. However there is a record, in the Parish Records for Winwick (discovered by pure chance when looking for something else) of the burial of Charles Potter, aged 1, the son of James and Ann Potter of Oldham. He was buried on 24th June 1832 having died of measles. On the same day Mary Byrom, wife of Henry Byrom, of Wigan, was buried, aged 53 (which fits with the baptismal record of Mary Cundliff in 1779), having died of apoplexy. This coincidence must throw some doubt as to whether Henry Byrom was married to Anne Cunliffe as suggested in the various family trees, and make Mary Cundliff the more likely wife for him. It appears that Charles Potter was buried on the same day as his grandmother. Further evidence for this hypothesis is that Henry Byrom was buried at the same church (St. Thomas, Ashton-in-Makerfield) on 26th November 1862, having died on 22nd November. The cause of his death is noted as "general decay". In my judgement the evidence points to Mary Cundliff being the wife of Henry Byrom and thus my ancestor.

The details relating to Thomas Byrom (1800-1882), who was a Mayor of Wigan, show him to be the son of this Henry Byrom, which would make him the elder brother of Ann Byrom who married James Potter. Another son was William Byrom, born 1804, who like Thomas and Ann was baptised at Winwick, all recorded as the children of Henry Byrom. That all of these various male Byroms were grocers also fits with this scenario.

St. Oswald's Church, Winwick where many members of the Byrom family were baptised, married and buried

The 1841 census indicates that Henry Byrom was living at High Street, Oldham with William Byrom (his son, born in 1804, according to his age recorded in the census return and consistent with the baptismal records for Winwick) – his occupation was a grocer's business. In the 1851 census Henry Byrom is described as "retired grocer" – living with his daughter and son-in-law (James and Ann Potter) at Chadderton (near Oldham) – his relationship to the head of household is given as father-in-law. He may have been simply visiting his family because he returned to his birthplace at some stage for the final years of his life. In the 1861 census Henry Byrom is recorded as living in his birthplace, Ashton-in-Makerfield. He died there in November 1862.

Henry Byrom's daughter, Ann Byrom (1802-1884,) was born on 13th June 1802 and baptised at Winwick on 11th July 1802. Her brother, Thomas Byrom (1800-1882), a grocer in Wigan, was elected Mayor of Wigan in 1848 and served as a Justice of the Peace. There is a memorial to him in Wigan Parish Church. A younger brother, William, mentioned above, was born in 1804. These three siblings were all baptised in the same church, as children of Henry Byrom. There is a record in the Parish records for Winwick of an illegitimate child called Mary born to Ann Byrom in 1820 who died an infant and who was buried on 24th April 1820 – the cause of death is given as "weakness". Ann Byrom married James Potter on 25th January 1827 at the parish church in Wigan, one of the witnesses being her brother Thomas Byrom.

Family trees on line named William Byrom (1733-1802) as Henry Byrom's father, and it was possible to confirm this from parish records. William Byrom was baptised at St. Thomas, Ashton on 4th July 1733, son of William Byrom. He married Ellen Birchall at Winwick on 21st October 1759. William Byrom's burial took place on 1st September 1802 at Ashton Chapel in the parish of Winwick. Some family trees on line show Ellen Claughton, d. 1815, as William Byrom's wife. However there are no parish records available to confirm this. Other trees name Ellen Birchall as his wife. There are parish records to confirm this so this must be regarded as the most likely conclusion. Ellen Birchall was baptised at Ashton on 29th December 1736 – her father is named as Nathan Birchall. Her marriage to William Byrom took place on 21st October 1759 at Winwick. Her burial took place at Ashton on 21st January 1814, the record stating that she was 78, the widow of William Byrom of Ashton and that she died of old age.

Tracing back from William Byrom, my 4th great grandfather, it was possible to identify his father as William Byrom (1710-1744) who was baptised at Winwick on 10th September 1710 and who married Sarah Gorse (d. 1764) at Wigan in 1731. The marriage record says that both parties came from Haddock, i.e. Haydock, within the parish of Winwick. Their deaths are recorded in the Winwick parish records in 1744 and 1764 respectively. William Byrom's father, my 6th great grandfather, was Henry Byrom (1682-1724) who was married to Ellin Deintith (b. 1763) – Henry Byrom died in Flanders in circumstances which are not recorded. Their marriage is recorded in 1706 at Winwick, as is Henry's baptism in 1682.

Henry Byrom's father, also named Henry (1660-1702), was married to Katherin Feilden (b. 1662). They were my 7th great grandparents. This Henry Byrom (one of many ancestors with that name) was the second son of Samuel Byrom (1634-1686). The establishment of this relationship is pivotal to making the link with the long line of Byroms which goes back as far as the Norman Conquest, because the details of this line contained in many family trees is corroborated by the evidence contained in the Byrom pedigrees researched by the Revd. Francis Raines.

Samuel Byrom and his wife Margaret Venables (b. 1637) were my 8th great grandparents, the last of my direct ancestors to live at Byrom Hall, Lowton in the parish of Winwick. Their eldest son and heir was John Byrom (1659-1695), my 8th great uncle, who was a barrister of Gray's Inn and the Member of Parliament for Wigan, elected in 1694, the year before his death. John Byrom inherited the bulk of the family wealth and estates. His son, Samuel Byrom (1685-1739), known as "Beau Byrom", inherited this at a young age, but unfortunately having been to university (Christ's College, Cambridge) he squandered his fortune in the fleshpots of London, where to quote The Revd. Francis Raines, author of the Byrom Pedigrees, he fell "into the hands of sharpsters and gamesters, the very bane and ruin of many young gentlemen when they first come from university, his estate was diminished, his reputation was lost." He lost all his money and was committed to the Fleet Prison for debt. Having lost his fortune he is believed to have died a beggar, but the details of his death are not known. "Beau Byrom" was my first cousin 7 times removed.

Other members of the family, including Henry Byrom, Samuel Byrom's second son, my 7th great grandfather, and his descendants remained in the Winwick area, but the family's wealth and influence was considerably diminished. A number of them are recorded in various trade directories as operating businesses in the Wigan district. Byrom Hall was acquired by one of the Manchester Byroms, a junior branch of the family descended from Raufe Byrom, a younger son of John Byrom (b. 1410) my 17th great grandfather.

The family trees on line traced back a further 20 generations of Byroms to Michel de Bures (1010-1090) who was my 28th great grandfather. He accompanied William, Duke of Normandy, the Conqueror, and fought at the Battle of Hastings and is recorded on the Falaise Roll as having done so. He was born in Bures, Normandy, which is not far from Bayeux. The castle at Bures, of which the remains still stand, was an important Norman stronghold. It was the location of one of the most infamous episodes in English history. King Henry II (who was as will be seen later my 25th great grandfather) was spending Christmas there with his court in 1170 when he is said to have uttered the words usually recorded, incorrectly, as "Who will rid me of this turbulent (or troublesome) priest?", as a consequence of which

Thomas Becket, Archbishop of Canterbury, was murdered by four heavily armed knights in Canterbury Cathedral on 29th December 1170. A more accurate account of what the King said, on learning of a provocative sermon preached by Becket in which he excommunicated those who had wronged him, is: "What miserable drones and traitors have I nurtured and promoted in my household who let their lord be treated with such shameful contempt by a low-born clerk!" The four knights appear to have believed that they were doing as the King wished.

The son of Michel de Bures was Ralph de Buron (1040-1107) who became the Lord of Horestan. He built Horestan Castle, near Derby during the reign of Henry I. The ruins still remain, much overgrown by trees. From him are descended not only the Byrom family of Lancashire but also the Byron family – these names evolved from Bures and Buron. The Lancashire Byroms settled in the Wigan area at some stage in the late 12th century, Geoffrey Byrom (1209-1257), my 23rd great grandfather, being known as Geoffrey Byrom de Glazebrook. Glazebrook is near Warrington, just south of the Winwick area, and the first Byrom mentioned in the Byrom Pedigrees is his grandson, Henry Byrome de Byrome (1260-1345), my 21st great grandfather, from whom the line of descent to Samuel Byrom referred to above is corroborated by several records referred to in the pedigrees. Henry Byrome de Byrome, referred to as Henry de Buyroum, was granted land in the Golborne area in the parish of Winwick in 1325.

The Arms of the Byrom family of Lancashire – Argent, a cheveron between three hedgehogs sable. The crest is a hedgehog or urchin and the motto "Arme a tous points" [Armed at all points]

In the next chapter I shall refer to a number of these Byrom ancestors, some of whom married into distinguished families which has led to the discovery of links to the Plantagenets and some well-known aristocratic families. This was clearly an important local family which acquired wealth and influence. Some of them were knighted. For the remainder of this chapter I shall confine myself to referring to the information about the family which emerges from the Byrom pedigrees researched by The Revd. Francis Raines and explain the link to the Byroms of Manchester and the famous John Byrom.

In the 14th century, in addition to the reference to Henry de Buyroum being granted land at Golborne in 1325, there is a record of Thomas de Byrom holding lands at Warrington adjoining Winnick, dated 1376. He appears to have been a younger son of Henry de Buyroum, and the brother of my 20th great grandfather, Simon de Byrom. Simon de Byrom (1320-1385) is recorded, as Symone de Byrom, in connection with a conveyance of land in the Haydock area in 1383.

Moving into the 15th century Simon de Byrom's son, Thomas de Byrom (1376-1432), my 19th great grandfather, is mentioned in land transactions in 1414 and 1422. His son, Henry de Byrom (1393-1477), who married Lucy Parr (1390-1477), a member of the Parr family of Warrington from which Catherine Parr, the last of King Henry VIII's six wives, was descended, is recorded in connection with land transactions in 1432 and 1434. The latter of these mentions his brother, Thomas, clerk. The term "clerk" in this context refers to a Clerk in Holy Orders and this is Dom. Thomas Byrom who was Prebendary of Lichfield from 1450 to 1466 and archdeacon of Nottinghamshire from 1461 until his death in 1476. Previously he had been Rector of Grappenhall, Cheshire, and of Warrington.

The head of the family in the next generation was John Byrom (b. 1410), my 17th great grandfather. He is mentioned in connection with several legal transactions between 1456 and 1467. He and his wife Margaret Levo or Lever had a number of children of whom the eldest, Henry, became the head of the family in the Winwick area and from whom my descent comes. A younger son, Raufe Byrom, moved to Salford during the reign of King Henry VII and "embarked in commerce" to quote The Revd. Francis Raines, founding the cadet branches of the Byrom family which lived in Manchester and Salford. They appear to have made considerable fortunes by trading as linen merchants and had strong connections with the Collegiate Church in Manchester, now Manchester Cathedral, where until it was badly damaged by bombing in the Second World War stood a Byrom Chapel. John Byrom, about whom there is a section below, was a famous member of this family who were significant benefactors to various institutions in the Manchester area and after whom various places in the city are named.

Returning to the Byroms of Byrom in the Winwick area, the next head of the family, my 16th great grandfather, was Henry (1438-1506), Raufe's elder brother. He appears to have been an important figure who is well documented in the records of the time. His marriage to Constance Abram (sometimes also referred to in records as Constancia Alburgham, b. 1425) brought him extra lands in Cheshire including a right to a ferry across the Mersey from Warrington to Latchford. He subsequently acquired from Sir Thomas Stanley, Earl of Derby further lands and another ferry from Runcorn to Chelwell which may refer to Thelwall, the name of the viaduct over which the M6 motorway crosses the River Mersey and the Manchester Ship Canal. Henry Byrom was present at a reception given by Sir Thomas Butler for King Henry VII at Bewsey Hall, Warrington, when the King visited his mother and step-father, the Earl of Derby, at Knowsley. There are family links to both the Butler family (known formerly as Boteler) and that of the Earls of Derby, the Stanleys, as will be seen in Chapters 25 and 26. Sir Thomas Butler's daughter, Margaret, married Sir Richard Bold (who were my 14th great grandparents, because their daughter Elizabeth Bold married a later Henry Byrom). Thus Sir Thomas Butler (1461-1522) was my 15th great grandfather and it is through the Butler link that I have been able to trace my ancestry to the Plantagenet kings.

There were a number of further generations of Byroms recorded in the Byrom Pedigrees in the Winwick area as land passed from father to son. John Byrom (1538-1593) was the second son of the Henry Byrom (1504-1559) who married Elizabeth Bold, but he inherited the family estates soon after his father's death because his elder brother, Thomas, died shortly after coming into his inheritance. This John Byrom was a justice of the peace who in 1584 was associated with other gentlemen of the County Palatine of Lancashire to defend Queen Elizabeth I from the Popish plots. One of the references to him is in connection with the right of patron of the Rectory of Grappenhall which the family held at this time. His son, Sir Henry Byrom (1563-1613), my 11th great grandfather, who married Katherine Gerard (1565-1613), was suspected in 1600 of harbouring a fugitive Catholic priest, but this was not proved. Katherine Gerard was a member of a well-known Catholic family which was very well connected to other Lancashire families some of whom will be mentioned in the next chapter.

Sir Henry's son was my 10th great grandfather Sir John Byrom (1585-1614). He married Isabella (or Isabel) Nowell (b. 1592) who came from another old Lancashire family, which can be traced back to the Norman Conquest. A direct ancestor of Isabella Nowell was Adelaide de Normandie, a sister of William the Conqueror, who was thus my 29th great grandmother. Her brother, William I, by a different line of ancestry, was my 28th great grandfather. So King William I was also my 30th great uncle and his sister was also my 29th great aunt! The Nowells were an important Lancashire family with a seat at Reed Hall near Burnley. Isabella Nowell was the daughter of Roger Nowell, the magistrate who hunted out and prosecuted the Lancashire Witches, also known as the Witches of Pendle, who were tried at Lancaster Castle in 1612 – Sir Roger Nowell (1560-1623) is therefore my 11th great grandfather. This is one of the earliest English criminal trials of which a detailed account exists in the form of a book written by the Clerk of the Court, Thomas Potts, entitled "The wonderfull discoverie of witches in the Countie of Lancashire" published in 1613. Roger Nowell had been High Sheriff of Lancashire in 1610. His grandson, also named Roger

Nowell (1605-1695), was a supporter of King Charles I in the English Civil War, raising an army at his own expense.

Lancaster Castle has the distinction of being the court which has been in longest continual use in England. It is interesting to note that two of the most famous trials held there (the Lancashire Witches Trials of 1612 and the Trial of the Birmingham Six for bombing a public house in Birmingham in the 1970s - the conviction was subsequently overturned following some of the evidence being held to be flawed) were prosecuted by two of my relatives, namely Roger Nowell and Patrick Russell QC, my uncle, later The Right Hon Sir Patrick Russell, a Lord Justice of Appeal [See Part III, Chapter 21]. The only member of the family to have sat there as a judge, so far as I am aware, is myself, and it is one of the courts over which as Resident Judge for Lancashire I held a supervisory jurisdiction.

The author, His Honour Judge Anthony Russell QC, Recorder of Preston 2006-2015

The author photographed in the magnificent Crown Court in Lancaster Castle

The next Henry Byrom (1608-1642), my 9th great grandfather, was at the age of five betrothed to Margaret Ireland, aged nine, the sixth child of Sir Thomas Ireland of Bewsy (Warrington). The marriage is recorded in the Parish Register at Warrington. However the marriage contract was annulled and later Margaret Ireland became the wife of John Jeffreys by whom she bore a son who became the notorious Judge Jeffreys. Henry Byrom married

Winifred Brotherton who came from a Lancashire Catholic family whose members were driven out of the county to Wales for their adherence to the Catholic faith. Henry Byrom was killed at the Battle of Edgehill in the English Civil War. He fought in the Royalist Army of King Charles I which won the battle.

Their son was Samuel Byrom (1634-1686) who married Margaret Venables (b. 1637), my 8th great grandparents. In 1670 Samuel Byrom sold the advowson of the Rectory of Grappenhall referred to earlier. He was the last of my Byrom ancestors to have lived at Byrom Hall. It is from his second son, Henry, that I am descended as set out earlier in this chapter and so we have come full circle into the 18th century.

John Byrom (1692-1763)

John Byrom is remembered as the poet who wrote the words to the Christmas Day hymn "Christians Awake! Salute the happy morn". Although a well-known person, mystery surrounds the birth of John Byrom. All references state that he was born on 29th February 1692 but some sources say he was born at Kersall Cell, Salford, and others say he was born at the site of what is now the Wellington Inn in the Shambles, Manchester, close to the Cathedral.

John Byrom as a young man

The parish records for the Collegiate Church in Manchester, now Manchester Cathedral, where John Byrom is buried, show him to be baptised on 29th February 1691/2, a somewhat ambiguous reference probably arising out of the fact that the year still officially commenced on 25th March, although many people regarded January 1st as a better starting date, as was soon enacted.

John Byrom is a distant relative of mine – a 6th cousin 11 times removed. The Manchester Branch of the Byrom family descends from John Byrom (1410-1441) who married Margaret Levo or Lever (d. 1441) my 17th great grandparents. He is the 6th great grandson of this couple, whose younger son Raufe Byrom (1442-1524 – my 17th great uncle) left the Wigan area and settled in Manchester. Through further generations descends John Byrom

(Adam, Henry, Lawrence, and three Edwards, the last of whom was John Byrom's father). This branch of the family were successful linen drapers and merchants and many of their members are buried in what is now Manchester Cathedral (then the Collegiate Church) in the Byrom Chapel, now known as the Jesus Chapel, although some records state that the Byrom Chapel was in fact what is now the Lady Chapel.

He was educated at the King's School, Chester where my brother and I were educated, Merchant Taylors School and at Trinity College, Cambridge where my brother, Nicholas Russell, read medicine 250 years or so later. John Byrom also studied medicine, at Montpelier, the leading medical school in Europe at the time, and subsequently became a Fellow of the Royal Society. He never practised medicine but was known as Dr. Byrom. He invented a form of shorthand which was widely used for many years, known as "The New Universal Shorthand".

On 14th February 1720 at Manchester Collegiate Church he married his cousin, Elizabeth Byrom. One of his children, Dorothy, known as Dolly, was given the poem "Christians Awake! Salute the Happy Morn" as a Christmas present on Christmas Day 1745, originally entitled "Christmas Day for Dolly".

His poems have been published – many of them are pithy epigrams such as his commentary on the celebrated feud between the composers Handel and Bononcini which ended when Bononcini left England in disgrace having been proved to have plagiarised a madrigal by Lotti.

> Some say, compared to Bononcini,
> That Mynheer Handel's but a ninny;
> Others aver, that he to Handel

> Is scarcely fit to hold a Candle.
> Strange all this Difference should be
> Twixt Tweedle-dum and Tweedle-dee!

For some time erroneously attributed to Jonathan Swift, this is now recognised as Byrom's work and it is the first recorded use of the phrase "Tweedle-dum and Tweedle-dee".

John Byrom's political views have attracted much comment and speculation. He has the reputation of having been a closet Jacobite. This may arise out of the fact that it was in Manchester in 1745 that Bonnie Prince Charlie was greeted with much celebration and his father, the Old Pretender, was proclaimed King as James III. John Byrom was in Manchester at the time (it was only a month before the composition of "Christians Awake!") and there were many adherents to the Stuarts in the town. The clergy of the Collegiate Church where Byrom worshipped (and where he and many members of the Byrom family are buried) were strong supporters of the Jacobite cause. Prince Charles Edward Stuart, the Young Pretender, attended Sunday Service at the Collegiate Church on 30th November 1745 before marching south to Derby from where the Jacobite army retreated later in December and the 1745 uprising faded away. Byrom must almost certainly have been in attendance at the Church Service and probably the blessing of the Prince's army which followed. However, John Byrom's supposed adherence to the Jacobite cause may be doubted when one considers a verse he composed in the form of a toast.

> God bless the King! (I mean our faith's defender!)
> God bless! (No harm in blessing) the Pretender.
> But who Pretender is, and who is King,
> God bless us all! That's quite another thing!

More recent research suggests that, moving in very influential social and intellectual circles, he may have been a secret agent, possibly a double agent. Occupying both camps was something he was accustomed to do in relation to his churchmanship – when St. Ann's Church, Manchester, was founded to provide a more Protestant, Hanoverian alternative to the High Church and Jacobite Collegiate Church, Byrom attended morning service at the Collegiate Church and the evening service at St. Ann's.

Certainly much mystery attaches to this remarkable man. Even after Byrom's death although his private papers had been carefully preserved, most of them were strangely destroyed in the 19th century giving rise to suggestions that he was involved in some sort of masonic society or even pursued occult interests. His appearance was striking, as the surviving images of him reveal – he was reputed to be the tallest man in the Kingdom.

JOHN BYROM.
Author of "Christians! awake, salute the happy morn."

John Byrom died in 1763 and is buried in what was the Byrom family's private chapel in the Collegiate Church, now Manchester Cathedral. His son Edward founded St. John's Church,

Manchester in memory of his father, but this church is now demolished. Edward Byrom was also the co-founder of Manchester's first bank. He died leaving no male heirs. Byrom Street and a number of other places bearing the Byrom name remain in the heart of what is now the legal hub of Manchester.

Chapter 25: Some Interesting Links

In the last chapter I recounted my discovery of the Byrom connection which enabled me to trace my ancestry through the Byroms back to the 11th century. If for no other reason than it gives you your name, the natural action when searching for one's ancestors is to concentrate on the male line. However the female line can be as interesting as I had already discovered, and as I researched it became clear that many of the male Byroms married wives who came from very distinguished families.

By reason of my role of Resident Judge for Lancashire before I retired in 2015 I had various duties concerning the Shrievalty of Lancashire. I was present at the annual swearing in of each High Sheriff and at a ceremony, unique to Lancashire, when the new High Sheriff hangs his or her shield in the Shire Hall at Lancaster Castle, where the Crown Court sits and where the Lancashire Assizes were held in the past. The hundreds of shields displayed dating back to the 12th century are a splendid display of heraldry. As I perused the names of my Byrom ancestors' wives I realised that many of them came from Lancashire families from which many of the High Sheriffs were drawn in earlier days, so pursuing researches into them was an interesting prospect. It is not surprising, when one thinks about it for a few moments, that the landed gentry was likely to mix socially with other landed gentry and that most marriages would be between people of the same class, in this case a somewhat limited pool. As I carried on my research I discovered that some of the High Sheriffs whose coats of arms were displayed in Lancaster Castle were themselves ancestors of mine. One such High Sheriff was Roger Nowell as revealed in the last chapter.

Sir Henry Byrom (1563-1613) and his wife, Katherine Gerard (1565-1613) were my 11th great grandparents. The Gerards were an important family from the same part of Lancashire as the Byroms, with a seat at Brynne in Ashton, south of Wigan. They had considerable holdings of land in the parish of Winwick. The Gerard family tomb is at All Saints Church in Wigan. Katherine Gerard's mother who married Sir William Gerard was Jane Joan Osbaldeston (1534-1583). I was able to discover that her father was Sir Alexander Osbaldeston (1487-1560) who was a High Sheriff of Lancashire. Osbaldeston is a village in the Ribble Valley, east of Preston, near where I had a house, and where Osbaldeston Hall still stands, although the last Osbaldeston to live there left in about 1750. The Osbaldeston family can trace its roots back to the reign of Edward the Confessor, shortly before the Norman Conquest, but it is believed to be even older. Sir Alexander Osbaldeston's wife was Ellen Tyldesley, the daughter of Sir Thomas Tyldesley (1461-1495) and Anne Radcliffe (1464-1536), who were my 14th great grandparents.

The Tyldesley family was an old and well-connected Lancashire family, and although I initially traced the link to them through family trees on line there is a pedigree drawn up in the late 16th century which could be referred to and used to confirm the information in the family trees. A general Internet search for the Tyldesley family revealed the existence of this pedigree. The Tyldesleys included some distinguished lawyers and at least one Member of Parliament. The Tyldesley family seat was at Myerscough Hall, north of Preston, where the family acted as loyal hosts to King James I. In 1651 Charles II also lodged there on his way from Scotland in an unsuccessful attempt to reclaim the throne of England from the Commonwealth. Myerscough College now occupies the site. The Tyldesley family were devout Roman Catholics and Royalist supporters and Sir Thomas Tyldesley was killed by Parliamentarian forces at the battle of Wigan Lane in 1651, the last armed conflict of the English Civil War.

The Radcliffe family is an even more distinguished family. Their seat was at Radcliffe near Bury, north of Manchester. This manor was acquired in the 12th century when the name Radcliffe was adopted by Henry de Radcliffe (1140-1190), my 25th great grandfather. His father was Nicholas FitzGilbert de Taillebois (b. 1100) whose ancestry can be traced back to Raoul de Taillebois born in Normandy in about the year 1000. Because several members of this family, who were my direct descendants, were knights who led men in various battles and wars their exploits are independently recorded in history books and various reference works on line so it has been possible to confirm the details in the family trees and to discover information about their lives. There are links from the Taillebois family to both the Norman and Plantagenet Kings and the pre-Conquest Saxon Kings.

For example, Sir John de Radcliffe (1356-1422), my 18th great grandfather, who was married to Margaret de Trafford (1358-1434), was a soldier who served Richard II, but during the troubles of that King's reign he became a supporter of the Lancastrian cause and subsequently served Henry IV and Henry V. He took part in the Battle of Agincourt and was present at the capture of Caen and the Siege of Rouen. In 1421 he was chosen to be made a Knight of the Garter, but he died before St. George's Day 1422 when the election would have taken place. He was awarded the family motto "Caen, Crecy, Calais". In addition to being a brave soldier, Sir John de Radcliffe was responsible for the introduction of Flemish Weavers beginning the long association of the Northwest of England with the textile industry. His grandson, my 16th great grandfather, Sir Alexander Radcliffe (1416-1475), was also a prominent supporter of the Lancastrian cause in the Wars of the Roses. In addition to the original family seat at Radcliffe the family became major landowners in Ordsall, Prestwich and Salford and they owned Wythenshawe Hall and Park in early medieval times.

The Taillebois family came to England with William the Conqueror. The name developed into Talbot, the surname of the Earls of Shrewsbury who are descended from the same family. This is an exceptionally important family with links to the Royal and Aristocratic families of pre-Conquest England and France from which the Plantagenet dynasty evolved and a family in which many of the great aristocratic families of England have their origins. However there are various anomalies in the early Taillebois descent, so some of the detail must be regarded as uncorroborated.

That Henry de Radcliffe (1140-1190), who was a younger son and who adopted the name Radcliffe where he had established his seat, was the son of Nicholas FitzGilbert de Taillebois, born about 1100, appears to be well documented. Nicholas FitzGilbert's father was named Gilbert, known as Sir Gilbert de Lancaster, fourth Baron Lancaster of Kendal, and his dates are recorded as 1089-1138. He was also known as Gilbert de Furnesio (Furness, the area of South Cumbria which was formerly the northern part of Lancashire). The third Baron Lancaster of Kendal was Sir Ketel of Kendal (b. about 1055) – it is not clear whether he was an elder brother of Sir Gilbert or his father. The dates are confusing and the records scant. My preferred solution is that they were brothers, but this is by no means clear. However there appears to be little doubt that they were descended from the second Baron Lancaster of Kendal, Sir Eldred (Aelfred) Taillebois of Workington, who was married to Aldgytha (b.1052).

Sir Eldred was the son of Ivo de Taillebois (1036-1094) about whom there is considerable information available, and his wife Aldgytha was the daughter of Ethelreda, a Princess of Northumberland who was a granddaughter of King Ethelred the Unready. Adopting my assumption that Sir Gilbert and Sir Ketel were brothers and not father and son, this means that King Ethelred the Unready (968-1016) is my 31st great grandfather and King Alfred the Great (852-905) my 35th great grandfather. King Egbert (788-825), regarded by some historians as the first king to rule the whole of England, would be my 37th great grandfather.

Ivo de Taillebois, first Baron of Kendal, (1036-1094) would be my 29th great grandfather. He is an interesting and well-connected figure who came to England with William the Conqueror. I have been able to discover a considerable amount of information about him from general searches on the Internet. He married Lucia of Mercia, Countess of Chester, Countess of Bolinbroke and Countess of Lincoln who was probably of Royal stock (1059-1141?). Ivo de Taillebois is believed to have been born in Caen, Normandy, or Anjou, although some historians say he was born in Lincolnshire. This latter theory may derive from the fact that in addition to being the first Baron of Kentdale (Kendal) he was Earl of Holland (by which name part of Lincolnshire was known).

Wherever he was born, he was a member of the family of the Counts of Anjou. His exact parentage is not known. Some records say he was the son of Fulke III, 5th Count of Anjou, but it is possible he was the son of Geoffrey II Martel, 6th Count of Anjou. Other records say he was the bastard half-brother of Fulke IV, the

7th Count of Anjou, which would make him the grandson of Fulke III. If this is correct, as seems more likely than his being in the legitimate line because of references in an ancient pedigree of the Counts of Anjou to his being on the sinister or left-handed (i.e. illegitimate) side of the family, then he was probably the bastard son of Ermengarde de Anjou, daughter of Fulke III, who was married to Geoffrey, Count of Gatinais. In this hypothesis the name of Ivo's father is unknown. Ermengarde is said to be a direct descendant of the Emperor Charlemagne, whose ancestry dates back according to some historians to Antenor, king of the Cimmerians, a people who lived in the land which is the modern Ukraine, last recorded in about 700 BC.

However it is also possible that Ivo Taillebois was a legitimate son of Geoffrey Count of Gatinais and Ermengarde of Anjou. His brother, Fulke IV, Count of Anjou, known as Fulke the ill-tempered, was the grandfather of Geoffrey Plantagenet (1113-1151), Count of Anjou from 1129. Geoffrey Plantagenet was thus the great nephew or half great nephew of Ivo Taillebois, which makes him my first cousin 28 times removed! He is also my 26th great grandfather by reason of my descent from the Plantagenets which is revealed in the next chapter. Geoffrey Plantagenet married Princess Matilda, daughter of King Henry I of England (ruled 1100-1135) and is regarded as the founder of the Plantagenet dynasty, also known as the House of Anjou. Their son was Henry II (ruled 1154-1189) who succeeded King Stephen (ruled 1135-1154) following the civil war in which Matilda, Countess of Anjou, also known as the Empress Matilda, contested the English Crown. King Henry II is therefore a second cousin 27 times removed as well as a 25th great grandfather and all subsequent members of the Royal Family can be claimed as (very) distant relatives by reason of this link.

Being born a bastard at this time had fewer social implications than in later periods. William the Conqueror was himself illegitimate, and was sometimes known as William of Normandy, the Bastard of Falaise. Ivo Taillebois is said to have fought alongside William the Conqueror at the Battle of Hastings in 1066. He was involved in the suppression of the rebellion led by Hereward the Wake, leading the King's Army at the siege of Ely in 1071, at which Ivo is credited with saving the King's life after Hereward shot an arrow through the King's shield, pinning it to his breast. Ivo Taillebois was Steward to King William II, William Rufus. Although clearly a great soldier and loyal servant to the Norman Kings various accounts of Ivo Taillebois reveal him to be one of the more unpopular Norman barons who abused the Saxons.

Before his marriage to Lucia of Mercia Ivo Taillebois was married to Lady Gondreda of Warwick, but there is no record of any children from this marriage. Lucia of Mercia's ancestry has been the subject of considerable speculation. One theory is that she was the grand-daughter of Lady Godiva (Godgifu) and Leofric Earl of Mercia, and that her father was Aelfgar, Earl of Mercia. This would make Lady Godiva a 31st great grandmother. Whoever Lucia's parents were, and the fact that she was called Lucia of Mercia implies a strong connection with the Earls of Mercia, she inherited considerable estates in Lincolnshire known as the "Honour of Bolinbroke". She married twice after the death of Ivo Taillebois, first to William de Roumare who became Earl of Lincoln, and, second, after his death, to Ranulf le Meschin, Earl of Chester.

The marriage of Sir Henry Byrom and Katherine Gerard in the late 16th Century was a most significant one in terms of tracing my ancestry because it led to these and other more direct Royal connections as will be seen. However before tracing those I shall explore another link to a closely related family to the Byroms, namely the Byrons. The families are in fact the same family, but the similarity of the names has caused some confusion in some of the family trees on line and a degree of unravelling the threads has been necessary. Katherine Gerard's great great grandfather (my 15th great grandfather) was William Gerard (b. 1470) who married Elizabeth Byron (1470-1526). Elizabeth Byron's ancestry can be traced back to Robert Byron (1180-1220) her 8th great grandfather and my 25th great grandfather, who married Cecilia Clayton (1180-1230). Robert Byron was the elder brother of Geoffrey Byrom (1184-1246) from whom my Byrom ancestors descend.

The Byrons settled in Clayton, now a suburb of Manchester, about three miles to the east of the city centre. The arms of the Byron family, to which the poet Lord Byron belonged, were incorporated in the arms of the Urban District of Droylsden in 1950 because the Byrons were the Lords of the manor of Droylsden. Clayton Hall, with origins in the 12th century, was the family home and its moat still exists beside St. Cross Church. The house also still stands although it has been rebuilt a number of times. The Byrons also owned Royton Hall and it was here that during the reign of Charles I Sir Clifford Byron had a hand cut off by an intruder he disturbed. Much of Royton, near Oldham, was owned by the Byron family until the early 17th century. In 1620 Clayton Hall was sold to Humphrey Chetham and his brother – Humphrey Chetham founded Chetham's School and Library in central Manchester, close to the Collegiate Church, now Manchester Cathedral. Chetham's School is now a world famous school of music. During the English Civil War Royalist cavalry were stationed at Clayton Hall. Afterwards, according to legend, Oliver Cromwell is said to have spent three nights at the Hall. In

1897 the Hall was acquired by Manchester City Corporation and it is occasionally open to the public.

When researching the Byrons I came across a record which was of particular interest to me in "A History of the Parish of Rochdale – Old Houses and Old Families" by Butterworth.

> "Towards the end of the thirteenth century by an undated charter, Richard the son of Andrew de Ormerod gave to John de Buron and Johanna his wife the homage and service due from William the son of Adam de Turnagh and a rental of xiii.d. from the lands called Quitacres…".

This is a reference to land at Whittaker, a hamlet near Littleborough to the east of Rochdale, where I now live, "quitacres" meaning "white acres", the derivation being Norse. "Kvit" is a modern day Norwegian word signifying the colour white. The John de Buron referred to is almost certainly John de Byron (1217-1279) the grandson of Robert Byron, the elder brother of Geoffrey Byrom from whom my Byrom ancestors descend – see the last paragraph but one. Other records indicate that John de Byron was married to a Joan, which is likely to be the Johanna referred to in the record. This means that by pure chance I live on land which was probably owned by my 23rd great grandfather more than 700 years ago! My house certainly dates back to Tudor times and it is believed that part of it may be considerably older.

Byron ancestors include Sir James Byron (1300-1351) and his wife Elizabeth Bernake (1302-1350), my 20th great grandparents, whose elder son Sir John Byron fought at the Battle of Crecy and took part in the Siege of Calais during the Hundred Years War. He died without issue and the line passed through his younger brother Sir Richard. Sir John Byron (1386-1450) my 18th great grandfather was Member of Parliament for Lancashire in 1421 and 1429. Sir Nicholas Byron (1406-1462) should be noted because of his marriage to Alice Boteler because another Boteler link led to a number of important connections, including the most direct and well corroborated route to the Plantagenets. Sir Nicholas and Lady Byron were my 17th great grandparents.

Before turning to explore the Boteler link I shall return to my Byrom ancestors. Henry Byrom (1504-1559) married Elizabeth Bold (1507-1545). They were my 13th great grandparents. The Bold family lived in Bold, Lancashire, near Widnes and Prescot, close to Byrom territory. The family seat was Bold Hall and the family acquired huge estates in Lancashire. Various Lancashire towns including Liverpool and Southport have streets called Bold Street and the Bold arms are incorporated in the coats of arms of the boroughs of Knowsley, Halton and St. Helens. The name is sometimes spelt Bould. It has been possible to trace the Bolds back from Elizabeth Bold to William de Bold (1129-1160) and his wife Alicia, my 27th great grandparents. In 1402 my 19th great grandfather Sir John de Bold (1360-1410) was the garrison commander who defended Caernarfon Castle against Owen Glendower. He was subsequently knighted and appointed Constable of the Castle. In 1407 he became High Sheriff of Lancashire. His son, Thomas (the younger brother of my 18th great grandfather Richard de Bold) fought alongside King Henry V at Agincourt in 1415.

Elizabeth Bold's parents, my 14th great grandparents were Sir Richard Bold (1462-1532) and Margaret Butler (1465-1537). Margaret Butler was a member of the Boteler family referred to earlier into which Sir Nicholas Byron married when he married Alice Boteler earlier in the 15th century.

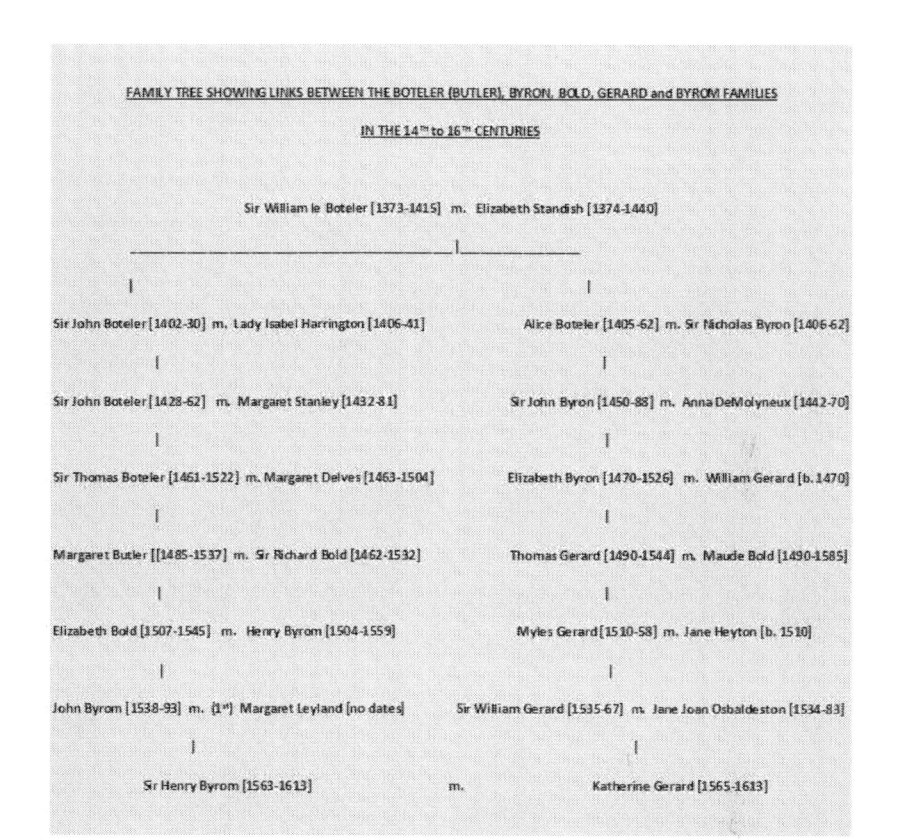

FAMILY TREE SHOWING LINKS BETWEEN THE BOTELER (BUTLER), BYRON, BOLD, GERARD and BYROM FAMILIES

IN THE 14TH to 16TH CENTURIES

Sir William le Boteler [1373-1415] m. Elizabeth Standish [1374-1440]

Sir John Boteler [1402-30] m. Lady Isabel Harrington [1406-41]	Alice Boteler [1405-62] m. Sir Nicholas Byron [1406-62]
Sir John Boteler [1428-62] m. Margaret Stanley [1432-81]	Sir John Byron [1450-88] m. Anna DeMolyneux [1442-70]
Sir Thomas Boteler [1461-1522] m. Margaret Delves [1463-1504]	Elizabeth Byron [1470-1526] m. William Gerard [b. 1470]
Margaret Butler [[1485-1537] m. Sir Richard Bold [1462-1532]	Thomas Gerard [1490-1544] m. Maude Bold [1490-1585]
Elizabeth Bold [1507-1545] m. Henry Byrom [1504-1559]	Myles Gerard [1510-58] m. Jane Heyton [b. 1510]
John Byrom [1538-93] m. (1st) Margaret Leyland [no dates]	Sir William Gerard [1535-67] m. Jane Joan Osbaldeston [1534-83]
Sir Henry Byrom [1563-1613] m.	Katherine Gerard [1565-1613]

The le Botelers (modern "Butler") were another very distinguished family with strong Lancashire links, the family seat being in Warrington, of which they bore the title Earls of Warrington. They had their origins in the d'Aubigny family which came to England with William the Conqueror. The main branch of the d'Aubigny family became the Earls of Arundel who from time to time played important roles in English history taking various surnames including Mowbray when the surname d'Aubigny was dropped by Royal command upon the creation of the Dukedom of Norfolk by King Richard II. The current Dukes of Norfolk, whose surname is FitzAlan-Howard are direct descendants. A FitzAlan ancestor, Sibyl (1285-1330) married

William le Boteler(1276-1330) and they were my 21st great grandparents.

The name le Boteler has its origins in the fact that members of the family held the office of Pincerna Regis or Chief Butler of England. The "Pincerna Regis" was the King's cup bearer and one of his most loyal confidants, and served as the Master Butler of the Royal Household. Various members of the le Boteler family in addition to those noted below have served as High Sheriffs of Lancashire. At some stage the modern spelling "Butler" was adopted.

In researching the ancestry of Margaret Butler I was led very seriously astray by a major error in many of the family trees on line prepared by others. Most of these indicated that that the Margaret Butler who was married to Sir Richard Bold was the daughter of the Earl of Ormonde and the Butlers of Ireland. From this assertion these trees traced a link to the Plantagenets. In fact Margaret Butler was a member of the Boteler/Butler family of Warrington, which seems more likely in any event because of geographical proximity to the Bold family also of Lancashire. The confusion probably arises from the fact that both Margaret Butlers appear to have died in 1537 and in each case the family name was formerly recorded as de Boteler – the English de Botelers being hereditary chief butlers of England and the Irish de Botelers being the hereditary chief butlers of Ireland!

It became clear that the link to the Plantagenets which depended upon Margaret Butler being of the Irish family was erroneous but further research into the ancestors of the English Margaret Butler revealed further interesting information and in particular a different route back through the de Bohun connection to the Plantagenets which is set out in the next chapter. This is well corroborated by information available in Burke's Peerage and various biographical articles on line. In fact there are also a number of connections to the Irish Butler family but these are more distant.

As will be obvious from the names referred to above, these families married into each other on several occasions. The family tree set out above indicates how the Botelers, Byrons, Bolds, Gerards and Byroms were closely connected to each other by marriage. Sir Henry Byrom and his wife Katherine Gerrard were 6th cousins. The discovery of the de Boteler link led to the exciting discovery that I could trace a direct link back through this connection to the Plantagenet Kings and thus to other Royal and Aristocratic Families and how this came about is revealed in the next chapter.

Chapter 26: A Connection to the Plantagenet Kings

It is said that because he had so many children, legitimate and illegitimate, almost all people with English blood in their veins will be descended from King Edward III. One calculation is that the probability of anyone with Anglo-Saxon ancestry being a descendant of King Edward III is 99.997%. However, it is not easy to prove the route by which this occurs, and indeed in my case, although there may be a route directly to Edward III, what I was actually able to discover from my researches was a direct line of ancestry back to his grandfather King Edward I resulting from my descent from Edward I's daughter, Elizabeth of Rhuddlan, the sister of King Edward II and aunt of Edward III. The period of the reigns of the three Edwards has always been of interest to me so it was a particular pleasure to make these discoveries. The relationships are not straightforward and it may assist in reading this chapter to make reference to the family tree below which traces the descent of Margaret Butler, who we met in the previous chapter, from her 7th great grandfather and my 23rd great grandfather, King Henry III.

As well as the Plantagenets themselves and their wives, along the way back to the Plantagenets we come across some well-known and lesser known but interesting characters about whom I shall reveal a little. From the point of view of tracing the ancestry most of the relationships are well corroborated by standard works of reference such as Burke's Peerage and the Dictionary of National Biography, and many historical writings. It should be noted that these relationships are very distant, twenty or more generations in the past, and through several female lines. So they would not entitle me or anyone else similarly related to claim an aristocratic title or to use a coat of arms of a distinguished ancestor. Peerages and baronetcies are, with a few special exceptions arising out of the individual grant, inherited by direct male descendants of previous holders. Similarly the right to use a coat of arms (more properly referred to as an armorial achievement) descends from the original grantee to direct male heirs and successors. Today many people choose to adopt a coat of arms given to someone with the same name but this is not proper. I have been granted my own arms, but this was as a result of my personal application to the College of Arms for a grant of arms, and the arms are peculiar to me, although there are some allusions to various of my family predecessors in the design of the shield and crest, such as the use of the Byrom hedgehog as part of the crest, but distinguished from the Byrom crest of a hedgehog alone by having a quatrefoil in its mouth (a device often associated with the Eyre family). The hedgehog stands on a low green mound to represent my Tuttle ancestry (tot hill).

The link to the Plantagenets is not as remarkable as it might appear at first blush. Assuming no duplication we each have in excess of 16 million 22nd great grandparents because each of our parents has two parents, so we have 4 grandparents, 8 great grandparents and so on. King Edward I who I have identified as my 22nd great grandfather is therefore one of about 8 million or so direct male ancestors in that generation. There will have been duplications because sometimes close cousins marry as we saw with my Eyre ancestors, and the further back in time one goes the more likely it is that distant cousins who have no knowledge of their relationship will marry and have children. For example, Sir Henry Byrom and his wife Katherine Gerrard were 6th cousins but probably unaware of this relationship. King Edward I was born in 1239 when the population of England was a little over 4 millon, so the likelihood is that almost everyone who was alive in England in the middle of the 13th century is a direct ancestor of mine, from which it follows that most people alive today with significant English ancestry are related to me, albeit in most cases very distantly. However it is unusual to have been able to trace what appears to be a clear line back to identifiable people in the Middle Ages, which was made possible because of the fortunate discovery that I am descended from the Byroms of Lancashire.

FAMILY TREE ILLUSTRATING MARGARET BUTLER'S DESCENT FROM KING HENRY III

King Henry III [1206-1272] m. Eleanor of Berenger [1217-1291]
|
King Edward I [1239-1307] m. Eleanor of Castille [1240-1290]
|
Princess Elizabeth of Rhuddlan [1282-1316] m. 2nd Humphrey de Bohun [1276-1321], Earl of Hereford and Essex
|
William de Bohun [1309-1360] m. Elizabeth de Badlesmere [1313-1355]
|
Elizabeth de Bohun [1345-1385] m. Richard FitzAlan [1346-1397], Earl of Arundel and Surrey
|
Elizabeth FitzAlan d'Arundel [1374-1425] m. Sir Robert Goushill [1360-1403]
|
Joan Goushill [1402-1456] m. Sir Thomas Stanley [1386-1458]
|
Margaret Stanley [1432-1481] m. Sir John Boteler [1428-1462]
|
Sir Thomas Boteler [1461-1522] m. Margaret Delves [1463-1504]
|
Margaret Butler [1485-1537] m. Sir Richard Bold [1462-1532]

My great aunt Marion Potter, the sister of my grandmother, who I mentioned in Chapter 22, was a great character. She was often referred to, quaintly, as a maiden aunt and she had a strong Lancashire accent. If I had been able to inform her that it was probable that she was descended from a princess, Elizabeth of Rhuddlan, and thus a direct descendant of Plantagenet Kings and Queens she would have responded by saying something like "Eeeh – well I go to the foot of our stairs." She was, like her sister my grandmother, a beautiful woman with a delicate complexion and luxurious white hair in old age. She was of the generation that rarely used first names even to people she knew well, always addressing my maternal grandmother and her sister, for example, as Mrs Eyre and Miss Tuttle.

To explore these connections it is probably most sensible to work backwards from Margaret Butler, my 14th great grandmother. As we have seen, she was the daughter of Sir Thomas Boteler (1461-1522) and Margaret Delves (1463-1504). She lived from 1485 to 1537, in the reigns of Kings Henry VII and VIII, she married Sir Richard Bold (1462-1532) and the family tree in the last chapter shows her relationship to my Byrom ancestors.

Margaret Butler's grandparents were Sir John Boteler (1428-1462) and Margaret Stanley (1432-1481). The Boteler family's origins have been mentioned in the last chapter. The family was very well-connected and linked to many great families including the Nevilles from which family the Earls of Warwick, including Warwick the Kingmaker, descended, as did Anne Neville, Richard III's queen. Sir Robert de Neville (1323-1413), who was through the Botelers my 19th great grandfather, was a Member of Parliament who held the office of Commissioner of Sewers, probably not an early example of concern for public health although interesting to note in connection with his 16th great grandson and my great grandfather Thomas Potter (1847-1904), the Sanitary Superintendent [see Chapter 23]! It is more likely to refer to an alternative meaning of the word "sewer" which was a term used to describe an officer who serves up a feast and arranges the dishes, such a personage being a member of the Royal Household.

Margaret Stanley (1432-1481) was the daughter of Sir Thomas Stanley (1405-1458) and Joan Goushill (1402-1456), my 17th great grandparents. Created the first Baron Stanley in 1456, Thomas Stanley was MP for Lancashire in the Parliaments of 1447-1451 and 1453-1454. From 1431-1436 he was Lieutenant Governor of Ireland. He held various other offices, including Chief Steward of the Duchy of Lancaster, Constable and Justice of Chester, and Lord Chamberlain. He was a Knight of the Garter. His eldest son Thomas was created Earl of Derby, a title still held by the Stanleys. His second son, William Stanley, was executed for treason in 1495 for his alleged part in the Perkin Warbeck conspiracy. Perkin Warbeck was a pretender to Henry VII's crown, claiming to be Richard, Duke of York, the younger of the Princes in the Tower.

For several generations the Stanleys were the rulers of the Isle of Man. In 1405 Sir Thomas Stanley's grandfather, Sir John Stanley, was granted the title King of Mann by King Henry IV as a fiefdom under the English Crown. The King of Mann was required to render homage to all future Kings of England and to give a tribute of two falcons on the coronation of each successive monarch. Several further generations of the family held the title and ruled the island, including Sir Thomas Stanley. From 1504 until 1765 the Stanleys were known as "Lord of Mann". In 1765 the title was revested in the Crown and today Queen Elizabeth II is the Lord of Mann.

Sir Thomas Stanley's wife Joan Goushill was the daughter of Sir Robert Goushill (1360-1403). Robert Goushill came from a wealthy Nottingham family with extensive estates in Nottinghamshire and Derbyshire. He did not enjoy his knighthood for long. He was knighted by King Henry IV at the Battle of Shrewsbury on July 21st 1403, at which the rebel army of Henry Percy (Hotspur) was defeated. The loss of life was enormous, estimated at three thousand killed or wounded. It was at the Battle of Shrewsbury that Henry, Prince of Wales, later King Henry V, received a serious headwound from an arrow the head of which was removed from his skull in which it had become embedded. The newly knighted Sir Robert Goushill was severely wounded in the side and was found by his servant who then murdered his master and stole his purse and ring. The servant was recognised and later captured and hanged for the crime. Robert Goushill was married to Elizabeth FitzAlan d'Arundel (1374-1425) and they were my 18th great grandparents.

As will be immediately apparent from her name Elizabeth FitzAlan d'Arundel was a member of the great FitzAlan family from which the Dukes of Norfolk, England's premier dukedom, descend. Members of this family have played prominent roles in English history being at the forefront of court and political life for centuries. The Earldom of Arundel is the courtesy title borne by the heir to the dukedom and is the oldest earldom in England dating back to the reign of King Stephen who created William d'Aubigny the first earl. The earldom passed to the FitzAlans as a result of the marriage of Isabel d'Aubigny to John FitzAlan (1200-1240), the Lord of Oswestry and Clun and when her brother Hugh, the last d'Aubigny Earl of Arundel, died without a male heir the title passed to her son, John FitzAlan (1223-1267), who was my 24th great grandfather. Elizabeth FitzAlan's parents were Richard FitzAlan, Earl of Arundel and Surrey (1346-1397) and

Elizabeth de Bohun (1345-1388), who were my 19th great grandparents.

Although I first traced my ancestry back to Henry III through Elizabeth de Bohun as indicated in the table above, there is also a line back to him through Richard FitzAlan as shown in the family tree below. Richard FitzAlan's mother, Eleanor Plantagenet, was the daughter of Henry, 3rd Earl of Lancaster, and thus, a direct descendant of the Plantagenet Kings, Henry III being her great great Grandfather. This means that both King Edward I and his brother, Edmund Crouchback, First Earl of Lancaster, are direct ancestors of mine. The relationships are very complicated and indicate how much inter-marriage there was in aristocratic families, and indeed in less noble families as has already been seen. Richard FitzAlan and his wife Elizabeth de Bohun were third cousins, sharing King Henry III as their 2nd great grandfather. Henry III can thus be shown to be my 23rd great grandfather by two routes, illustrating the duplication point to which I referred earlier.

Eleanor Plantagenet was the daughter of Henry Plantagenet, 3rd Earl of Lancaster (1281-1345) and Maud de Chaworth (b 1282) – my 21st great grandparents. Her brother Henry, 4th Earl of Lancaster, was the father of Blanche of Lancaster who married John of Gaunt, the fourth son of Edward III, the father of King Henry IV (Henry Bolinbroke) who usurped the throne from Richard II, commencing the Wars of the Roses. The father of Henry, 3rd Earl of Lancaster was Edmund, 1st Earl of Lancaster, 1245-1296, (who married Blanche of Artois, 1248-1302) – they were my 22nd great grandparents. The 2nd Earl of Lancaster, Thomas, Henry's elder brother had rebelled against King Edward II and was implicated in the murder of Piers Gaveston. He was condemned in a trial at Pontefract Castle presided over by the King and executed in 1322.

Edmund 1st Earl of Lancaster (known as Edmund Crouchback) was a younger son of Henry III who is, as has been noted, a 23rd Great Grandfather of mine, by two different routes. The Lancaster Inheritance, now the Duchy of Lancaster, derives from the grant of the Lancaster estate in 1265 by Henry III to Edmund Crouchback, and I was privileged to be present at a ceremony to mark the 750th anniversary of this grant in the presence of HM Queen Elizabeth II at Lancaster Castle in May 2015 in my capacity of Recorder of Preston and the Resident Judge for Lancashire. Every British Monarch holds the title "Duke of Lancaster" and in the County of Lancashire is known as such, and when the loyal toast is proposed Lancastrians will toast: "The Queen, Duke of Lancaster". Edmund's wife, Blanche of Artois, was the daughter of Robert of Artois, 1216-1250 and Maud of Brabant, 1224-1288, and the grand-daughter of Louis VIII, King of France, 1187-1226 and Blanche of Castille, 1188-1252. Thus Louis VIII of France is a 24th Great Grandfather which links me to the Capetian Kings of France and through them back to the Emperor Charlemagne, to whom my ancestry can be traced by another route as is noted elsewhere.

To return to Richard FitzAlan he was Admiral of the West. He won a number of naval victories which earned him great popularity. However he fell out with King Richard II and was implicated in a conspiracy to depose the King, for which he was tried and condemned for High Treason and beheaded in 1397. The general populace revered him as a martyr and his tomb in the Church of the Augustin Friars, Bread St., London became a site of pilgrimage. Thomas Cromwell rented a house from the Friars and lived there from about 1525. After the dissolution of the monasteries, Thomas Cromwell acquired further property on the site of the Augustin Friary, known as Austin Friars, establishing one of the largest houses in London where he lived until his downfall and execution.

FAMILY TREE ILLUSTRATING RICHARD FITZALAN's DESCENT FROM KING HENRY III

King Henry III [1206-1272] m. Eleanor of Berenger [1217-1291]

|

Edmund Crouchback, 1st Earl of Lancaster [1245-1296] m. Blanche of Artois [1248-1302]

|

Henry Plantagenet, 3rd Earl of Lancaster [1281-1345] m. Maud de Chaworth [b. 1282]

|

Eleanor Plantagenet [1315-1385] m. Richard FitzAlan, Earl of Arundel & Surrey [1313-1374]

|

Richard FitzAlan, Earl of Arundel & Surrey [1346-1397] m. Elizabeth de Bohun [1345-1385]

Elizabeth de Bohun came from yet another distinguished family. The de Bohuns can be traced back to Humphrey with the Beard (so called because being unshaven was unusual at the time) who died before 1113, a 29th great grandfather. His son, also Humphrey (d.1123), was the first to be known as de Bohun. The third Humphrey de Bohun (d.1164-5) sided with the Empress Matilda in the Civil War which ensued when Stephen usurped the throne following the death of Henry I, Matilda's father. His grandson, Henry de Bohun, the first de Bohun Earl of Hereford, (1176-1220) was one of the rebel barons who were instrumental in securing King John's agreement to the Magna Carta in 1215. He was one of the 25 barons appointed to enforce the charter and as a result was excommunicated by the Pope. Subsequently readmitted to the Church he died on pilgrimage to the Holy

Land. Henry de Bohun was married to Maud FitzGeoffrey de Mandeville (1177-1236), the daughter of Geoffrey FitzPiers, Earl of Essex, Chief Justiciar to King John. Their son, Humphrey de Bohun (1208-1275) who was godfather to Prince Edward, later King Edward I, acquired the Earldom of Essex following the death of his mother when the Mandeville line expired.

Geoffrey FitzPiers was an interesting character who played an important role in English history. He was a prominent member of the government during the reigns of King Richard I, the Lionheart, and King John, and from the last year of the reign of King Richard until his death in 1213 he was the principal minister holding the office of Chief Justiciar. He was High Sheriff of Northamptonshire from 1184-1189 under King Henry II and he also was appointed a justice of the forest during that reign.

When King Richard went on crusade shortly after his coronation, Geoffrey FitzPiers was appointed one of the five justices of the King's Court (a near equivalent of a modern day high court judge) – as a justiciar he was also one of the advisers to the Crown, or a minister in today's terms. He was one of the earliest Royal Justices who went on Assize when Henry II began the practice of sending justices around the country on Assize. It has been suggested by some historians that he was the author of the treatise on laws which bears the name of Ranulph de Glanville, which means, if correct, that he was one of the most important and distinguished lawyers in English legal history.

In 1198 he was appointed Chief Justiciar, thus becoming the chief minister. He retained this office until his death in 1213 during the reign of King John. The role as chief minister gradually became performed by the Chancellor and when King Edward I reformed the judiciary the Justices of the King's Bench were headed by a

Chief Justice, now the Lord Chief Justice. The Chief Justiciar may thus be regarded as the forerunner of both the offices of Prime Minister and Lord Chief Justice. He occupied judicial office for a total of 28 years, fifteen of which were as head of the law and principal minister of the kingdom, serving three Kings, Henry II, Richard I and John.

In addition to his considerable legal and political skills, he was an accomplished soldier having defeated the Welsh king Gwenwynwyn in 1198. At his coronation in 1199 King John conferred the Earldom of Essex upon Geoffrey FitzPiers who was connected with the former earls through his mother, and through his wife Beatrice de Say who was also a member of the Mandeville family. Geoffrey FitzPiers was my 26th great grandfather.

Effigy of Geoffrey de Mandeville, first Earl of Essex in the Temple Church, London

Geoffrey Fitzpiers's grandfather Geoffrey de Mandeville, thus my 28th great grandfather, was created the first Earl of Essex in

1140 by King Stephen. Geoffrey de Mandeville changed allegiance following Stephen's capture in 1141 and acknowledged the Empress Matilda as his sovereign lady. However when Stephen was released he returned to his original allegiance, but not for very long because he ended his days in rebellion against King Stephen as an outlaw in the Isle of Ely dying of an arrow wound in 1144. He was buried in the Temple Church in London where his effigy can still be seen.

Two more Humphrey de Bohuns succeeded to the Earldom of Essex, followed by Humphrey de Bohun (1276-1322), Earl of Hereford and Essex who married Elizabeth Plantagenet (1282-1316), the daughter of King Edward I (1239-1307) and Eleanor of Castille (1240-1290). This Humphrey de Bohun was thus the brother-in-law of King Edward II. Humphrey de Bohun and Elizabeth Plantagenet were my 21st great grandparents.

Humphrey de Bohun was a renowned soldier who was one of several Earls and Barons who laid siege to Caerlaverock Castle in Scotland in 1300. He took part in many other Scottish campaigns under both Edward I and II including the Battle of Bannockburn in 1314 after which he was betrayed when taking refuge with other Englishmen at Bothwell Castle and taken prisoner. Edward II, his brother-in-law, ransomed him in exchange for Robert the Bruce's Queen, Elizabeth de Burgh, his daughter Marjorie Bruce, two Scottish bishops and other prisoners.

Subsequently he became one of the barons who rebelled against Edward II, opposing the ascendency of the Despenser family, for whom he had a particular dislike because he had lost some of his Welsh estates to them. He was killed on 16th March 1322 in battle at Boroughbridge, Yorkshire, in the civil war which ensued. His death was gory. He led the fight on the bridge but underneath the bridge was a pikeman of the troops loyal to the King who thrust his pike upwards through the planks of the bridge, skewering the Earl of Hereford through the anus. His dying screams are said to have caused the rebel forces to panic and retreat.

Earlier he had opposed the influence of Piers Gaveston , the first favourite of Edward II. This was a reversal of friendship because Humphrey de Bohun had gained a reputation as an elegant fop who loved the tourney and he and Gaveston and other young barons and knights, with the permission of the Prince of Wales (later Edward II), left one of Edward I's Scottish campaigns with which they had become bored to take part in a tournament in France. Despite this apparent flippancy he maintained high principles and he insisted that the King should obey Magna Carta and other safeguards against monarchic tyranny. He was a leader of the reform movement that promulgated the Ordinances of 1311, to restrain Edward II and reaffirm Magna Carta, and fought to ensure compliance with them.

A great granddaughter of Humphrey de Bohun and Elizabeth Plantagenet, through their son William de Bohun, was Eleanor de Bohun (1366-1397) who married Thomas of Woodstock, Duke of Gloucester (1354-1397) the youngest son of Edward III, who was murdered at Calais in 1397.

Princess Elizabeth Plantagenet (1282-1321) was the daughter of Edward I and sister of Edward II, who was born in 1284. Also known as Elizabeth of Rhuddlan, she was the youngest daughter of Edward I and Eleanor of Castille. She was first married to John I, Count of Holland, at Ipswich in 1297. John I died two years later. She married Humphrey de Bohun at Westminster Abbey on 14th November 1302. They had eleven children of whom four died in infancy, including their last child Isabella shortly after whose birth Elizabeth died, and with whom she is buried in Waltham Abbey.

The fifth son of Humphrey de Bohun and Elizabeth Plantagenet was William de Bohun (1309-1360) who married Elizabeth de Badlesmere (1313-1355), my 20th great grandparents. William de Bohun had a twin brother, Edward. William was a close confidant of King Edward III having assisted in the arrest of Roger Mortimer, who was de facto ruler of England following the deposition of Edward II whose Queen, Isabella, known as the She-Wolf of France, was Mortimer's mistress. William de Bohun was a distinguished soldier, serving in Scotland and in France. He was a commander at the Battle of Crecy and the Battle of Morlaix. He was present at the naval victory of Sluys. He was an early Knight of the Garter (created a Knight in 1349, the year after the Order was founded) having been created Earl of Northampton in 1337.

Elizabeth de Badlesmere was the daughter of the first Baron Badlesmere. Previously she had been married to Roger Mortimer's son and heir, Edward Mortimer. Elizabeth de Badlesmere's father was Sir Bartholemew Badlesmere (1275-1322), First Baron Badlesmere and her mother was Margaret de Clare (1287-1333) who were my 21st great grandparents. A distinguished soldier in the armies of both Edward I and Edward II, Bartholemew Badlesmere was created a baron by Edward II in 1309. Initially loyal to the king Lord Badlesmere was one of the barons who rebelled against King Edward II and he was convicted of treason and hanged, drawn and quartered by order of the King in 1322. The Badlesmeres were another important Norman family.

A sister of William de Bohun was Eleanor de Bohun (1304-1363) who married first James Butler (1304-1337) first Earl of Ormonde (the head of the Irish Butler/Boteler family). She married James Butler in 1327. Following his death in 1337 she married Thomas de Dagworth, Lord Dagworth, in 1337. Thomas de Dagworth died in an ambush in Brittany in 1352. Her descendants include Anne Boleyn and Catherine Parr, the second and sixth wives of King Henry VIII, the Dukes of Beaufort, Newcastle, Norfolk, and in addition to the Earls of Ormonde, the Earls of Desmond, Shrewsbury, Dorset, Rochester, Sandwich, Arundel and Stafford.

My 19th great grandmother Elizabeth de Bohun, who married Richard FitzAlan, was the daughter of William de Bohun and Elizabeth de Badlesmere. Each of them was a great great grandchild of King Henry III so they were third cousins.

Thus I have been able to trace my ancestry back to the Plantagenet Kings. This means that Edward I, Henry III, John, Henry II, Henry I and William I are all direct ancestors. So also are two remarkable women, firstly Matilda, daughter of Henry I, known as the Empress Matilda because of her first marriage to the Holy Roman Emperor Henry V, who subsequently married Geoffrey Plantagenet, Count of Anjou, and secondly Eleanor of Aquitaine, the wife of Henry II, the son of Matilda and Geoffrey Plantagenet. It is possible through these Royal connections to trace ancestry to the French Royal Kings of the House of Capet which ruled France from the 10th to the early 14th century and through them back to the Emperor Charlemagne. I have been able to discover that there are also numerous Scottish Kings, Scandinavian Kings and pre-conquest Saxon Kings in my ancestry, all of whom are ancestors of the Plantagenets and their wives.

Of English monarchs, using the same links, it has been possible for me to establish the following more distant relationships in addition to the direct ancestors mentioned above: Henry V is my

2nd cousin 17 times removed, Henry VI is my 3rd cousin 16 times removed, Edward IV and Richard III (who were brothers) are my 5th cousins 16 times removed, Henry VII is my 4th cousin 15 times removed, Henry VIII is my 5th cousin 14 times removed and Edward VI, Mary I and Elizabeth I are my 6th cousins 13 times removed!

Once one can get back to famous ancestors such as those mentioned in this chapter the task of tracing ancestors is rather easier than with the less famous characters discovered in the earlier chapters in this book because these are well-documented people who are to be found in history books and works of reference. This means that the research is in some respects less rewarding. The relations of the Plantagenet Kings can be followed up easily by any reader who wishes to do so. However I feel privileged that I have been able to establish these links, acknowledging that it was the good fortune of being able to trace my Byrom ancestry which enabled me to discover these interesting ancestors. The concluding part of this book is a commentary on my findings.

The table which follows, tracing my ancestry back to Rollo, regarded as the first Duke of Normandy, is an illustration of one of my lines of descent resulting from my discoveries which includes Royal and Aristocratic forebears.

Anthony Patrick Russell and Nicholas John Russell - Descent from Rollo, First Duke of Normandy

[The first named and underlined person is the son or daughter of the previously named couple – early dates are usually only approximate]

1. <u>Rollo (Rolf) the first Duke of Normandy</u> (860-931) m. Poppa de Rennes (872-925) – Great x 33 Grandparents
2. <u>William I, Duke of Normandy</u> (900-942) m. Sprote de Bretagne (911-940) – Great x 32 Grandparents
3. <u>Richard I, Duke of Normandy</u> (933-996) m. Gonnor de Crepon (936-1031) – Great x 31 Grandparents
4. <u>Richard II, Duke of Normandy</u> (963-1027) m. Judith de Bretagne (982-1017) – Great x 30 Grandparents
5. <u>Robert I, Duke of Normandy</u> (999-1035) and Harlette de Falaise (1003-1050) [*not married – William the Conqueror was their illegitimate son*] – Great x 29 Grandparents
6. <u>King William I (the Conqueror)</u> (1025-1087) m. Matilda [*daughter of Baldwin V, Count of Flanders*] (d. 1083) – Great x 28 Grandparents
7. <u>King Henry I</u> (1070-1135) m. 1st Matilda [*daughter of Malcolm III King of Scotland*] (d. 1118) – Great x 27 Grandparents
8. <u>The Empress Matilda</u> (1103-1167) m. 2nd Geoffrey Plantagenet, Count of Anjou (1113-1151) – Great x 26 Grandparents. [*Matilda was the daughter of King Henry I - she was first married to the Holy Roman Emperor, Henry V*]
9. <u>King Henry II</u> (1133-1189) m. Eleanor of Aquitaine (1122-1204) - Great x 25 Grandparents
10. <u>King John</u> (1167-1216) m. Isabella of Angouleme (1180-1245) - Great x 24 Grandparents
11. <u>King Henry III</u> (1206-1272) m. Eleanor of Berenger (1217-1291) - Great x 23 Grandparents
12. <u>King Edward I</u> (1239-1307) m. Eleanor of Castille (1240-1290) - Great x 22 Grandparents
13. <u>Princess Elizabeth Plantagenet</u> [*Elizabeth of Rhuddlan*](1282-1316) m. 2nd Humphrey de Bohun (1276-1321) 4th Earl of Hereford and 3rd de Bohun Earl of Essex - Great x 21 Grandparents
14. <u>Sir William de Bohun KG</u> [*created 1st Earl of Northampton*] (1309-1360) m. Elizabeth de Badlesmere (1313-1355) - Great x 20 Grandparents

15. Elizabeth de Bohun (1345-1385) m. Richard FitzAlan KG [11th Earl of Arundel and 9th Earl of Surrey] (1346-1397) - Great x 19 Grandparents
16. Elizabeth FitzAlan d'Arundel (1374-1425) m. Sir Robert Goushill (1360-1403) - Great x 18 Grandparents
17. Joan Goushill (1402-1456) m. Sir Thomas Stanley KG [created 1st Baron Stanley, titular King of Mann] (1386-1458) - Great x 17 Grandparents
18. Margaret Stanley (1432-1481) m. Sir John Boteler (1429-1463) - Great x 16 Grandparents
19. Sir Thomas Boteler (1461-1522) m. Margaret Delves (1463-1504) – Great x 15 Grandparents
20. Margaret Butler [Boteler] (1485-1537) m. 2nd Sir Richard Bold (1462-1532) - Great x 14 Grandparents
21. Elizabeth Bould [Bold] (1507-1545) m. Henry Byrom (1504-1559) – Great x 13 Grandparents
22. John Byrom (1538-1593) m. Margaret Leland [Leyland] (dates not known) – Great x 12 Grandparents
23. Sir Henry Byrom (1563-1613) m. Katherine Gerard (1565-1613) – Great x 11 Grandparents
24. Sir John Byrom (1585-1611) m. Isabella Nowell (b. 1592) – Great x 10 Grandparents
25. Henry Byrom (1608-1642) m. Winifred H Brotherton – Great x 9 Grandparents
26. Samuel Byrom (1634-1686) m. Margaret Venables (b. 1637) – Great x 8 Grandparents
27. Henry Byrom (1660-1702) m. Margaret Brotherton (1660-1720) – Great x 7 Grandparents
28. Henry Byrom (1682- 1724) m. Ellin Denteith (b. 1673) – Great x 6 Grandparents
29. William Byrom (1710-1744) m. Sarah Gorse (d.1764) - Great x 5 Grandparents
30. William Byrom (1735-1802) m. Ellen Birchall (1736-1814) – Great x 4 Grandparents
31. Henry Byrom (1777-1862) m. Mary Cundliff (1779-1832) – Great x 3 Grandparents
32. Ann Byrom (1802-1884) m. James Potter (1802-1851) – Great x 2 Grandparents
33. Thomas Potter (1847 - 1904) m. Mary Elizabeth Oldham (1860 - 1931) – Great Grandparents
34. Elsie Potter (1888 - 1948) m. Sidney Arthur Russell (1884-1953) - Grandparents
35. Michael Hibberd Russell (1921-1987) m. Pamela Eyre (1920-2011) - Parents
36. Anthony Patrick Russell (b. 1951) and Nicholas John Russell (b. 1953)

Part V – Some Thoughts And Conclusions

Chapter 27. Kings and Princes, Saints and Sinners - some further Royal Connections

When I embarked upon this project I had no idea where it would take me. I thought that with a bit of luck I could go back to the early 19th century and possibly a bit further, but the prospect of delving into the Middle Ages and beyond never occurred to me. As I have said previously the discovery of the Byrom link was a wonderful find. Initially I was simply pleased to have confirmation that the fact that my uncle's name of Byrom was significant, rather than chosen on a whim. To then discover that the Byrom families of Wigan and Manchester had the same origins which meant that the famous John Byrom was a distant relative was a further bonus, particularly as my professional chambers in Manchester when I practised at the Bar were on Byrom Street, named after him. The discovery also shows that history passed from one generation to another by word of mouth can be reliable, because some members of my family always said that there was a distant connection to John Byrom.

However when further researches revealed all the links mentioned in the last few chapters showing descent from Kings and Queens and some leading aristocratic families the sense of bringing history to life was most exciting, and the tracing of Royal ancestry, albeit at a very distant degree caused me some amusement as well as considerable interest. It led to much reading about these people and a desire to discover more about some of the lesser known characters. The discovery of the story of Sir Robert Goushill and his few days of knighthood was a tale I would never have heard about were it not for a search of his name. Although the gory fate of Humphrey de Bohun on the bridge at the Battle of Boroughbridge in 1322 is mentioned in some history books it is as a footnote which never registered until I knew that he was an ancestor. Geoffrey FitzPiers, despite my having studied legal history in some depth, was unknown to me until I discovered his name as an ancestor, yet he was a highly distinguished and able lawyer who deserves to be better known. Although I was aware that the Royal and aristocratic families of Europe were closely connected and there was much intermarriage, until I saw for myself the numerous links I had no idea how extensive this was.

In the last chapters I mentioned the important link to the Plantagenets, but this led to finding links to many other Royal personages. To set out all the detail of who begat whom would create a rather dull list, but I have been able to trace connections to many Anglo-Saxon Kings as far back as King Egbert (771-839), my 37th great grandfather, who include Alfred the Great (35th great grandfather) and Ethelred the Unready (31st great grandfather). There are several links by marriage to the French

Royal House of Capet, which enables me to trace my ancestry back to the Emperor Charlemagne (742-783), my 36th great grandfather. This in turn leads to the Rurik Dynasty of Russia who ruled Russia until the late 16th century and who include Ivan the Terrible and Boris Godunov – through Anne of Kiev, the daughter of Yaroslavl the Wise, Grand Prince of Kiev and Novgorod, who was married to King Henri I of France (1008-1060), my 29th great grandparents. By reason of the marriage of King Henry I of England, my 27th great grandfather, to Matilda of Scotland there is considerable Scottish Royal ancestry back to Kenneth MacAlpin (810-859), including Donald II, known as Donald the Madman, Malcolm I (Dangerous Red MacAlpin), Duncan I who was slain by MacBeth, and Malcolm III who slew MacBeth. Malcolm III's queen, Margaret Atheling, the great granddaughter of Ethelred the Unready, was canonised as a saint. She is one of several of my direct ancestors who were canonised, for several of Charlemagne's direct ancestors were also saints, including Saint Arnulf, Bishop of Metz, who is the Patron Saint of Brewers. Saint Arnulf was my 41st great grandfather, who lived between 582 and 640 – he was married to St. Clothilde, and because he was a deacon and not a priest there was no bar on marriage, and in those days a deacon could become a bishop.

In addition to these Royal links, through the Dukes of Normandy there are links to the Scandinavian Royal families of Norway, Jutland, Sweden and Denmark. These include Sigurd Ragnarsson "Snake Eye" (776-812), King of Denmark and Sweden, a 37th great grandfather, who is said to have perished in a snake pit in Northumbria at the hand of King Ella of Northbumbria. Charlemagne's ancestry has been traced back to the Roman Empire and earlier. Several of his ancestors were Kings of Cologne including Sigobert the Lame (445-509) whose son

Chloderic became known as Chloderic the Parricide having sent assassins to murder his father. Chloderic was my 45th great grandfather.

The recent identification of the body discovered in the car park in Leicester as that of Richard III, the last Plantagenet King of England, and that he suffered from scoliosis, fascinated me. I suffer from scoliosis and when I saw the pictures of the skeleton I realised that Richard III's spinal deformity was very similar to my own, although in my case extensive surgery has eased the problem. Scoliosis can run in families, and my father, a doctor and someone with his own interest in Richard III, said to me fifty years ago when I was diagnosed with scoliosis that he believed the King suffered from the disease, which explained the accounts of him as having a hunchback (being known as "Crookback Dick"), but also that he was mobile and able to act as a soldier, and he suggested that perhaps I was related to Richard III in some way. My father, who died in 1987 at the age of 66, would have been delighted to have had his diagnostic theory confirmed and that by my researches Richard III was his 5th cousin 15 times removed.

The re-interment of the body of King Richard III in Leicester Cathedral in 2015 was a remarkable occasion – the only burial of a medieval king to have been televised! It was a very poignant event, but for me there was a pleasing coincidence. One of the hymns sung at the service was "There's a wideness in God's mercy" to the tune Corvedale, composed by a good friend of mine, Maurice Bevan, who was for many years a Vicar Choral at St. Paul's Cathedral. We sang the hymn at Maurice's funeral and that of his wife. I think he would have been very proud that his beautiful tune was used on this day. Had I known at the time of my distant relationship to the king I would have applied for a ticket to attend his reinterment, but alas my researches had not progressed to that extent then.

Some may regard the interest in such distant Royal relatives as somewhat self-indulgent. For my part although I do enjoy the fact that I have made the connection I recognise that these are very obscure links. However many people are interested to discover their origins, and it is fascinating to find out what your roots are, as the popularity of the television programme "Who do you think you are?" proves.

The Marquis of Ruvigny and Raineval, a Swiss aristocrat, set about compiling a complete table of the descendants of Edward III, entitled "The Plantagenet Roll of the Blood Royal". He commenced this Herculean task in about 1900 and his work extends to four large volumes – it is by no means complete. The descent I have discovered is, of course, from Edward I, two generations earlier, but the Marquis makes two points in his introduction which are worthy of note. "Even if Edward I may be justly termed the father of the British people, it is quite a different thing to be able to trace the line…birth alone entitles one to a place in the Plantagenet Roll, for on one side at least there must be a strain of gentle blood through which it is possible to trace ancestry back to the feudal and crusading days. One whose name occurs in this Roll can trace an ancestry back to William the Conqueror and Alfred the Great, to St. Louis and the Emperor Charlemagne." "Every Royal descent necessarily implies the possession of distinguished historical personages as ancestors – men and women who meet us in the pages of history, kings, warriors, statesmen, Knights of the Garter, canonised saints and so forth. And if it is sometimes urged that, after all, the quantity of Royal blood that flows in any person's veins must be infinitesimally small, the same holds true of the blood of our paternal ancestors; we only have one-half of our fathers' blood, one-quarter of our grandfathers', one-eighth of our great-grandfathers' and so on."

Sir Anthony Wagner, a former Garter King of Arms, has written that of Her Majesty the Queen's 128 5th great grandparents, one was a plumber (George Carpenter, 1713-1782) and another a landlord of an inn in Stamford (Bryan Hodgson, d. 1785). These are ancestors via her mother, Elizabeth Bowes-Lyon, the Queen Mother.

Because Fletcher Christian, who led the Mutiny on the Bounty, was descended from Edward I, through his daughter Joan of Acre, Countess of Gloucester, and the fact that there was so much intermarriage between the families of the mutineers and the Tahitian women who went and inhabited Pitcairn Island, almost every Pitcairn Islander and Norfolk Islander descended from them is a descendant of King Edward I, and thus all of them will be cousins to myself, my brother and my Russell/Potter/Byrom relatives who are descended from another daughter of Edward I, Elizabeth of Rhuddlan – see the information about the Plantagenet and de Bohun descent in Part IV of this book. So Royal ancestry can occur in many ways, and of course even Royalty may throw up some unexpected ancestry!

When I was putting the finishing touches to this book the genealogy site to which I subscribe posted some information about one of my maternal lines of ancestry in relation to the Wilton family [See Chapter 9: The Langmaids of Polperro]. The ancestry appears well-researched and corroborated in several respects, thus passing my balance of probability test. This established that a direct ancestor of Marian Willton, who married John Langmaid in 1654 and who was my 8th great grandmother, was Elizabeth of Rhuddlan, daughter of King Edward I, who was as has already been seen, a direct ancestor of mine through the Byrom family link via William de Bohun. So I am directly descended through both my father and mother by different routes from the Plantagenet Kings, and in particular King Edward I.

This provides further proof, if it were needed, that Edward I can be regarded as the father of the English people. The daughter of Elizabeth of Rhuddlan from whom this particular line descends was Margaret de Bohun (1311-1391), a sister of William de Bohun, who married Hugh de Courtney (1303-1377), 2nd Earl of Devon. They had at least 16, possibly as many as 18, children, one of whom became Archbishop of Canterbury and Lord Chancellor [William Courtney 1342-1396]. Many English people will, inevitably given the number of children born to this couple, have some descent from this union. Another lesson to be drawn from this discovery, as I have said elsewhere, is that genealogical research should never be regarded as closed and as more material becomes readily available on the Internet new, interesting and sometimes surprising information may come to light. It also reinforces how useful membership of a genealogy website can be and that it is a good idea to store your own family tree on the site so that when new information about your relatives becomes available you are alerted to it.

Chapter 28. Other less glamourous ancestors

However my researches uncovered some other less famous yet interesting characters from years gone by, and I have found this as interesting as the discovery of the Royal ancestry . Of these, the best known is John Byrom [Chapter 24]. It was always claimed that he was connected to the family, hence my uncle's name of Byrom, but no member of the family knew how this came about. The discovery that the Potters, always thought of as the most humble of the branches of the family, were the connection to the well-known figure was itself a surprise, even more so when it became established that the Potters were direct descendants, through the Byroms, of Royalty and Aristocracy. John Byrom was a most interesting man and, despite being well-known, something of a mystery. Clearly a highly intelligent and accomplished polymath, as his academic career, his writings and his inventiveness indicate, a Fellow of the Royal Society, and a great wit and raconteur, yet there are many question marks over him. Was he a secret Jacobite? Was he a spy or government agent? Did he have masonic or occult interests? Why were most of his papers destroyed in the 19th century? The fact that he was educated at the same school as my brother and myself, something that had escaped me until my recent researches, was one of those coincidences that sometimes crop up in life which give one cause for thought.

The Revd. John Eyre [Chapter 13] was an ancestor completely unknown to me until recently. It was a general search of his name on the Internet which uncovered his story and what an interesting one it proved to be – the classic tale of a young man over-indulging and then repenting and living a devout life. St Francis of Assisi comes to mind. Unlike the prodigal son John Eyre does not appear to have become reconciled to his father. What a sad contrast is the fate of Samuel "Beau" Byrom, losing all his inherited wealth and dying a beggar.

Thomas Eyre [Chapter 12], my 3rd great grandfather, must have been an interesting character. What was it that took him to London at the end of the Napoleonic Wars where he met his wife, Isabel Murphy? An apprenticeship? Was he looking for work? The ending of the long wars with the French resulted in economic depression and social unrest. Perhaps he had served in the Army or Navy or was a merchant seaman. At the time of his marriage in 1815 Thomas Eyre was aged 24, so it is likely he had been working for some time, but we do not know what he was doing. He had several occupations, ending up as an accountant and collector of taxes, not the most popular of jobs. His children had a variety of careers and five of them emigrated to Australia and New Zealand. The letter he wrote to his daughter Maria is a fascinating document, in parts stern, in other parts loving and tender and containing much gossip. What a wonderful glimpse into the past for my long lost Antipodean cousins who have the original! In this age of instant communication one can appreciate from that letter how moving to the other side of the world was truly cutting oneself off from one's family, friends and community. Two centuries earlier members of the Tuttle family, because of their devout Protestant beliefs, made a similar break with their roots by becoming early settlers in North America.

The trial of John Langmaid [Chapter 9] came as something of a shock. When I embarked upon my researches I was humourously advised that I would probably come across the odd illegitimate ancestor. In fact there are remarkably few examples of bastards in my ancestry, a distinguished exception being William the Conqueror! Of course other bastards have been discovered amongst my ancestors, such as the cruel and notorious King John, but familial illegitimacy is not the cause for him being regarded as such! However I had not expected to find that a fourth great grandfather stood trial at the Old Bailey resulting in a sentence of death, although mercifully pardoned. For me, as a lawyer, the trial was interesting. The full record reveals that it was fair, the evidence was compelling and although at that time a defendant could not give evidence in his own defence John Langmaid was well represented by a barrister. This discovery led to my reading, with great interest, about the history of smuggling in Cornwall and particularly Polperro in which my Langmaid ancestors played a significant part. The discovery of so much Cornish ancestry on my mother's side through both her parents was as considerable a surprise to me as it would have been to her.

The name Evan Victor Creak was known to me from a very early stage as one of my great grandfather's nephews, and I knew from my great grandmother's journal that his wife's name was Marie and that she had died in 1924. What I did not know until a very late stage in my researches as a result of making searches of all my known relatives on a genealogy website was that Marie had German origins, something which probably made life rather difficult at the time of the First World War and its aftermath, and that her father was Felix Carl von Goldstein [Chapter 3] who had such an interesting career in India, distinguishing himself at the time of the Indian Mutiny. This is a very good example of how the genealogy websites coupled with general Internet searches can uncover a great deal of long forgotten family history.

William John Stephens [Chapter 16] is another example of someone about whom a great deal could be discovered from an examination of the census returns, and the naval records augmented by general historical searches about his ship and the history of the time, to build upon what little was known of him from the family records. So it was also with Henry Russell, my great grandfather, the census returns indicating where he studied to become a teacher in addition to where he lived as a child, how his parents appear to have bettered themselves, and how his family progressed [Chapter 19]. As the information became revealed these people came to life.

Rural life in Dorset where the Hibberd, Sweetapple, Hart and other families connected with them lived for centuries in little villages suddenly became closer. Trade assumed an importance that I had not quite appreciated. In times when people did not move far from their homes and mobility which we take for granted today was very limited, it is obvious that every little village required its butcher, baker, and candlestick maker, not to forget in the larger places such as elegant 18th century Truro, the Peruke makers and cordwainers, and grocers, drapers, milliners and corset makers in Lancashire and Suffolk. Many of my ancestors carried out in their localities what were for those days essential tasks. Today we can obtain most of our needs with a few clicks on the computer!

For me these revelations of social history through these ancestors, most of whom would have remained unknown but for this research, have been of as much interest as the discovery of royal and saintly connections.

Chapter 29. Some Themes which have emerged

In the course of my researches I identified in excess of 750 direct ancestors, as far back as a 51st great grandparent born in 302 AD, Teutomer, a Frankish general reliably claimed as an ancestor of Charlemagne. This is, of course, a very small proportion of the whole, because when one goes back 20 or 30 generations the number of direct ancestors amounts to millions, since the total doubles with every generation until duplication reduces the number as one approaches the origins of the human race. An enterprising American amateur genealogist claims to have traced his ancestry back to Adam and Eve! He has worked out his relationship to King Henry II as that of 25th great grandson, the same as my own according to my researches. Thus all his earlier direct ancestors in the line beyond Henry II would bear the same relationship to me, which raises the entertaining possibility that my ancestry can also be traced back to Adam and Eve, who if he is correct would be my 153rd great grandparents. By his reckoning Joseph of Arimathea would be a 78th great grandfather and Mark Anthony a 75th great grandfather. Other ancestors along the way include Noah, Abraham, Isaac and Jacob, King Priam of Troy, Aenias, the Roman Emperors Tiberius, Nero and Claudius, Boudica and Old King Cole. Who knows? He may be correct!

One surprising and genuine discovery was that apart from the Potter/Byrom ancestry which was very firmly based in South Lancashire and a bordering part of Cheshire, my ancestors for many generations came from three rural areas in the South of England, those linked with the Tuttles from Norfolk and Suffolk, those linked with the Eyres and their connections from Cornwall and latterly Devon, and those associated with the Russells and Hibberds and their linked families from Hampshire and Dorset. As I have indicated I knew of the East Anglian connections of my Tuttle ancestors, but it was particularly interesting to discover the Cornwall and Dorset connections about which I and all my relatives who I have known personally knew nothing. This in turn emphasised something which is obvious when one thinks about it but perhaps not always thought about, namely how until the nineteenth century resulting from the Industrial Revolution and the growth of the railways in particular, the population was basically immobile remaining in the same area for many generations. Thus the Byroms and Potters remained in the Winwick area of South Lancashire for several centuries, making the move of Henry Byrom and James Potter to the Oldham area in the early 19th century, albeit only twenty miles or so, quite an unusual occurrence. The Eyres remained in Cornwall until various of the children of Thomas Eyre took the major step of emigrating to Australia and New Zealand in the middle of the 19th century. The Hibberds and the various associated families came from a few little villages in Dorset for many generations. The Oldhams and Fullaloves lived in Longdendale in North East Cheshire for many years. And the Tuttles remained in East Anglia until the 20th century.

It is also obvious that immobility was not confined to geographical factors. It was also social. It is clear from all my researches that my ancestors usually married within the same class, whether it was the aristocracy, the landed gentry, the rural farmers or the tradesmen. Again this is a well-known fact, but it is interesting to find real evidence of this from one's own ancestors. This can be illustrated in the Byrom family for example, because two of my direct Byrom ancestors married into the Parr family, the name Brotherton crops up twice as a Byrom wife, and the Boteler/Butler, Trafford, Bold, Radcliffe and Tyldesley names occur again and again. But the same was so in less distinguished families. Amongst my father's Hibberd ancestors in rural Dorset the Sweetapples, Lockyers and Horders recur, and we have seen how in the Eyre family second cousins married each other. However the difference between the prosperous Byrom family and the poorer Hibberds is that, although from a limited social circle, the families into which the Byroms married came from across Lancashire and from further afield, whereas those into which the Hibberds married were from villages no further than a few miles apart and in many cases from the same village.

The fate of the Byrom wealth, squandered by Beau Byrom, shows how easily family circumstances can alter. Social history is littered with similar tales of wealthy families suddenly finding that fate has dealt them a blow. Similarly from relatively humble origins wealth can be acquired, as with Henry and Ebenezer Tuttle whose business skills brought them considerable fortunes or, as in the case of Laura Eyre, some clever investing can transform a situation. Many of my direct ancestors were second or later sons, so if there was family wealth, given that usually the principal beneficiary of any family wealth would be the eldest son, who would definitely inherit any title, it is not surprising that there is little evidence of any inherited wealth in recent times. Similarly substantial wealth would not usually pass throught the female line if there was a son to inherit it.

There are some interesting unanswered questions. What took Thomas Eyre to London in 1815? What were the influences on the Revd. John Eyre which caused him first to become something of a rake and then to convert to the religious life with such a considerable impact on the evangelical movement? What drove Henry Tuttle to break away from his humble origins as the son of a hawker, to move to Lowestoft and establish such a successful business? Henry Russell also broke away from his background to take up a profession – teaching. What influences fostered this ambition in him? What was it that caused John Langmaid to take up a firearm and threaten Crown officers? In the trial he was said to have been of good character. Smuggling is one thing, threatening to kill a Government official quite another. Did his son leave Cornwall and move to Suffolk to work for the Revenue Service to escape the ignominy of being known as the son of a convicted felon? The Russell and Potter families knew of their Hibberd and Byrom links as is clear from the naming of my father and his elder brother, yet neither of the brothers knew what was the reason for their second names. Is this an indication that in the mid-20th century although communication and knowledge became more widespread this was at the expense of the loss of information passed on within families and by word of mouth? Were objects such as family bibles which would often contain details of family history regarded as less important in an increasingly ephemeral age?

The family history uncovered emphasises two significant periods of emigration, namely the colonisation of North America in the 17th century and of Australia in the 19th. My maternal grandmother, although not knowing the details, was aware of an American connection in the Tuttle family and of an Australian connection in the Eyre family of her husband. Passing on history by word of mouth is something of a lost art these days.

The Byrom family was clearly once very well-connected, but the Byroms themselves did not make a great mark. There are no Byrom High Sheriffs of Lancashire although almost every family into which they married produced at least one. The family had significant wealth until the early 18th century, but Byrom Hall is not one of the great houses of the area. Rebuilt in 1713, Nikolaus Pevsner gave the staircase a short mention but he considered nothing else about it worthy of note. Whilst the Leghs and the Gerards have chapels and monuments in the parish church at Winwick, of the Byroms, although many members of the family were associated with the church, there is no sign, except perhaps a forgotten gravestone, worn and overgrown with the passage of time, waiting to be uncovered again.

The Tuthills of Norfolk were also once a very well-connected and land-owning family, but by the time of the end of the 18th century, apart from the memorial to John Tuthill in the church of St. George Colegate, Norwich indicating that he was a merchant, the family appears to have gone into something of a decline. Inherited wealth tends to pass to elder sons, so it may be that the surviving Tuttles came from younger brothers and the elder Tuttle brothers, like John Tuthill, died without sons so the wealth passed to the daughters and into other families through their marriages .

The Eyres appear to have been a respectable middle class family for generations – many members were tradesmen and merchants in Cornwall. The family was sufficiently wealthy at the end of the 18th century to send two of Thomas Eyre's brothers to Oxford University, both of whom became clergymen, as had their uncle, the Revd John Eyre, who was educated at Cambridge [Chapter 13]. Thomas Eyre himself was clearly a talented man becoming a tax collector and accountant.

The Potters were also tradesmen, grocers and drapers, in the Wigan area, a notch or two below the Byroms, and it is interesting to note Thomas Potter becoming a local government officer. Public service is a theme which does run through several branches of the family, even today, with magistrates, councillors, at least three mayors, no fewer than four judges, several doctors, officers in the armed forces and teachers cropping up in many of the constituent families in the 20th century. When my uncle was a judge of the Court of Appeal there were three other part time judges in the immediate family all of whom, including myself, subsequently became full-time judges. There are other lawyers who have practiced in various fields, and further lawyers in the next generation. My brother followed our father into the medical profession becoming a consultant physician and two of our cousins became consultant psychiatrists. Others have married doctors and there are several members of the medical profession in the next generation. In that next generation are several teachers. One of my nephews pursues a successful career as an Army officer. In the latter part of the 20th century and this one the family must be categorised as professional. The Russell family, from relatively humble origins, was at the forefront of this transformation to professionalism with Henry Russell's training as a teacher at a time when teacher training as such was in its infancy.

Time and again in various branches of the family are found butchers, grocers and drapers, perhaps proving that the English are indeed a nation of shopkeepers, but reinforcing the fact that with limited mobility and a population living in many small towns and villages, every community needed these trades.

One of the facts that struck me as interesting as the researches progressed is that my ancestry is very English – there is hardly a single input of any other nationality in many generations. My ancestry is also basically predominantly and unashamedly middle class. In the 19th and early 20th century the census records reveal that many of my forebears, although none lived in particularly grand circumstances, had domestic servants in their households. My mother, brought up in the suburb of Purley in Surrey in the 1920s and 30s, the daughter of a bank manager, remembered there being a live-in servant when she was a child, and for the whole of her life there was a family tradition that we had boiled eggs for breakfast on Sunday because when she was a child the family's cook went to church on Sunday mornings for the early service so my grandmother took responsibility for breakfast. My mother continued with this practice and I do so to this day, although the reason behind the tradition ceased before the Second World War. In my own childhood, although my mother did not work, she had domestic help in the week – for many years this was in the person of Mrs Lloyd who before the Second World War had been a live-in maid in our house, not a grand house but a suburban five-bedroomed Edwardian house built by an architect for his own use. My bedroom was the maid's room which Mrs Lloyd had once occupied. Nowadays, except for the very wealthy, live-in domestic servants do not exist, and most domestic cleaners are supplied by an agency.

Something which surprised me was the age to which many of my ancestors survived. I was expecting the average life of my ancestors to be quite short, because we have all been given to believe that life was harder in times gone by and lives were generally shorter. However although the average mortality rate was undoubtedly considerably higher in past eras than it is today, account must be taken of the fact that the infant mortality rate was particularly high which significantly affected the overall figure. Those who survived into adulthood had a good chance of living relatively long lives, particularly if they came from the middle or upper classes. Although several of their siblings lived well into adulthood and reached good ages the sad tale of the three Potter children buried in the grave at Ashton [see Chapter 23] reinforces how precarious life as an infant was. On the two pages of the parish records where Charles Potter's burial is recorded there are the details of 16 burials in a three and a half week period between 24th June and 18th July 1832. Of these, 10 burials were of children aged 3 or less – 5 died from measles including Charles Potter, 2 from smallpox, 1 from croop and 1 from whooping cough, and the remaining child died a few days after birth from weakness. 2 of the adults died from cholera.

As my researches progressed I became increasingly aware of how much can be discovered with the facilities available on the Internet, but how important it is to keep an open mind and not assume that everything found there is correct. It is all too easy to tick off a name on an index list, without delving further, taking for granted that a line of ancestry is thus firmly established. Seeking corroborative evidence and discovering more than one source is very important to help arrive at firm conclusions about ancestry, and the examination of a parish record or the census return is an enjoyable and rewarding experience in itself. Adopting this approach also means that a better picture of the ancestor and his or her life can be built up. The general search of a name can sometimes reveal the most interesting information about people who made a mark even in a small way. Searching "Langmaid family Cornwall" led to the discovery of the trial of John Langmaid, and searching the Old Bailey records on line led to finding the transcript of the trial. It is interesting to look up known addresses to discover if the house still exists, read about the history of a place where an ancestor lived or the church where an ancestor was baptised, married or buried – there may be a reference to a relative or a monument of a relative in the church or graveyard. All this gives one a clue as to not only who one's ancestors were but the sort of lives they lived. In this regard a careful examination of the parish and census records, including reading entries about other families living in the vicinity, can be very revealing.

Another aspect of the research which became increasingly clear was that to confine oneself too narrowly can be very restrictive. It is instinctive when doing such researches to concentrate upon the male line. It is, after all, the father whose name is usually passed on to his descendants, but as my findings have shown it can be the maternal line which leads to the more interesting results. I was fortunate to discover a long and well-documented line of male Byrom ancestors all living in the same locality for centuries, but it was their wives and the families from which these women descended which enabled me to discover the links set out in previous chapters.

As I have already said the high probability is that anyone with predominantly English ancestry is descended from the Plantagenets, but it was my good fortune to be able to trace the connections of a well-connected family back to the 12th and 13th centuries which enabled me to prove a line of descent from the medieval kings. It was pure good luck arising out of the identification of Henry Byrom as my 3rd great grandfather which led to these discoveries. But for the fact that he was residing in the same household as his daughter and son-in-law James and Ann Potter on the date of the 1851 census, which was the first to require the relationship of every resident to the head of the household to be stated, this connection would not have been made. Henry Byrom was quite an old man in 1851, aged 74, so he may have been living with his daughter. However he may have been no more than a visitor to the address – his address in the previous census was not far away in Oldham, but by 1861 he was living in his birthplace, Ashton-in-Makerfield. The discovery enabled me to identify James Potter's wife Ann as having the surname Byrom which was the key to tracing their marriage record and other parish records, leading to the discovery of the Byrom family, explaining my uncle's second name and revealing the interesting connections set out in the last few chapters. Had Henry Byrom not been residing with his daughter and son-in-law on the night of 30th March 1851 when the census took place, the likelihood is that none of this would have been discovered and the use of the name Byrom would have remained a family mystery. The chance of establishing with any degree of proof which of the many James Potters who were born in Lancashire at the relevant time was my relative without this clue seems remote, and the likelihood is that without it a dead end would have been reached in the early 19th century.

I had some further good fortune in that several of my family names are unusual which made tracing the links rather easier than was the case with my Russell or Potter names which are more widespread. For example in the 1841 census 653 people with the name Byrom (including variants such as Byram) were recorded for the whole of England whereas there were over 11,000 Potter entries and over 13,000 Russells. Of the 653 Byroms well over half were living in Lancashire. There were 6 people named Henry Byrom living in Lancashire in 1841 according to the census records, and 66 named James Potter. Good luck is an important asset for the genealogist, as is having ancestors with uncommon names.

Some may disagree, but I believe that it is important to know about one's roots and the influences which may have come into play affecting one's own upbringing and those of one's relatives not only of the present generation but also the preceding generations. To learn about one's antecedents is instructive – it is certainly interesting. As this book shows, in my own family are some remarkable characters – John Byrom, The Revd. John Eyre, Henry and Ebenezer Tuttle, Air Marshal Sir Geoffrey Tuttle, Wing Commander Anthony Eyre, Leslie Appleton, Felix Carl von Goldstein, Angela Mortimer, and Lord Justice Russell to name those who achieved some distinction in a variety of fields and John Langmaid who achieved notoriety. There are the links to the Kings and aristocracy of the Middle Ages and earlier, who even though their influence can only be infinitesimally small, if characteristics are in any way inherited, may have had an effect upon the character of ancestors and of course oneself.

It may be regarded by some as unduly vain or narcissistic but having discovered my roots in this way I applied to the College of Arms for a grant of arms. This was granted, and incorporated into the arms are references to various aspects of my ancestry in the form of the Byrom hedgehog as the dominant object in the crest, standing on a green mound to note my Tuttle (tot-hill) ancestry, and holding a gold quatrefoil in its mouth which is an emblem of the Eyres. In the shield the dominant colour is red to represent my Russell surname, and the red portion of the arms is reminiscent of the tau cross, the emblem of St. Anthony of Egypt – this could therefore be read as representing my name, Anthony Russell. In the shield there are allusions to my profession and judicial appointments by the use of ermine and the sword of justice, entwined around which is a serpent bringing to mind a rod of Aesculapius to represent the medical profession of my father and brother; and the emblem of the paschal lamb couchant (lying down) is a reference to a number of aspects of and influences on my life, including the city of Preston of which I was the Recorder for just short of a decade (and Recorder of the Preston Guild of 2012 which takes place every 20 years), the University of Central Lancashire of which I am an Honorary

Fellow, and the Honourable Society of the Middle Temple of which I am a Master of the Bench. My chosen motto is: "Steadfast in Adversity". Reading a coat of arms is yet another way of discovering information about a person or family. My coat of arms is illustrated on the front cover of this book.

Researching this information took up a great deal of time, but it was an exciting exploration resulting in some interesting discoveries. This book gives an indication of what can be uncovered and after two years or so of research, most intensively in the final six months, which was a most enjoyable and rewarding journey, I believe I can properly say that I think I now know who I am! If some readers are enthused to carry out a similar exercise then one of the objects of this book will have been achieved.